THE WORLD BANK ANNUAL REPORT 1995

THE WORLD BANK, WASHINGTON, D.C.

ZB
WB
A56

Photo Credits   Cover photographs: Curt Carnemark and Ray Witlin
                  Regional photographs: Curt Carnemark and Franck Charton
Design   Book Design: Joyce Petruzzelli, Graphic Design Unit, The World Bank Group
                  Cover Design: Brian Noyes, The Magazine Group
                  Typography: Graphic Design Unit, The World Bank Group
Editorial   Peter C. Muncie, Office of the Publisher, The World Bank Group

ISSN: 0252-2942
ISBN: 0-8213-2884-0

This Annual Report, which covers the period July 1, 1994, to June 30, 1995, has been prepared by the executive directors of both the International Bank for Reconstruction and Development (IBRD) and the International Development Association (IDA) in accordance with the respective by-laws of the two institutions. James D. Wolfensohn, president of the IBRD and IDA and chairman of the boards of executive directors, has submitted this Report, together with accompanying administrative budgets and audited financial statements, to the board of governors.

The executive directors would like to take this opportunity to render tribute to Lewis T. Preston and express appreciation for the outstanding leadership he provided to the World Bank Group from September 1, 1991 until his untimely death on May 4, 1995. During that period the Bank's membership became nearly universal, and the challenges facing the Bank Group were greater than ever. They acknowledge in particular Mr. Preston's role in reemphasizing the reduction of poverty in the developing world as the Bank's central objective, in promoting investment in people, in enhancing the quality of the Bank Group's assistance to its member countries, in developing partnerships with the public and private sectors, and in making the Bank a more open, flexible institution, better equipped to respond to the vast challenges its diverse membership will face in the years to come.

Annual reports for the International Finance Corporation (IFC), the Multilateral Guarantee Agency (MIGA), and the International Centre for Settlement of Investment Disputes (ICSID) are published separately.

Executive Directors	Alternates
Ibrahim A. Al-Assaf	Ibrahim M. Al-Mofleh
Khalid M. Al-Saad	Mohamed W. Hosny
Marc-Antoine Autheman	Arnaud Chneiweiss
Ali Bourhane	Luc-Abdi Aden
Andrei Bugrov	Eugene Miagkov
Marcos Caramuru de Paiva	Armando Montenegro
Huw Evans	David Stanton
Fritz Fischer	Erika Wagenhöfer
Jean-Daniel Gerber	Jan Sulmicki
Leonard Good	Winston Cox
Enzo Grilli	Helena Cordeiro
Eveline Herfkens	Sergiy Kulyk
Ruth Jacoby	Jorgen Varder
Bimal Jalan	Mushfiqur Rahman
Abdul Karim Lodhi	Kacim Brachemi
Leonard K. Mseka	Joaquim R. Carvalho
Peter W.E. Nicholl	Christopher Y. Legg
Atsuo Nishihara	Rintaro Tamaki
Julio Nogues	Carlos Steneri
Jan Piercy	Michael Marek
Walter Rill	Philippe Peeters
Suwan Pasugswad	Khin Ohn Thant
Jorge Terrazas	Roberto Jimenez-Ortiz
Zhang Shengman	Zhu Guangyao

August 1, 1995

The World Bank, which consists of the International Bank for Reconstruction and Development (IBRD) and the International Development Association (IDA), has one central purpose: to promote economic and social progress in developing nations by helping raise productivity so that their people may live a better and fuller life. This is also the aim of the International Finance Corporation—which works closely with private investors from around the world and invests in commercial enterprises in developing countries—and the Multilateral Investment Guarantee Agency (MIGA)—which was established to encourage direct foreign investment in developing countries by protecting investors from noncommercial risk. Collectively, the World Bank, the IFC, and MIGA are known as the World Bank Group.

Of the four institutions, the IBRD, established in 1945, is the oldest and largest. The IBRD is owned by the governments of 178 countries that have subscribed to its capital. Under its Articles of Agreement, only countries that are members of the International Monetary Fund (IMF) can be considered for membership in the IBRD. Subscriptions by member countries to the capital stock of the IBRD are related to each member's quota in the IMF, which is designed to reflect the country's relative economic strength.

The IBRD makes loans only to creditworthy borrowers. Assistance is provided only to those projects that promise high real rates of economic return to the country. As a matter of policy, the IBRD does not reschedule payments, and it has suffered no losses on the loans it has made. It has earned a net income every year since 1948.

The IBRD obtains most of its funds through medium and long-term borrowings in the capital markets of Europe, Japan, and the United States. It also borrows funds at market-based rates from central banks and other government institutions. The IBRD's solid standing in the markets is based upon the combination of conservative lending policies, strong financial backing by its members, and prudent financial management.

Apart from borrowings, significant amounts also come from the IBRD's paid-in capital, from its retained earnings, and from the flow of repayments on its loans.

The International Development Association was established in 1960 to provide assistance to the poorer developing countries on terms that would bear less heavily on their balance of payments than IBRD loans. IDA's assistance is concentrated on the very poor countries—mainly those with an annual per capita gross national product of less than $696 (in 1993 U.S. dollars). By this criterion, about sixty countries are eligible.

Membership in IDA is open to all members of the IBRD, and 158 have joined. The funds lent by IDA come mostly in the form of contributions from its richer members, although some developing countries contribute to IDA, as well. IDA's resources have also been augmented by frequent transfers from the net earnings of the IBRD.

IDA credits are made only to governments. They have to be repaid over a period of thirty-five to forty years. They carry no interest, but there is an annual service charge of 0.5 percent on the disbursed amount of each credit. Although IDA is legally and financially distinct from the IBRD, it shares the same staff, and the projects it assists have to meet the same criteria as do projects supported by the IBRD.

The success of the Bank's operations depends upon the trust it has established with borrowers, and this trust is based on the experience and technical skills the Bank has demonstrated over the years in working with its member developing countries.

Under its Articles of Agreement, the Bank cannot allow itself to be influenced by the political character of a member country: Only economic considerations are relevant. It also seeks to ensure that the developing country gets full value for the money it borrows. Bank assistance, therefore, is untied in that it may be used to purchase goods and services from any member country.

The IFC was established in 1956. Its function is to assist the economic development of developing countries by promoting growth in the private sector of their economies and helping to mobilize domestic and foreign capital for this purpose. One hundred sixty-five countries are members of the IFC. Legally and financially, the IFC and the World Bank are separate entities. The IFC has its own operating and legal staff, but draws upon the Bank for administrative and other services.

In its project-financing role, the IFC provides loans and makes equity investments. Unlike most multilateral institutions, the IFC does not accept government guarantees for its financing. Like a private financial institution, the IFC prices its finance and services, to the extent possible, in line with the market, while taking into account the cost of its funds, and seeks profitable returns. The IFC shares full projects risks with its partners.

MIGA, the newest member of the World Bank Group, was established in 1988. It has as its principal responsibility the promotion of investment for economic development in member countries through guarantees to foreign investors against losses caused by noncommercial risks and through advisory and consultative services to members countries to assist them in creating a responsive investment climate and information base to guide and encourage the flow of capital.

MIGA is also an entity separate from the World Bank. Like the IFC, it has its own operating and legal staff but draws upon the Bank for administrative and other services. MIGA currently has 128 members.

The year 1994 marked the fiftieth anniversary of the Bretton Woods institutions. The world has changed a great deal in the past fifty years. During the past decade alone, a significant transformation has taken place in the way nations organize their economic activity. For many developing countries, private flows have become the most important source of financing. Economic activity throughout the world is rapidly becoming integrated, creating a truly global economy.

These changes have increased both the scale and complexity of the development agenda, radically altering the context in which the World Bank carries out its activities. In response, the Bank is also changing. Its overarching goal continues to be the reduction of poverty; increasingly, its task is that of a partner helping countries design and implement policies that expand markets and strengthen their economies to improve the quality of life for people everywhere *(see accompanying box)*.

The Bank has a vital role to play in managing the rapid changes in the new global economy across a continuum of different country needs with a flexible array of interventions. These include the use of its guarantee powers, which became a standard operational tool during fiscal 1995.

At the one end of the continuum of change is the growing number of countries able to attract private capital flows. Here, the Bank's major role is to assist with the medium- and long-term aspects of change management: ensuring the robustness of financial and institutional frameworks and helping to secure social integration through support for health, education, and safety nets. While serving its shareholders—member governments—the Bank, at the same time, has strengthened its partnership with the private sector in these countries, acting as a strategic bridge to channel resources to them in ways that fuel economic growth.

Further along the continuum, there are the many countries that have not yet become part of the new global economy of expanded trade and capital flows. Here, the Bank's role is to help them implement sound economic policies and investments in people and infrastructure, begin to attract private capital, and become integrated with the global economy. IDA's role in helping achieve and manage these changes in the poorest countries is particularly important.

At the other end of the continuum are those countries facing severe economic and social stress, where basic government itself has collapsed or is in danger of doing so. Here, clearly, there is a need for much more thinking by all concerned on what needs to be done. Working with other institutions, there is potential for the Bank to do more, within the framework of its Articles of Agreement, in areas such as demobilization and building the institutions necessary for long-term development and stable governance.

Perhaps nothing has changed more rapidly in the 1990s than the financing structure for development. Aggregate net flows to developing countries have more than doubled in the past five years, and private sector financial flows have quadrupled. In 1994, for the fifth year in a row, net total resource flows to developing countries from the developed world reached a record level—an estimated $227 billion *(see Appendix 11)*. As in previous years, the increase was due entirely to growth in private flows, and this increase was divided fairly evenly between foreign direct investment and private loans. Record levels of private flows are the result of development success, and they reflect a number of related factors, including economic liberalization in an increasing number of countries, a renewed emphasis on private markets in the provision of goods and services, and respectable rates of economic growth in many developing countries.

Despite the volatility (as seen early in 1995) in foreign capital flows, foreign direct investment (FDI) seems not to have been affected greatly. FDI

GUIDING PRINCIPLES IN A CHANGING WORLD

The Bank Group can continue to serve its members effectively in a rapidly changing world only if it becomes more flexible, cost-conscious, and efficient, Bank president Lewis Preston told the institution's governors in October 1994 during the annual meetings of the Bretton Woods institutions.

The need for the Bank to be flexible was also on the minds of most of the thirty-four speakers at a Madrid conference—"Fifty Years after Bretton Woods: The Future of the IMF and the World Bank"—which was held on the eve of the annual meetings, and which brought together financial officials, academics, think tank experts, as well as staff from the Bank and the IMF. A remark by Manmohan Singh, India's minister of finance, was typical: "Institutions must necessarily adapt to changing circumstances, and the Bretton Woods institutions are no exception to this rule."

In his address to the Bank's governors, Mr. Preston said that six principles would guide the Bank's response to a changing world: greater selectivity ("a more sensible sharing of tasks within the international system is required"); increased collaboration with all the Bank's partners, from the private sector to nongovernmental institutions; deepening client relationships ("country ownership of policies and projects is crucial"); measuring success by results; cost effectiveness; and excellent financial management.

The unfinished development agenda remains enormous—and so, too, is the need for an institution that has fifty years of development experience, a close relationship with virtually every developing country, and a committed staff of development professionals. And that was perhaps the clearest message to emerge from the meetings: The need for a flexible, efficient Bank Group is greater today than ever before.

flows into developing countries in 1994 are estimated at $80 billion, an increase of 13 percent over 1993. As in the past, a few countries received the bulk of the flows, with China accounting for almost 38 percent of the total. Direct investment often comes in tandem with transfers of know-how, market access for products and services, and other development ingredients.

As well as adapting to the new means by which development is being financed, the Bank also faces serious questions in the minds of the publics and their parliaments in its member countries. There are budgetary pressures that have impacted official aid flows, forcing difficult choices between bilateral and multilateral priorities. Furthermore, part of the conceptual foundation upon which the case for assistance flows has long rested is eroding: Some doubt the purpose of assistance in the wake of the Cold War's end; others doubt that large multilateral lenders can ever be effective.[1]

The case for development is compelling, however. Over the past five decades, average per capita incomes in developing countries have more than doubled. The GDPs of some economies have quintupled. Life expectancy has increased by more than 50 percent. There has been a "green revolution" in South Asia, an "economic miracle" in East Asia, Latin America has largely overcome its debt crisis, and substantial gains in health and literacy have taken place in Africa.

Within this diversified global context, it is vitally important that the Bank be a cost-effective, responsive, and flexible institution able to deliver timely, high quality advice, supported by financing for the implementation of programs and projects.

---

1. During fiscal 1995, a special task force was created by the Development Committee to assess the implications of economic change on the development priorities, instruments, operations, and management of five multilateral development banks and to consider whether improvements could strengthen their impact on the development process. The five banks are the World Bank, the Asian Development Bank, the African Development Bank, the Inter-American Development Bank, and the European Bank for Reconstruction and Development.

The Task Force on the Role of the Multilateral Development Banks, as it is called, will also evaluate procedures and practices for coordination among the multilaterals and other members of the development community, and consider whether it is possible to make any improvements on a regional, country, or sectoral basis.

The task force, which is headed by Abdlatif Yousef Al-Hamad, director general and chairman of the Arab Fund for Economic and Social Development, is expected to present its report to the Development Committee toward the end of calendar 1995.

In this respect, the support received from the Bank's board of governors at the October 1994 annual meetings in Madrid was highly encouraging. All shareholders expressed strong interest in the future direction of the Bank Group and strong appreciation for its services.

The first exploratory meeting on the eleventh replenishment of IDA resources (IDA-11), held in Madrid in October 1994, was very constructive. The IDA Deputies reaffirmed their strong support for a multilateral approach to assisting the world's poorest countries. Three subsequent meetings of Deputies were held in the first half of 1995 *(see accompanying box)*. Clearly, however, the fiscal constraints that a number of donors are experiencing make it essential that efforts be redoubled to conclude a significant replenishment of IDA resources.

The steady growth of the IFC has also continued to receive the strong endorsement from the Bank Group's shareholders. Requests for IFC support are growing rapidly—and this is likely to continue as more and more member countries move to strengthen their private sectors.

Encouraging support was also received for the institutional changes that the Bank has undertaken over the past several years under the leadership of the Bank's late president, Lewis T. Preston, and with the guidance and advice of the Bank's executive board. Those changes include the increasing country and client focus of the Bank's work, the changing composition of the lending program, the stress on ownership and participation by project stakeholders, the emphasis on implementation and results on the ground, and the strengthening of the Bank's skills mix.

Shareholders also noted with approval how much the Bank has changed. For example, it is now among the world's largest investors in areas such as education, health care, family planning, and environmental protection in the developing world. It is one of the largest investors in private sector development. It is also among the

DISCUSSIONS BEGUN ON THE IDA-11 REPLENISHMENT

The four IDA replenishment meetings in fiscal 1995 took place in an environment of budgetary pressure for some donors and, therefore, of growing uncertainty about the likely adequacy of the replenishment. Nevertheless, IDA Deputies were in agreement that poverty reduction remains IDA's central goal and that labor-intensive growth and environmental sustainability are important supporting goals. They noted that IDA's borrowers have urgent and substantial needs for financing to achieve these goals. Although they expressed serious concern about the funding outlook, they intend to continue discussions in the coming months to seek a significant replenishment level.

Deputies discussed several aspects of IDA's lending activities and programs. They endorsed the existing strong linkage between a country's IDA lending level and its performance on economic policy and project implementation. They agreed that the country-assistance strategy (CAS) is an important means of ensuring that IDA's principal goal of poverty reduction is pursued effectively and that it is tailored to specific country conditions. Deputies urged that CAS papers draw more explicitly on IDA's analytical work, especially poverty assessments and public expenditure reviews.

The issue of debt sustainability for heavily indebted poor countries gained increasing prominence during the year. IDA Deputies discussed possible expansions to IDA's menu of options to assist these countries and encouraged IDA management to propose to the board of executive directors, in the course of fiscal 1996, specific additional measures for countries facing debt-sustainability problems and a significant burden of multilateral debt. Throughout the year IDA monitored the situation of these countries. As agreed with the executive board, CAS papers for these countries are now to include an enhanced treatment of their long-term financial prospects and of their debt sustainability.

Deputies discussed how IDA can further encourage the growth of private sector economic activities in its borrowing countries and they noted the importance of overall economic policies in this context.

Deputies also discussed lending projections for the IDA-11 period (fiscal 1997–99), noting these projections are anchored in the assistance strategy for each country. They anticipate continued discussions later in the year of the lending projections, the overall size of the replenishment, and the burden-sharing among donors.

WORLD BANK OPERATIONAL AND FINANCIAL OVERVIEW, 1991–95

(millions of US dollars unless otherwise noted; fiscal years)

Item	1991	1992	1993	1994	1995
IBRD					
Commitments[a]	16,392	15,156	16,945	14,244	16,853
Disbursements[a]	11,431	11,666	12,942	10,447	12,672
Net disbursements to current borrowers, excluding prepayments[a]	2,909	2,594	3,289	963	2,238
Net disbursements to all borrowers, including prepayments[a]	2,109	1,833	2,331	-731	897
Net income	1,200	1,645	1,130	1,051	1,354
Financial return on average investments	9.23%	8.07%	6.09%	3.56%	5.71%
New medium- and long-term (MLT) borrowings after swaps[b]	10,883	11,789	12,676	8,908	9,026
Average cost of new MLT borrowings after swaps	8.06%	6.69%	5.97%	5.03%	6.32%
Subscribed capital	139,120	152,248	165,589	170,003	176,438
Statutory lending limit	152,327	168,368	183,312	189,189	198,988
Loans and callable guarantees outstanding	90,648	100,968	104,606	109,468	123,676
As a % of statutory lending limit	60	60	57	58	62
Headroom	61,679	67,400	78,706	79,721	75,312
Liquidity ratio	51%	48%	48%	51%	46%
Reserves-to-loans ratio	11.2%	11.7%	11.7%	13.9%	14.3%
IBRD/IDA Joint Activities					
Administrative expenses	964	1,074	1,236	1,389	1,409
IDA					
Commitments	6,293	6,550	6,752	6,592	5,669
Disbursements[a]	4,549	4,765	4,947	5,532	5,703
Net disbursements	4,274	4,441	4,581	5,110	5,205
Development credits outstanding	45,478	52,304	56,158	62,810	72,032
Accumulated surplus	598	1,363	1,194	1,365	1,995

a. Excludes guarantees and loans to the IFC.
b. Includes disbursements from the Special Fund.

most "open" and accountable development institutions in the world through expansion of its disclosure of information and establishment of an independent Inspection Panel.

Governors were particularly supportive of the steps taken to make the Bank Group more flexible, leaner, and cost-conscious. Steps include being more selective in what it does—despite the increasing demands placed upon it by member countries—and doing more to maximize the strengths of its partners; enhancing budget discipline and cost-consciousness; and improving transparency so that problems can be identified—and rectified—as early as possible.

Against this background, the Bank posted a strong record of performance in fiscal 1995. Commitments by the IBRD amounted to $16.9 billion, up $2.6 billion over the fiscal 1994 total. A major increase was posted in the Europe and Central Asia region, which saw commitments rise from $3.7 billion for forty-two projects to $4.5 billion for fifty-eight projects. IDA commitments, of $5.7 billion, fell by $923 million from the previous year, mostly the result of a downturn in commitments to the Africa and South Asia regions.

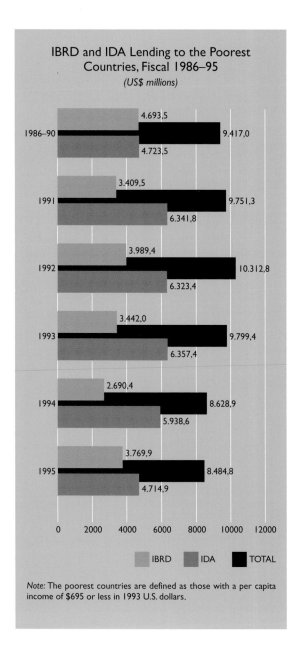

IBRD and IDA Lending to the Poorest Countries, Fiscal 1986–95

(US$ millions)

1986–90
- 4.693,5
- 9.417,0
- 4.723,5

1991
- 3.409,5
- 9.751,3
- 6.341,8

1992
- 3.989,4
- 10.312,8
- 6.323,4

1993
- 3.442,0
- 9.799,4
- 6.357,4

1994
- 2.690,4
- 8.628,9
- 5.938,6

1995
- 3.769,9
- 8.484,8
- 4.714,9

0 2000 4000 6000 8000 10000 12000

■ IBRD ■ IDA ■ TOTAL

Note: The poorest countries are defined as those with a per capita income of $695 or less in 1993 U.S. dollars.

The Bank demonstrated its flexibility and responsiveness to diverse client needs in a number of dramatic ways during the year: through approval of $1 billion in finance to support financial sector reform in Mexico; emergency assistance to Russia to contain and clean up a massive oil spill 1,000 miles northeast of Moscow near the Arctic circle; financing of emergency recovery programs in Burundi and Rwanda; and provision of emergency assistance to Haiti to halt that country's economic and social deterioration.

Assistance to the poorest countries—those with a per capita gross national product of $695 or less (in terms of 1993 United States dollars) totaled $8,485 million—$3,770 million from the IBRD and $4,715 million from IDA *(see accompanying figure)*.

Gross disbursements by the IBRD of $12.7 billion were substantially higher than in the previous year. IDA disbursements amounted to $5.7 billion, an increase of $171 million over the total for fiscal 1994.

On the financial side, the IBRD borrowed the equivalent of $9,026 million in the world's financial markets. Its net income was $1,354 million. In addition, late in the fiscal year, the executive directors of the Bank, moving to respond to the expressed needs of the Bank's clients, agreed to expand the single currency loan program beyond its two-year pilot phase. The addition of the single currency loan option allows borrowers to select any currency or composite currency for which there is sufficient borrower demand and in which the IBRD can efficiently borrow from the market.

Efforts continued to reduce the debt burden of severely indebted poor countries through support for policy reform, provision of IDA credits, extraordinary IDA allocation for countries engaged in debt workouts, "Fifth Dimension" allocations, funding from the Debt-reduction Facility for IDA-only Countries to reduce commercial debt, and technical assistance for debt management.

Through the Fifth Dimension program, which is financed out of IDA reflows, additional IDA allocations are provided to IDA-only countries that have outstanding IBRD debt, are current in their debt service to the IBRD and IDA, and have an IDA-supported adjustment program. These allocations are in proportion to the IBRD interest due in that year. In fiscal 1995, the program provided supplemental IDA allocations totaling $185.8 million to fourteen countries.

The Debt-reduction Facility provides low-income countries with grant funds to reduce their commercial debt that is public, external, noncollateralized, and unguaranteed. The facility is financed through contributions from the

IBRD's net income and from donors. Eight operations have been completed (for Bolivia, Guyana, Mozambique, Niger, São Tomé and Principe, Sierra Leone, Uganda, and Zambia); they utilized $79.6 million in IBRD resources from the facility and $74.3 million in co-financing to extinguish about $1 billion in principal. Eight additional operations—in Albania, Ethiopia, Guinea, Mauritania, Nicaragua, Senegal, Tanzania, and Viet Nam—are currently under preparation.

While twenty-five countries have "graduated" or phased out their reliance on World Bank lending, the Republic of Korea became the first country ever to progress from being a purely concessional borrower from IDA to being an IDA donor and an IBRD graduate. Korea reached the milestone with the signing on March 3, 1995, of its two final loan agreements with the IBRD.

Eritrea joined the IBRD on July 6, 1994, bringing the total membership of the IBRD to 178. At the end of the fiscal year, action was pending on membership in the IBRD for Bosnia-Herzegovina, Brunei Darussalam, and the Federal Republic of Yugoslavia (Serbia/Montenegro).

Eritrea and the Azerbaijan Republic became members of IDA on July 6, 1994 and March 31, 1995, respectively, increasing IDA's membership to 158. At June 30, 1995, action was pending on membership in IDA for Bosnia-Herzegovina, Brunei Darussalam, Ukraine, and the Federal Republic of Yugoslavia (Serbia/Montenegro).

The board of executive directors is responsible for the conduct of the general operations of the Bank and performs its duties under powers delegated to it by the board of governors. As provided in the Articles of Agreement, five of the twenty-four executive directors are appointed by the five member governments having the largest number of shares; the rest of the board is elected by the other member governments, who form constituencies in the election process every two years.

The executive directors consider and decide on the IBRD loan and IDA credit proposals made by the president and they decide policy issues that guide the general operations of the Bank and its direction. The executive directors are also responsible for presentation to the board of governors at its annual meetings of an audit of accounts, an administrative budget, and the *Annual Report* on the operations and policies of the Bank, as well as any other matters that, in their judgment, require submission to the board of governors.

During fiscal 1995, the executive directors met 131 times in formal board meetings and another 67 times in seminars, informal sessions, and as the Committee of the Whole. In addition, most of the executive directors serve on one or more of five standing committees: Audit Committee, Committee on Development Effectiveness, Budget Committee, Personnel Committee, and Committee on Executive Directors' Administrative Matters. The executive directors' Steering Committee, an informal advisory body, also meets regularly.

In addition to the meetings and committee work, groups of executive directors at times travel to borrowing countries in order to learn firsthand—through talks with government officials and inspection of Bank-supported projects—about country circumstances and special problems. In fiscal 1995, a group visited several transitional states in Eastern and Central Europe—Albania, former Yugoslav Republic of Macedonia, Moldova, and Ukraine.

Shaping Policy

The board of executive directors has an oversight role that covers virtually all Bank policy. It considers initiatives proposed by the president, so its role cannot be separated from most of the Bank activities covered in this report.

However, the executive directors also exercise an important role in shaping Bank policy and its evolution as they work for changes in direction, emphasis, and/or improvements in Bank results. It is in this role that the directors represent shareholder governments and their changing perspectives of the Bank. These policy initiatives normally reflect needs perceived by shareholders and involve a process of consensus building, both among directors and with Bank management.

Many of the changes in Bank policy that grow from initiatives by the executive directors occur gradually over a period of years, such as the increasing emphasis on environmental issues, governance, institution building, and the role of the private sector in development; the discussion by the board of Bank country-assistance strategies (CASS); the opening up of Bank disclosure policy; and the renewed interest in lending for both infrastructure and human-resource development.

Other initiatives by the executive directors occur more rapidly, such as the creation in 1994 of the independent Inspection Panel that reports to the board. And in fiscal 1995, for example, as a result of the shock effects of the Mexico peso crisis, many directors pressed for considerably more lending to strengthen financial institutions in countries affected by the crisis. The directors were also active in discussions of how to ease the debt burden of low-income countries.

Accountability and Development Effectiveness

For some years the executive directors have been encouraging the Bank to become more efficient and show more accountability as an institution while encouraging more accountability by staff and management within. Both areas of concern moved forward considerably under President Lewis Preston, who appointed the Task Force on Portfolio Management upon taking office. The task force report (the "Wapenhans Report") resulted in a major policy shift for the institution toward results-oriented supervision and implementation in the field, along with an increased emphasis on the quality of projects and operations. The "cultural change" process is still not complete, and the executive directors are active informally and in board committees in helping to shape an appropriate personnel policy, as well as a new field office policy, to complement the implementation focus.

The executive directors are involved in the budget process of the institution at various points. They discuss planning directions informally with management, which cover both planned expenditures and areas of policy and operational emphasis. The directors' Budget Committee discusses various aspects of the budget over the course of the year. The streamlining of the Bank to reduce its administrative costs, as well as improve other efficiency matters, had been stressed for some time. In fiscal 1995, President Preston announced an initiative to reduce the administrative budget by 10 percent to 12 percent over two years.

The executive directors' concern for accountability was further reinforced in fiscal 1995 by their review of recommendations of the Ad Hoc Committee on Board Procedures, which had been approved two years earlier by the board. The revised board procedures were an attempt to define more explicitly the accountability of the board for policy and operational oversight and set standards for the CAS papers prepared by management. The Bank's lending strategy for most borrowing countries is discussed by the board every two years, and that for the largest borrowers is discussed every year. In the 1995 review, the directors made it clear that the quality and comprehensiveness of the CAS papers still needed improvement, particularly regarding coverage of social and poverty concerns and countries' potential problems and opportunities related to the external environment. Directors also made it clear that they would continue to monitor closely the quality of Bank projects.

In another move to improve Bank accountability, the directors created the Committee on Development Effectiveness (CODE), which

became a reality in fiscal 1995. The new committee's mandate combines oversight of the work of the Operations Evaluation Department (OED), formerly a function of the Audit Committee, with a new directive to deal with issues related to the effectiveness of on-the-ground results of Bank operations.

The CODE also oversees the responses of Bank management to OED's findings and recommendations. In fiscal 1995, the CODE's findings and recommendations were reviewed by the full board, as were the fiscal 1994 annual report of the director general (DGO), Operations Evaluation, the annual review of evaluation results, and the evaluation work program for fiscal 1996.[1]

The Inspection Panel complements the Bank's existing systems for quality control in project preparation and implementation. As such, it helps the executive board in its governance of the Bank. In fiscal 1995, the executive directors discussed the panel's procedures in the context of its first requests for inspection.

The executive directors have spearheaded the Bank's focus on beneficiary participation, which was given a boost by the Wapenhans Report's finding that beneficiary participation in the design and implementation of projects greatly enhanced projects' chances of success. The directors more recently have led the way in defining participation as direct beneficiary participation, rather than accepting nongovernmental organizations (NGOs) as proxies for beneficiaries since their interests are not necessarily the same. (It is recognized that NGOs may have a role to play in helping the direct beneficiaries organize themselves.)

The Private Sector

Again, the private sector focus has grown out of several years of consensus building by the executive directors. It aims for development driven by the private sector, with an appropriate public sector role in the guidance and regulation of the private sector. The private sector is now a recognized area of emphasis for the Bank,

---

1. For details on the activities of the Operations Evaluation Department, see pages 44–45.

although there is not yet a formal, comprehensive policy other than the view that the Bank should complement, not displace or compete with, the private sector. Efficiency and accountability themes permeate this policy area also, particularly since the IFC still has the most private sector experience in the Bank Group. Closer coordination and information-sharing among the Bank, the IFC, and MIGA have been outgrowths of the emphasis on the private sector.

Another outgrowth of both the private sector emphasis and the desire for more efficiency was the decision to mainstream Bank guarantees as an operational tool. Again, several years of experience with a pilot program helped achieve consensus among the executive directors on a dramatic departure from what had been Bank policy for half a century. Although the Articles of Agreement mention guarantees, they have been used only sporadically and have never found a widespread role in Bank operations. In fiscal 1995, however, the board agreed that the Bank's guarantee could be used much more, given a number of conditions, to attract private capital and the private sector, particularly to large infrastructure projects. Since the IFC and MIGA are also involved in guarantees, directors stressed the need for careful coordination and collaboration among the parts of the Bank Group, as well as with bilateral export credit agencies.

Appointing a New President

In March 1995 the executive directors unanimously appointed James D. Wolfensohn to become the Bank's ninth president. He was appointed for a term of five years that began on June 1, 1995.

Human Resources Development

Evidence that human capital development—the focus of the Bank's vice presidency of Human Resources Development and Operations Policy (HRO)—is critical for overall economic and social development is not new. What is new is that the awareness of its importance has gone beyond the confines of academic scholars and social reformers and has entered into the thinking of mainstream decisionmakers.

There is a growing demand from developing countries for Bank support in the area of human-resources development; both lending and nonlending services have grown rapidly during the first half of the 1990s.

The past fifty years have witnessed the Bank's evolution from an organization created for the reconstruction of postwar Europe into a modern institution seeking partnership with its clients in expanding markets and strengthening economies to improve the quality of life for people everywhere, especially the poorest. And while the Bank's fundamental objectives remain the same, its approach to development has evolved over time as new challenges have emerged and lessons have been learned.

Bank lending for human-resource development has increased sharply from an average of about 5 percent of the total in the 1980s to 15 per-

cent in the period fiscal 1993–95. The Bank is now the single largest source of external finance for investment in human capital in developing countries—with support increasingly going to the provision of effective primary services in education and health, where the impact on poverty reduction and growth is the greatest.

Bank lending for education has exceeded $2 billion in each of the past three fiscal years; since 1986, the Bank has lent more than $800 million to fifty-one HIV/AIDS projects in nearly forty countries; and in the past two fiscal years, the Bank has lent almost $1 billion in support of population and reproductive health objectives.

The core issues at the World Summit on Social Development (Copenhagen, March 1995) were consistent with current Bank priorities and lending directions, including the expansion of social sector lending and more systematic attention to safety nets and social impacts in the design of economic reform programs. At the summit, the Bank announced plans to increase social spending by 50 percent over the next three years. At a time when foreign aid flows are contracting, it committed itself to providing $15 billion for basic social needs and a further $5 billion for water-supply and sanitation programs. Lending for basic social needs during fiscal 1995 alone

amounted to $3,907 million: $2,097 million for education-sector projects; $1,162 million for projects and components in the population, health, and nutrition sector; and $648 million for projects in the social sector.

Despite this shift in the pattern of lending, the task ahead remains large. The Bank's long-term vision in the area of human-capital formation is to help developing countries reach the point where inadequate investments in people no longer hold back growth or keep people in poverty. However, it remains a challenge to persuade some countries that the social sectors are not "soft." In fact, they are "hard," and there is no doubt that early and substantial investment in people allows economic growth to benefit a larger share of the population, thus effectively reducing both poverty and inequality.[1]

The challenge of development in the broadest sense is to improve the quality of life in the poorer countries of the world. Although a better quality of life generally calls for higher incomes, it involves much more than that: It involves quality education, higher standards of health and

1. The rate of return to primary education investment in developing countries is 18 percent—a much higher return than from most investments in the industry and infrastructure sectors.

nutrition, a cleaner environment, and more eco-nomic opportunities.

Experience shows that this improvement in the quality of life results by moving simulta-neously on two parallel tracks: economic re-forms, to provide stability and an enabling envi-ronment for growth, and investments in people—education, health, nutrition, family planning. The two reinforce each other, and to-gether, they can form a "virtuous circle" of development.

Successful countries, in fact, have moved on both these tracks. There is no—and can be no—delinking of economic reforms and effective social policy. Economic growth is crucial. No country has achieved sustained improvements in living standards without it. But investing in people to create human capital—which is the main attribute that people draw on in order to live more productive lives—is equally critical to raising living standards.

The HRO vice presidency was established in 1993 to address the full range of issues related to human-resources development, poverty re-duction, and operations policy. Within the vice presidency, two sector departments—Education and Health, and Poverty and Social Policy—ad-dress social sector issues. Each department has a team-based management structure, and the work programs of each are organized into eight thematic areas. The first four are along the con-ventional sectoral lines: education and training, health, population and reproductive health, and nutrition. The other four deal with cross-cutting interlocking issues: poverty and social safety nets; social security and labor markets,[2] gender analysis and policy,[3] and early childhood devel-opment.

The vice presidency's third department, the Operations Policy Department, is unique in that it has a perspective over the entire opera-tional complex. It is responsible for portfolio-management functions, issuance of operational directives, procurement activities, technical as-sistance oversight, Bank relations with nongov-ernmental organizations (NGOs), participatory development, work related to the Development Committee, Bank/UN relations, public sector management and governance, and computer in-formation services.

Poverty-reduction activities. In the area of poverty and social assistance, the Bank's annual report on its poverty-reduction activities[4] found that 25 percent of total Bank investment lend-ing in fiscal 1994 (43 percent of total IDA invest-ment lending) was directly targeted to the poor; these investments supported activities to in-crease the productivity and economic opportu-nities for the poor, to develop their human re-sources, and to provide social safety nets. The evaluation noted further that the quality of country-assistance strategy (CAS) statements also improved, while the Bank continued to extend and improve its use of participatory techniques in its analysis and lending. Eleven poverty as-sessments were completed during the period under review, and much additional economic and sector work supported poverty-reduction efforts at the country level.

The report went on to say, however, that a fundamental constraint exists to evaluating the effectiveness of the Bank's efforts at reducing poverty. Experience has shown that it is virtu-ally impossible to disentangle the aggregate "on-the-ground" impact of the various actions taken in a given country by any one donor from those taken by other donors or by the government. It is possible (but difficult), nonetheless, to assess the aggregate effect of all factors and of specific projects. Monitoring poverty levels in many countries is constrained, however, by a lack of reliable data. The report recommended, there-

2. A 1994 policy research report, *Averting the Old Age Crisis: Policies to Protect the Old and Promote Growth*, makes a strong case for reforming existing pension systems and designing new ones in ways that both protect the old and encourage economic growth. The HRO vice presidency is working with the Bank's six operational regions to help countries design affordable, administratively feasible social security and social insurance programs that would not have an adverse effect on work incentives or labor demand.

3. In late 1994, a two-day conference, cosponsored by the Bank and the Inter-American Development Bank, was held to update staff of the two institutions on recent research into gender issues. Leading academics were invited to share their findings as a way to sensitize staff to consider economic and poverty issues from a more gender view-point, to make staff aware of the cutting edge research on gender issues now being carried out by academics, and to build a bridge on gender work between donor institutions and the academic community.

4. World Bank. 1995. *Poverty Reduction and the World Bank: Progress in Fiscal 1994*. Washington, D.C.

fore, that the Bank and other donors expand their assistance to build capacity for poverty monitoring, for only by systematically capturing data can the on-the-ground impact of government and donor-supported efforts to reduce poverty be assessed.

In the context of the tenth agreement to replenish IDA resources (IDA-10), the Bank committed itself to increase steadily the share of both social sector and poverty-targeted investment lending during the three-year IDA-10 period relative to IDA-9 (fiscal 1991–93), where justified by the country-assistance strategy; to include specific poverty-reduction measures in the design of adjustment operations whenever feasible; and to complete poverty assessments for all major IDA recipients by December 1994.

Lending during fiscal 1995 for projects in the Bank's program of targeted interventions (PTI) was 32 percent of total investment lending *(see Table 2-1)*. IDA commitments for the PTI, as a share of IDA investment lending, amounted to 54 percent. Projects are included in the PTI if they include a specific mechanism for targeting the poor or if the proportion of the poor among project beneficiaries significantly exceeds their proportion in the overall population.[5]

Of the twenty-seven adjustment operations approved during fiscal 1995 (not including three debt-reduction loans), fourteen, or 52 percent, were poverty focused.[6]

By June 30, 1995, poverty assessments had been completed for thirty-three IDA-recipient countries out of sixty-nine countries that have recently received IDA credits. Assessments are under way in another twenty-six IDA countries. Despite the fact that the IDA-10 agreement did not define what was meant by "major IDA recipients," poverty assessments were undertaken during the year in ten countries that are both large and active IDA borrowers—Albania, Burkina Faso, Côte d'Ivoire, Kyrgyz Republic, the Lao People's Democratic Republic, Nicaragua, Nigeria, Tanzania, Togo, and Yemen.

Population, health, and nutrition. Intensified efforts during the past two years in activities related to population and reproductive health culminated in the publication in fiscal 1995 of two reports on population and women's health that were widely disseminated at the International Conference on Population and Development (September 1994, Cairo).[7]

Speaking at the conference, the late World Bank president Lewis Preston noted that if the development community does not deal with rapid population growth, poverty will not be reduced and development will not be sustainable.

During fiscal 1995, the Bank published an HRO-authored report, *Enriching Lives: Overcoming Vitamin and Mineral Malnutrition in Developing Countries*,[8] which reported that millions of lives around the world could be saved and the quality of life of hundreds of millions markedly improved—very inexpensively—by eradicating three vitamin and mineral deficiencies in people's diets.

The three vitamins and minerals are vitamin A, iodine, and iron—so-called micronutrients. More than 2 billion people are at risk from micronutrient deficiencies, and more than 1 billion are actually ill or disabled by them, causing mental retardation, learning disabilities, low work capacity, and blindness. It costs little to correct these deficiencies through fortification of food and water supplies. In a country of 50 million people, this would cost about $25 million a year. That $25 million would yield a fortyfold return on investment.

The Bank is involved in micronutrient projects in thirty countries. Micronutrient investments by the Bank in fiscal 1995 amounted to an estimated $71 million.

5. A description of each project in the PTI that was approved during fiscal 1995 can be found in the project summaries in Section Four of this *Annual Report*. The PTI projects are marked by [§].

6. A description of each poverty-focused adjustment operation that was approved during fiscal 1995 can be found in the project summaries in Section Four of this *Annual Report*. These operations are marked by [†].

7. World Bank. 1994. *Population and Development: Implications for the World Bank.* Development in Practice Series. Washington, D.C.; World Bank. 1994. *A New Agenda for Women's Health and Nutrition.* Development in Practice Series. Washington, D.C.

8. World Bank. 1994. *Enriching Lives: Overcoming Vitamin and Mineral Malnutrition in Developing Countries.* Development in Practice Series. Washington, D.C.

TABLE 2-1. PROGRAM OF TARGETED INTERVENTIONS, 1993–95

(millions of US dollars; fiscal years)

	1993	1994	1995
Total World Bank PTI lending	4,674	4,441	5,437
As share of investment lending (%)	27	25	32
As share of all Bank lending (%)	20	21	24
Total number of PTI projects	72	63	75
IDA PTI lending	2,137	1,853	2,423
As share of IDA investment lending (%)	41	43	54
As share of all IDA lending (%)	32	28	43
Number of IDA PTI projects	44	35	48

NOTE: *Investment lending is defined as all lending except for adjustment, debt and debt-service reduction operations, and emergency-reconstruction operations.*

Health-sector reform is at the center of the Bank's project and sector work in most middle-income countries and in an increasing number of low-income countries, as well. *World Development Report 1993, Better Health for Africa: Experience and Lessons Learned,* and other major studies provide the basic framework for health-sector reform efforts. Because borrowers and donors alike look to the Bank for leadership in this field, substantial additional resources during the past fiscal year were devoted to health-sector reform activities.

One critical area of growing attention in Bank-supported projects is the nurturing and development of the next generation: the children of the developing world.

Three million children in developing countries die every year because of lack of clean water; 12 million children under the age of five die of various other causes; and 130 million children do not have access to primary education. More than a million children are blind because they do not get enough Vitamin A. Another 50 million are seriously impaired, both mentally and physically, because their diets lack iodine. In low-income countries, more than half of young children are anemic, leading to a vicious circle of poverty: Malnourished mothers give birth to low-birthweight babies, who become the most likely candidates to perpetuate poverty.

Evidence confirms that health, nutrition, and educational interventions early in childrens' lives yield high returns. The Bank is one of the leading international financiers in the field of early childhood development: Since 1990, lending in support of early childhood development has involved fourteen projects or project components in sixteen countries.

Support to education. The Bank today accounts for about a quarter of all external support to the education sector. Since its first education project was approved in 1962, the institution has continuously expanded its financing of education projects, in both absolute and relative terms, as part of its mission to reduce poverty. Cumulative lending for education amounts to $21,579 million through more than 500 projects in more than 100 countries.

This volume of finance gives the Bank a leadership role among donors. Compared with spending on education by low- and middle-income country governments and peoples, however, external financing plays a minor role. A conservative estimate of public spending at 4 percent of GNP and private spending at 2 percent yields a total annual education expenditure of $270 billion for all low- and middle-income countries. All external finance together, however, amounts to only 2.2 percent of this total, and World Bank financing to only about 0.8 percent. This low share means that the Bank's principal contribution must be to provide advice designed to help governments develop education policies suitable for the circumstances of their countries.

A report—*Priorities and Strategies for Education: A World Bank Sector Review*—synthesizes the Bank's work on education since the 1980 publication of its education-sector policy paper and considers options for the Bank's borrowers. The report was discussed by the executive board late in the fiscal year and was amended after taking into account directors' comments.

It concludes that reforming education financing and management of education means redefining the role of government in six key ways, with appropriate priorities depending on country circumstances. They are: a higher priority for education in general; greater attention to the linkages between learning and labor market outcomes; focusing public investment on basic education, coupled with more reliance on private financing for higher education; increased attention to equity issues; greater involvement at the household level to improve the accountability of educational systems; and more autonomous institutions.

These six key areas of education-system reform will be supported by World Bank projects in the context of the principles that the Bank adopted in 1994 at the time of its Fiftieth Anniversary to guide its future operations: greater selectivity, partnership, client orientation, results orientation, cost effectiveness, and financial integrity.

Participatory development. The Bank continues to encourage governments to support participatory development approaches. The participation of directly affected stakeholders in Bank-supported projects—that is, those people, particularly the poor and marginalized, who may be expected to benefit or lose from Bank-supported operations—is increasing. A preliminary review of fiscal 1995 operations reveals that eighty-six out of a total of 242 new projects included influential forms of participation by directly affected stakeholders.

Evidence of the positive effects of participation is growing. A recent study of people's participation in environmental assessments in Latin America found several instances where important environmental effects and mitigation measures were only identified through broad public consultation and discussion. Similarly, a review of economic and sector work (ESW) in Africa found that "by far" the most striking and generalized attribute to successful ESW had been the increasing involvement of the government, local consultants, and stakeholders in its preparation and discussion.

Following the executive directors' endorsement of a plan of action to mainstream participation, several initiatives were undertaken during fiscal 1995. A Senior Managers' Oversight Committee was established to oversee the mainstreaming of participation in Bank operations. One of the first tasks of the committee was to review Participation Action Plans prepared by each operational region. These plans specify procedures and plans for integrating participatory approaches in lending operations and ESW.

The first in a series of Bankwide training courses in stakeholder participation took place during the year. The regions have also undertaken several staff-training initiatives: The India Department has developed a course on stakeholder participation, and the Africa region has held a training and information seminar on systematic client consultation.

The $2 million Fund for Innovative Approaches in Human and Social Development (FIAHS), set up late in fiscal 1994, enabled the regions to strengthen their capacity to use participatory approaches and social assessment methods by hiring thirteen social scientists to provide technical support in these areas. The FIAHS also provided support for the use of participatory approaches or social assessments in forty-eight projects and in ESW. The fund's resources, which were exhausted before the end of the year, will be replenished in fiscal 1996.

Bank relations with NGOs. In fiscal 1995, 41 percent of projects approved by the Bank plan to involve NGOs *(see Table 2-2)*. Two trends evident during the past year were increased NGO involvement at an earlier stage in the project

TABLE 2-2. PATTERNS IN WORLD BANK-NGO OPERATIONAL COLLABORATION, FISCAL YEARS 1974–95

	Total 1974–92		1993		1994		1995	
	No.	%	No.	%	No.	%	No.	%
By region (number of projects)								
Africa	236	n.a	31	41*	38	63*	33	57*
East Asia and Pacific	53	n.a	12	27*	22	51*	12	29*
South Asia	68	n.a	11	42*	15	79*	12	67*
Europe and Central Asia	10	n.a	2	7*	10	24*	17	29*
Latin America and the Caribbean	71	n.a	14	28*	24	50*	22	42*
Middle East and North Africa	21	n.a	3	16*	5	31*	4	29*
Total	459	n.a	73	30	114	50	100	41
By sector (number of projects)								
Adjustment related (including social funds)	35	8	5	7	12	11	9	9
Agriculture/rural development	172	37	14	19	36	32	29	29
Education	47	10	6	8	10	9	14	14
Environment	25	5	13	18	5	4	6	6
Industry/energy	41	9	8	11	13	11	8	8
Infrastructure/urban development	67	15	8	11	24	21	15	15
Population, health, and nutrition	64	14	16	22	14	13	19	19
Rehabilitation/reconstruction	8	2	3	4	—	—	—	—
Total	459	100	73	100	114	100	100	100

n.a. = Not available.
— = Zero
* Refers to percentage of NGO-involved projects in all World Bank-approved projects in the region.

cycle, especially in the assessment of potential environmental and social impacts of Bank-financed activities, and increased NGO involvement in ESW. For example, NGOs have played an active role in assisting many governments in preparing participatory poverty assessments and national environmental action plans (NEAPS). These NGO inputs contribute valuable alternative perspectives and provide a vehicle for further government-NGO collaboration.

Throughout the year, the Bank organized a number of workshops with NGOs and government representatives on the Bank's project cycle and the various procedures that take place within each segment of the cycle. These workshops help improve NGOs' understanding of the Bank's activities and encourage their active participation in the Bank's operations. At the same time, a task force, composed of NGO representatives and Bank staff, was established to find ways to identify—and overcome—obstacles to Bank-NGO collaboration at the operational and policy level. On the Bank's side, to assist task managers in better understanding the benefits and challenges of working with NGOs, the Operations Policy Department published a practical guide, "Working with NGOs," which identifies key issues for successful collaboration.

Policy dialogue with NGOs during fiscal 1995 focused on issues related to the ongoing negotiations over the eleventh replenishment of IDA resources (IDA-11). The World Bank-NGO Committee organized three regional NGO meetings—

in Colombia, Ethiopia, and India—at which participants stressed the need for a full IDA replenishment. In April 1995, representatives from a diverse group of NGOs met with IDA Deputies and conveyed their strong support for IDA. They also asked that IDA assistance be more carefully targeted on efforts to reduce poverty and that increased emphasis be placed on removing constraints that prevent the poor from benefiting from economic policy reforms. NGOs also strongly supported the establishment of the Consultative Group to Assist the Poorest, through which the Bank will directly finance NGOs working in the microfinance field *(see Box 2-1)*.

Numerous consultations with NGOs were held throughout the year in preparation for the World Summit on Social Development in Copenhagen and the forthcoming World Women's Conference in Beijing.

The Bank's Economic Development Institute (EDI) is forming a network of trainers, consisting in large part of NGO staff, to work with grassroots entrepreneurs in developing countries. The program enhances their organizations' capacity to train microentrepreneurs, monitor and evaluate projects, and deliver gender and social analysis training. The German-based NGO, Transparency International (TI), has been instrumental in EDI's work on governance issues. TI and EDI are working closely together in South Africa and Uganda to train senior government officials (and inform the general public and journalists) on issues relating to governance.

Environmentally Sustainable Development

The establishment in January 1993 of a central vice presidency for environmentally sustainable development (ESD) explicitly recognized that development could be achieved and sustained only through the integration of economic, social, technical, and ecological dimensions.

In the intervening thirty months, ESD has played a major role in promoting integrative approaches to development. Challenges have included (a) reconciling the objective of long-term sustainability with that of medium- and short-term cost effectiveness and (b) defining sector-by-sector and topic-by-topic Bank policies and practices that are consistent with the objective of sustainable development. In carrying out its mandate, ESD has promoted best practice, provided quality guidance, facilitated innovation, and disseminated information. Awareness that the relationships among sectors are complex stimulated ESD to give greater emphasis during fiscal 1995 to cross-sectoral linkages and institutional partnerships.

Advancing environmentally sustainable development by breaking barriers between disciplines and sectors is a unique challenge. Four dimensions to this challenge are: natural resources and ecosystem management, food security, urbanization, and infrastructure.

Natural resources and ecosystem management. Population growth continues to strain natural resources, natural habitats, and ecosystems.

Food security. Access to, and availability of, food are major problems in many areas of the developing world. Given the limited possibilities for expansion of agricultural areas, increasing food security requires that the efficiency of food production within a sustainable biological and institutional framework be increased. Efficiency increases, in turn, require promoting the development and adoption of new technologies and farming systems that increase productivity, conserve or enhance the resource base, and are accessible to poor producers.

Urbanization. Ninety percent of the population growth that will take place over the next twenty-five years will be generated in urban areas. Rapidly growing cities pose formidable challenges for urban management, investment policy, and institutions. Building on the lessons learned from past successes and failures in urban management, special efforts are needed to mobilize a combination of private and public sector initiatives to provide affordable housing, efficient municipal services, and a healthy urban environment.

Institutional and physical infrastructure. New partnerships between public and private sectors must be developed to provide adequate infrastructure services.

ESD has taken up these four challenges by contributing to well-formulated Bank projects through its support to the six operational regions, by formulating policies and disseminating best practices, training staff, and building partnerships.

Support to operations. ESD provides direct operational support through its (a) participation in "cutting edge" operations in new fields; (b) production and dissemination of best practice papers, which are highly effective in supporting operational work; and (c) review of sector work and best practices prepared elsewhere in the Bank.

ESD, for example, chaired a task force that recommended an operational strategy for Argentina's provinces that promotes a clearer and more efficient match of expenditure responsibilities and revenue authority; greater accountability of public authorities to their constituents; and sustainable financing of investments, including participation of private capital markets. Support was also provided for the formulation and implementation of Bank strategy in areas such as the expanding role of local government and private sector participation in infrastructure and its financing in Brazil, India, Mexico, Peru, South Africa, Uganda, and Uzbekistan.

Assistance was also given in implementing the Water Project for Municipalities in Low-income Areas in Brazil; technical and institutional solutions in the areas of service levels, delivery systems, and targets were tested. Preliminary lessons indicate that water and sanitation infrastructure can be more cost effective if stakeholders are involved at the various stages of the project cycle. The project is financing about $100 million in water supply and sewerage investments in eleven cities in different regions of Brazil.

During the past year a new study analyzed the difficulties encountered in the transition in Ukraine from collective farming to other types of organizations in the wake of that country's land-reform and farm-restructuring program. Several constraints were identified, including insufficient capital, inadequate market supply of farm inputs, and legal and political uncertainty. Given the importance of farm privatization and agricultural reform elsewhere in the former Soviet Union, similar studies will be carried out in other countries.

ESD helped develop an early warning flood-protection component in the Yangtze Water Basin Project in China. It also played an active role in the appraisal of the recently approved Liepaja Environment Project in Latvia and the Klaipeda Environment Project in Lithuania and provided similar support to the Haapsalu and Matsalu Bays Environment Project in Estonia. These three projects, all of which involve pollution control and environmental management, constitute the Bank's first investments in support of the Baltic Sea Environment Program. In the Aral sea region, support is being given in the areas of water-resources management, the environment, and water supply and sanitation.

Reviews of CAS documents are a major priority. In reviewing the documents, ESD strives to help Bank operational staff better understand the linkages between poverty and the environment and to view social, environmental, cultural, and agricultural concerns as more interrelated. Direct contact with country departments is established in the formative stages of preparing the various CAS documents, and specific recommendations on the treatment of environmental, agricultural, and infrastructure issues are made at that time. To maximize its contribution to the formulation of CAS documents, ESD focused its efforts on fourteen countries where its experience and knowledge were deepest and where there was the most potential impact from its contribution.

Policy and best practice. Policy and best practice papers are written with practical application to operations in mind and incorporate lessons learned from previous policy and best practices work. The recently completed Municipal Development Sector Review, for example, examined the Bank's efforts to improve the efficiency and responsiveness of urban service delivery in developing countries. The study concluded that three elements are crucial to the reform of urban service delivery: a clear division of responsibilities among levels of government; revenue reform (which means, generally speaking, that local governments need more financial autonomy to carry out their assigned tasks); and balancing central regulation and local accountability. These conclusions point to the need for the Bank to go beyond a focus on the internal administration of particular cities; it should also emphasize reforms in the relationship between the central government and local jurisdictions as part of institutional reforms designed to improve service delivery.

The Forest Policy Implementation Review reported on changes in analytical work and in lending operations in the three years following the adoption of the Bank's new forest policy. It recommended only minor shifts in emphasis in the Bank's work on forests and forest policy. The review suggested that (a) forest resources have to be better targeted to reduce poverty, (b) forest conservation and utilization have to be reconciled, and (c) policy and institutional reform are needed to set the stage for private investment consistent with poverty reduction and environmental protection.

The paper, "Economywide Policies and the Environment," analyzed the specific links between economywide policies and environmental issues and argued that there are significant payoffs for both the Bank and its borrowers in attempting to better understand the links and act on them. The report concluded that removal of price distortions and promotion of market incentives and other features of adjustment-related reforms generally contribute to both economic and environmental gains.

"National Environmental Strategies and Action Plans: Key Elements and Best Practice," distributed to the Bank's executive directors in April 1995, was written to assist governments in preparing, revising, and updating their NEAPs by suggesting a variety of analytical methods and best practices. This paper reflected international consultation involving country representatives and NGOs in London in November 1994.

By the end of fiscal 1995, fifty-seven active IDA borrowers had completed NEAPs or equivalent documents, and NEAPs for sixteen IBRD borrowers had either been completed or were in advanced stages of preparation. NEAPs provide a basis for the Bank's dialogue with borrowers on environmental issues, describe a country's major environmental concerns and problems, and formulate policies and actions to address whatever problems are identified. The borrower is responsible for preparing and implementing its NEAP.

The latest annual report on the environment—published in early fiscal 1996—provides a "green accounting" of the Bank's lending portfolio in the three years following the United Nations Conference on Environment and Development, held in Rio de Janeiro in June 1992. It documents the lessons learned in implementing the rapidly growing portfolio of environmental loans and the progress being made in assuring that the Bank's lending is environmentally sustainable. Almost 10 percent—or some $6.5 billion—of the Bank's cumulative portfolio during that period has been devoted to projects with environmental objectives.

As an agency that finances infrastructure projects and promotes market-based economic development, the Bank has been a target of criticism from a number of environmental groups. The Bank listens to such criticism and, over the past few years, has built up strong interactions with environmental specialists and activists. Consultations are now mandatory for all environmental assessments, and the Bank has benefited from inputs from qualified environmental groups during the preparation of most of its policy papers. The vice president, ESD, has consulted with environmental NGOs on a bimonthly basis for the past two years.

ESD also expanded its focus on social aspects of development by helping to mainstream attention to social concerns and participatory approaches to development, providing technical support on social issues, and exploring additional areas of social analysis. One significant development in this area was the publication of the "World Bank Sourcebook on Participation." The sourcebook was written to help mainstream participatory approaches into Bank

work; as such, its primary audience is Bank task managers and other Bank staff.

The sourcebook, which draws on the experience, talent, and contributions of more than 200 Bank staff, shares the experiences of selected Bank task managers who have used participatory approaches in Bank operations. It explores what it means to use participatory processes to plan and decide upon implementable and sustainable activities and attempts to answer questions task managers have about using participatory planning and decisionmaking. Copies of the sourcebook were presented to more than 750 development practitioners in Bangladesh, Denmark, Germany, India, Italy, the Philippines, and the United Kingdom.

Other areas of the fiscal 1995 work program included (a) completion of a review of integrated approaches to river-basin planning, development, and management and (b) preparation of "Energy Use in the Transport Sector," which deals with the concept of energy intensity of transport modes and the role energy policies play in affecting demand for transport.

Progress was also made in incorporating more fully the environmental costs and benefits in the economic analysis of projects through (a) development of a training program, (b) mainstreaming environmental externalities and economywide dimensions into a selected number of projects that were in the early stages of the project cycle, (c) collaborating with other Bank units in writing or revising operational directives that deal with environmental matters, and (d) publication of "Monitoring Environmental Progress," a data-rich publication that aims to promote a participatory process in determining how indicators of environmentally sustainable development are compiled and used.

Global Environment Facility. The Global Environment Facility (GEF) is a financial mechanism that provides grant and concessional funds to developing countries for projects and activities that aim to protect the global environment and thereby promote environmentally sound and sustainable development. GEF resources are available for projects and other activities that address climate change, biological diversity, international waters, and depletion of the ozone layer. Activities addressing land degradation, primarily desertification and deforestation, as they relate to the four focal areas, are also eligible for funding.

The GEF was established in 1991 as a pilot program. In March 1994, seventy-three participating governments ("participants") concluded negotiations to restructure the facility and replenish its Core Fund with more than $2 billion for a three-year period. The governance structure of the GEF consists of a council, assembly, and an independent secretariat headed by a chief executive officer.

The Bank has three principal roles in the GEF: It (a) is the trustee of the GEF Trust Fund; (b) acts as an implementing agency; and (c) provides administrative support for the GEF secretariat.

As trustee, the Bank is expected to mobilize resources for the fund, manage fund financial resources, maintain appropriate financial records and accounts, provide for their audit, and monitor the application of budgetary and project funds. As one of three implementing agencies (the Bank, the United Nations Development Programme (UNDP), and the United Nations Environment Programme (UNEP)), the Bank is expected to "draw upon its investment experience in eligible countries to promote investment opportunities and to mobilize private sector resources that are consistent with GEF objectives and national sustainable development strategies."

One of the objectives of the Bank in meeting its responsibilities as implementing agency is streamlining and mainstreaming the project cycle of Bank-implemented GEF projects with regular Bank project processing. Efforts were made during the year toward achieving this objective. First, the Bank's executive board is now reviewing and approving Bank-implemented GEF projects in the same manner as it does Bank projects. Second, GEF processing procedures are now aligned closely with Bank investment-processing procedures. In addition, operational directives have been adjusted to ensure that global environmental externalities are identified and quantified (wherever feasible) and that global environmental concerns are addressed in CASs (wherever appropriate). To this end, a start has been made on a longer-term program to integrate the global environment dimension with the Bank's sector work. Third, Bank-implemented GEF operations will be equally subject to the Bank's annual portfolio-performance review.

Through the end of fiscal 1995, 148 projects worth $869 million had been endorsed by the GEF participants and the new council. Of this total, sixty-three projects for $558 million were allocated for World Bank GEF investment projects. The allocation of the Bank's GEF project resources, by focal area, is 50 percent for biodiversity, 30 percent for climate change, 12 percent for international waters, 7 percent for the reduction of ozone-depleting substances, and 1 percent for multiple thematic areas.

Strengthening agricultural research. During fiscal 1995, the Consultative Group on International Agricultural Research (CGIAR) vigorously pursued its program of renewal and rededication that had been launched at its 1994 mid term meeting in New Delhi. The program seeks to clarify the vision of the CGIAR, reform its research agenda, reform its governance and operations, and secure stable financial support for its mission.

At a ministerial-level meeting of CGIAR members, held in Lucerne, Switzerland, on February 9–10, 1995, new orientation, governance, and financing arrangements for the CGIAR were endorsed. The CGIAR is an informal association of forty-three governments, international organizations, and private foundations supporting an international research system for agriculture, forestry, fisheries, and natural resource management in developing countries. It is jointly sponsored by the Bank, the UNDP, and the Food and Agriculture Organization of the UN (FAO). During the past year, UNEP was invited to become a fourth sponsoring member.

Côte d'Ivoire, Egypt, Iran, and Kenya joined the CGIAR at the Lucerne meeting. With Colombia, which joined a few months earlier, total developing country membership in the group is now fourteen. Members hailed the broadening membership as an important step towards equitable North-South ownership of the research system. The delegates also supported efforts to render the system more open and to strengthen its links to national research systems in both developed and developing countries. Global and regional fora of farmers' groups, universities, NGOs, and other groups will be held to ensure that the system's research agenda reflects the needs of its member countries.

A program launched in mid 1994 under the Bank's leadership to stabilize the CGIAR's finances in both 1994 and 1995 attracted additional donor support, thereby ensuring full funding for the group's core research agenda—approximately $270 million in each of the two years.

Training, workshops, and seminars. Staff training plays an important role in ESD's delivery of services to support Bank activities. Sixty-nine separate training courses were conducted during the year, covering the full range of ESD activities. Environment-related courses included economic analysis of environmental valuation, participation and social assessment, economywide policies and the environment, and environmental management and planning. Agricultural seminars in areas such as water resources, agricultural and rural development, food production and integrated pest management, and rural finance were organized. Infrastructure-related training included courses on private sector participation, enabling strategies for housing policies, urban services delivery, and municipal management.

Building partnerships. Efforts to build partnerships with others, both inside and outside the Bank, were supported by a wide range of activities during the past year, including participation in the Cairo Conference on Water Resources (November 1994), organization of the Second Annual Environmentally Sustainable Development Conference (September 1994), and frequent instances of technical cooperation with other donor agencies and governments. Agricultural partnerships were firmed up by strengthening links with the UNDP, the FAO, the International Fund for Agricultural Development, the agricultural departments of regional development banks, international agricultural research centers, and key NGOs.

Speakers at the Second Annual ESD Conference (whose theme was the "Human Face of

the Urban Environment") called for new approaches to meet today's urban challenges of economic development, poverty reduction, and environmental protection.

The 900 environmentalists, development practitioners, and policymakers attending the three-day conference heard the late World Bank president Lewis Preston confirm the institution's dedication to reducing urban poverty, which is an essential precondition for reducing urban environmental degradation.

Private Sector Development

Developing countries increasingly recognize the critical role of the private sector in development and the need to create the conditions for business to prosper. They are transforming their economies from state-dominated to competition-oriented markets. This transformation includes cutting out public sector investment better suited to the private sector and stepping up financial sector reform. And they are doing more to facilitate private funding of infrastructure projects; such investment is crucial for promoting growth and reducing poverty. All this requires a more favorable and competitive business environment, based on thorough legal, regulatory, and institutional reforms.

The Bank Group is unique in its capacity to work with developing country governments and the private sector to promote investment, jobs, growth, and so, to reduce poverty. It has the credibility to act as an honest broker between government and business. Its global reach enables it to gather and disseminate cross-country experience. It has access to the highest levels of government almost anywhere. And its advice is frequently backed by substantial investment—through its readiness to play a catalytic role, it helps attract investment from a variety of official and private sources to countries and projects that otherwise would be regarded as too risky.

In fiscal 1995, the Bank Group's efforts in private sector development were focused on helping countries create a more favorable environment for private business, catalyzing funding for private enterprises (especially in support of long-term investments in infrastructure), as well as directly supporting private sector development and helping developing countries to reform and strengthen their financial sectors.[9] Specifically, privatization remained a central focus of the Group's assistance, as did banking reform. At the same time, the Bank worked with governments, local institutions, and communities (as well as with the private sector) to forge partnerships to sustain reforms and manage economic development more effectively. The year also saw extensive Bank Group involvement in helping some Latin American countries deal with immediate crises in their banking sectors.

The Bank Group supports about $25 billion of private-sector finance a year, or 10 percent of all investment by private enterprise in developing countries. The Bank's financial intermediation loans of close to $2 billion a year support $4 billion in private investment. The IFC—through its loans, equity investments, and credit lines, provides $2.9 billion a year, and with a much bigger multiplier of about 6 to 1, supports roughly $18 billion worth of investment. MIGA's guarantees are currently running at more than $600 million a year, supporting about $2.5 billion in private sector investments. In addition, World Bank adjustment loans and credits of $5.3 billion help create a competitive and attractive business climate and promote financial sector reform.

Catalyzing infrastructure finance: World Bank guarantees. Developing countries currently spend an estimated $200 billion a year on infrastructure—a figure beyond the means of governments and multilateral agencies. East Asia alone may have to spend more than $1 trillion on infrastructure between now and the end of the decade. Such large-scale, long-term funding requires increasing reliance on private developers, operators, and financiers. Through various measures and instruments, such as guarantees, the World Bank helps governments and entrepreneurs tap international and local capital markets for long-term infrastructure funding.

9. The Bank Group's private sector development activities are carried out in the three major institutions of the Group—the World Bank, the IFC, and MIGA. Private sector development work is a major component of the work programs of many World Bank units—notably, the Finance and Private Sector Development vice presidency, the Cofinancing and Financial Advisory Services vice presidency, the Development Economics and Chief Economist vice presidency, and the six operational regions.

BOX 2-2. INTO THE GUARANTEE MAINSTREAM

The Bank's guiding principle in providing guarantees is to cover the minimum risk possible to make a project financeable. To this end, mainstreaming established two types of guarantees—the partial risk guarantee and the partial credit guarantee.

Partial risk guarantees *are used mainly for limited recourse project finance, where lenders attach more importance to the revenues and assets of a project that the sponsor's credit. Most build, own, and operate (BOO) projects are financed under these arrangements. In these cases, guarantees can cover risks associated with government contractual commitments to a project, for example, the stability of the regulatory regime, tariff formulas, and risk of nonpayment by a publicly owned utility.*

Partial credit guarantees *allocate risks differently. The World Bank guarantees repayment, but only for a part of the term of the financing. The purpose is to improve borrowing terms through a length-*

ening of maturity, and hence, the guarantees generally apply to later repayments. They can also apply to a limited number of interest payments, or a combination of both.

Government counterguarantees are required from the host government when the Bank provides its guarantees. Though the counterguarantee adds an additional layer of processing, it reinforces the government's commitment to the project. The counterguarantee indemnifies the Bank for any payment it makes under its guarantee.

Guarantees carry fees. The standby fee, covering the period of the guarantee when it is not callable, is 25 basis points yearly on the outstanding amount guaranteed. When the guarantee is callable, the fee is set between 40 and 100 basis points, depending on the risk coverage. All fees above 25 basis points are paid to the government, so that the net cost for a Bank loan or guarantee is the same.

The ability of entrepreneurs to obtain debt financing is often constrained by lenders' concerns over the risks to project cash flow necessary to service the debt. These concerns are also linked to regulatory and legal issues, such as setting tariffs, the convertibility of revenues to service foreign currency debt, and the contractual performance of public sector utilities or energy suppliers. Much of the Bank's policy and sector work has thus aimed at improving the business environment and reducing these risks, but until reforms take root, private financial markets are reluctant to provide sufficient credit without official and multilateral guarantees. For that reason the Bank moved in fiscal 1995 to mainstream its guarantee operations.

The World Bank's guarantee instrument was revitalized and amended to catalyze the flow of private capital to infrastructure projects when the executive directors approved a proposal, "Mainstreaming of Guarantees as an Operational Tool of the World Bank." The new guarantee initiative replaces the Expanded Cofinancing Operations (ECO) Program by broadening country eligibility to any Bank borrower, modifying fees, and simplifying procedures. Though large pools of equity capital are potentially available for investment in private sector infrastructure projects, debt financing has been constrained because private lenders are unwilling to assume certain sovereign risks. A World Bank partial risk guarantee helps address this constraint by protecting lenders from these risks *(see Box 2-2)*.

Bank partial credit guarantees can also enhance borrowing terms, as well as increase flexibility in terms of currencies and markets. In China, for instance, partial credit guarantees for the public sector Yangzhou and Zhejiang power projects drew in private financing with much longer maturities and lower costs than would have been possible without the guarantee. Other completed operations include a partial risk guarantee for Pakistan's Hub Power Project, one of the largest private sector projects in the developing world; a partial credit guarantee for the Leyte-Luzon Power Project in the Philippines; and a contingent loan with characteristics of a guarantee for the financing of the private

sector Rockfort Power Project in Jamaica, with MIGA providing political risk insurance. Several guarantees are currently in the pipeline, covering all regions. And from an initial focus on power projects, sector coverage of guarantees has expanded to include water and toll road projects. Most of those in the pipeline cover private sector projects.

As part of the mainstreaming effort, an information and education campaign was launched. A brochure on Bank guarantees was distributed widely, and seminars were held outside and inside the Bank. Country missions explained the potential of guarantees to policymakers and representatives of both public and private sectors. An internal training program on project finance techniques and Bank guarantees was also set up.

Financial sector reform and innovative lending for private sector development. To meet the growing range of demands for support of private sector investment, the Bank continued in fiscal 1995 to deliver innovative operations to support local financial institutions and markets. Financial sector adjustment loans totaled $1.2 billion, and financial intermediation loans amounted to $1.8 billion. The adjustment loans help create a competitive financial sector, and the intermediation loans feed it. Such operations provide support to a wide range of financial intermediaries strong enough to access growing private capital.

There has been a steady change in the complexity of the Bank's financial sector loans. A few years ago, most addressed policy issues, such as interest rate and credit policy. Today, the issues are more institutional, such as strengthening banking supervision, regulations, and accounting.

This shift is well illustrated by the banking components in the sequence of financial sector operations in Mexico. The $500 million Financial Sector Adjustment loan, approved in June 1989, focused mainly on interest-rate policy, while the $23.6 million Financial Sector Technical Assistance Project, approved in fiscal 1995, supported the improvement of off-site supervision. Meanwhile, the $1,000 million Financial Sector Restructuring Program, approved in June 1995, involves the definition of comprehensive bank-failure resolution mechanisms and is much more detailed in specifying how the accounting, auditing, and supervision functions are to be upgraded.

The Bank is also moving into new areas—payments systems and capital markets, for instance. Current and future operations—in China, Mauritius, Russia, and Viet Nam—include financial and technical assistance to help modernize payments systems to reduce delays and risks in transferring funds and to link these systems to those used for clearing and settling securities transactions.

Innovative operations in support of local financial institutions and markets were also approved. The hallmark of these operations is the provision of support to a wide range of financial intermediaries strong enough to access growing private capital—except where systemic risks cannot easily be overcome. In India, highly rated banks are now authorized to take foreign currency deposits from Indian sources. With assurance from a Bank-funded backstop facility that rollover funding can be obtained even during times of market distress, those domestic banks can extend foreign currency credits to exporters whose growth demands such investment.

In Moldolva, enterprises can now obtain pre-export finance from private financial intermediaries and trading companies with the benefit of a Bank-financed local guarantee unit that provides insurance against changes in export regulations and other specified political events.

Much of the future growth (and poverty reduction) in low-income developing countries will be generated by small businesses that now have little or no access to financing. The Bank, therefore, has started to work with institutions that have a track record in lending to rural and urban microenterprises and whose operations are sustainable, replicable, and based on strong resource mobilization.

Microfinance programs that succeed in reaching large numbers of poor and female entrepreneurs have four characteristics:
- their financial services are tailored to the needs of poor entrepreneurs;
- their operations are streamlined to reduce unit costs;
- their clients are strongly motivated to repay their loans through the use of peer group guarantees and other incentives; and
- their interest rates and fees reflect the full cost of service delivery.

The Bank allocated (in fiscal 1994) $2 million from IBRD net income to the Grameen Bank of Bangladesh—whose highly successful program lends primarily to poor women—to assist similar credit programs in other countries. It is also in the process of establishing a microfinance program under the aegis of the Consultative Group to Assist the Poorest under which up to $30 million of IBRD income transfers will be made available to successful microfinance programs during the next two to three years.

Making the business environment attractive. In itself, private ownership is not enough. It is real competition among private owners that creates benefits for all. That requires mobility of capital, labor, and knowledge, and increasingly, access to technology. Governments can foster this with simple, transparent, and uniformly applied incentives, laws, and regulations—so-called second-generation reforms. In fiscal 1995, Bank support for these reforms continued broadly in four areas:
- establishing a legal environment that defines and enforces property rights and allows property to be freely traded;
- reforming public institutions so that rules for businesses are administered in a predictable and open way and at least cost;
- reforming regulatory regimes so that product, capital, and labor markets are better aligned with the needs of a competitive, outward-oriented economy; and
- improving the efficiency and customer responsiveness of various service providers (utility companies, for example).

In Senegal the $40 million Private Sector Adjustment and Competitiveness Credit has been designed to improve the investment climate and facilitate and enhance the private sector supply response to a new, favorable exchange rate through a liberalized and more competitive en-

BOX 2-3. FIAS: FOSTERING FOREIGN FUNDING

The Foreign Investment Advisory Service (FIAS) advises governments that want to attract more and better foreign direct investment. The advice is on policies, programs, and institutions that governments use to regulate their relationships with private direct investors. In its advice, FIAS tries both to promote investor-friendly environments and the development interests of the host country.

Over the years, FIAS has seen its advice adopted in most of the eighty-five countries where it has worked. During the year just completed, this advice included ways for The Gambia to restructure its foreign investment policies, a strategy for Zimbabwe's investment-promotion agency, suggestions for structuring investment-promotion agencies in Bolivia and Peru, and an evaluation of Kazakhstan's foreign investment laws. New initiatives included advice on policies governing foreign investment in China's infra-

structure sectors, policies to promote linkages between foreign investors and domestic firms in Indonesia and the Philippines, and a diagnosis of both policy and institutional constraints to foreign direct investment in the West Bank and Gaza. Altogether, FIAS completed twenty-six advisory projects during the year.

The services of FIAS are likely to continue to be in great demand. An increasing number of developing countries want to tap the booming pool of international direct investment flows. As countries make basic improvements in their investment laws and institutions, they find that more complex issues and new opportunities call for continuing policy and institutional changes. FIAS has been able to help with both the basic, as well as with the more complex, policy and institutional issues.

vironment, improved conditions for increased export opportunities, and increased competitiveness through lower costs of production and of maritime transport. And in Bolivia, the Bank supported regulatory reforms that eased the way for private entry into the infrastructure sector.

Private sector assessments for thirty-four countries were either carried out or were in progress by the end of fiscal 1995. These assessments describe the structure of the private sector in a country, identify constraints to its development, and suggest economically efficient ways of overcoming hurdles. In several cases (in Colombia, Côte d'Ivoire, Egypt, Hungary, Morocco, the Philippines, and Sri Lanka), assessment findings have been systematically discussed with the governments and a variety of private sector participants in order to foster a self-sustaining dialogue between the two.

Complementing the Bank's work in private sector development, the Foreign Investment Advisory Service (FIAS), run jointly by the Bank and the IFC, continued to help developing countries shape policies and institutions conducive to foreign direct investment *(see Box 2-3).*

Enterprise reform and privatization. More than twenty of the Bank's private sector development loans approved in fiscal 1995 had

privatization as a key component, as governments seek to strengthen market forces, encourage investment, and ease budget deficits. In the past decade, the value of medium-sized and large enterprises privatized around the world exceeded $300 billion. In Russia alone, more than 15,000 businesses, employing 15 million workers, have been transferred into private hands, creating 40 million shareholders. Today, more than half the output of the Czech Republic, Hungary, and Poland is produced by private businesses. China's town and village enterprises (which are essentially private) have shown that small and medium-sized firms can be dynamic forces for economic growth.

In Bolivia, the Regulatory Reform and Capitalization Technical Assistance Project, approved in fiscal 1995, and a Capital Adjustment Credit, currently under preparation, will help the government to privatize firms in six major sectors—telecommunications, electricity, oil and gas, railways, aviation, and mining—through a unique process of capitalization. Shares worth about $2 billion are being distributed to pension accounts for all Bolivian adults, stimulating savings and the savings ethic. Another $2 billion of new funds are available for investment by the privatized Bolivian companies—allowing them to leverage $6 billion or so of debt, if they need it. Lessons from these and other groundbreaking operations, as well as from the emerging problems of postprivatization assistance, are being rapidly disseminated and incorporated into the design of future operations.

The Bank was also active in providing direct technical assistance to help governments organize and implement their privatization plans. For larger activities requiring a sustained effort, such assistance was carried out by large teams with substantial field presence, focusing on detailed design and implementation. The development of this new type of service marks an effort to respond more flexibly and promptly to government needs and is provided as a complement to Bank operations and the overall Bank–government dialogue. In some of the more complex cases, budgetary funds were leveraged with cofinancing grants of various types.

Dissemination and partnerships. During fiscal 1995, a study was completed on the special problems of private sector development and privatization—and on measures that might be taken to address them—in lower-income countries. The report, "Private Sector Development in IDA Countries," concluded that the central challenge was for government to cut risk and minimize transaction costs and instill confidence in the private sector. Its recommendations: Cut the debilitating losses of the state enterprise sector, equip the banking sector to function effectively and provide needed financing to deserving enterprises, and reduce barriers to competition and undertake regulatory reform.

As part of the supervision of a privatization-assistance loan to Russia, a Bank investigation of the privatization process was published in fiscal 1995.[10] The study concluded that Russia's mass privatization program was successful in rapidly transferring ownership but that there was an acute need for other reforms—in the areas of law, land, corporate governance, shareholder protection, creditor rights, and the social safety net. All of these are being tackled in one way or another, but most urgent is the development of capital and securities markets.

Private sector development and privatization mean little unless there is widespread support for reform within a country. The Bank has thus been supporting private–public partnerships with a view to building consensus on reforms and changing attitudes towards entrepreneurship and profit-making. Private–public partnerships are also being used to identify constraints to reform and to generate solutions. In Egypt, for example, local business associations and other groups participated in discussions to develop consensus within the country on specific reforms.

In fiscal 1995, the Bank intensified its efforts to establish networks and close relationships with a wide variety of partners involved in private sector development, especially in developing local capabilities and fostering entrepreneurship. The $70 million Private Sector Adjustment Credit in Ghana is helping the government develop and use local accounting and investment-banking expertise in privatizations. In Congo, staff from the Bank's Private Sector Development Department are providing training and advice to the newly formed Privatization Committee on how to build consensus on privatization, prepare privatization packages, and evaluate tender offers. The Bank is also encouraging learning-by-doing and is helping local firms gain access to international expertise. Thus, in Kazakhstan, it is funding a pilot project that supports study-tour training so that enterprise managers can learn from the experiences of successful firms in the United States and elsewhere.

Over the years, the role of the Bank in infrastructure has shifted from one that exclusively involved financing to one that also encourages reform, private provision, and private investment. This is especially true for telecommunications, the sector moving fastest from public ownership to private provision and investment. As Bank lending to the sector has

10. Liberman, Ira, and John Nellis, eds. 1995. *Russia: Creating Private Enterprises and Efficient Markets.* Studies of Economies in Transformation Series, Number 15. Washington, D.C.: World Bank.

fallen off, there has been a large increase in nonlending advisory and other services. In addition, there has been a commensurate increase in the Bank's lending for informatics, which totaled on the order of $1 billion in fiscal 1995. Many Bank projects today have an informatics component.

Increasingly, private sector development calls for closer cooperation with outside agencies. In energy, for instance, a framework memorandum of understanding was reached between the Bank and the United States-based Electric Power Research Institute to cooperate in areas such as clean power technology and renewable energy. Similar memoranda were agreed to with the International Energy Administration on energy efficiency and conservation and with the U.S. Renewable Energy Laboratory. Links with NGOs continued to be strengthened: Meetings in London, the Hague, and Washington covered energy and the environment and rural and renewable energy.

In industry and mining, the Bank cosponsored—with the United Nations Conference on Trade and Development, the International Council on Metals and the Environment, and UNEP—an international conference on Development, Mining, and the Environment. The conference provided a forum for nearly 300 participants from a broad range of stakeholders to share ideas, perspectives, experiences, and solutions for sustainable mining sector development. The conference proceedings and results were summarized on video for wide distribution.

Links are being forged with Keidanren, the Japanese industrial association. Links of this type, which are also being developed elsewhere in the world, will help the Bank reach a broader group of business leaders, managers, and professionals and so inform them about the Bank Group's involvement in private sector development. Possible joint activities include thematic seminars with broad international coverage and country-focused discussions on private investment issues.

The Bank has also teamed up with the U.S. National Research Council. The first fruits of this partnership came out of a November 1994 symposium, "Marshalling Technology for Development," which highlighted the leapfrogging opportunities and pitfalls of the technology revolution for developing countries. The symposium provided a unique opportunity for the council and the Bank to share their complementary expertise in technology and development. A similar partnership is being planned with European technology experts, with the help of the European Union.

The Bank itself has begun to use technology more strategically in disseminating private sector development best practices—for example, through a recent teleconference on competitiveness policy, which reached several thousand participants in El Salvador, India, Mozambique, and Senegal.

Commitments

World Bank commitments (IBRD and IDA combined) amounted to $22,522 million in fiscal 1995, an increase of $1,686 million (8 percent) over fiscal 1994's total *(see Table 3-1)*. Commitments by the IBRD were $16,853 million, while IDA commitments totaled $5,669 million equivalent (SDR3,829 million).

The biggest increase in commitments was in the Latin America and the Caribbean region, where fifty-two projects were approved for a total of $6.1 billion. Comparable figures for the previous year were forty-eight projects for $4.7 billion. Lending volume also increased greatly in the Europe and Central Asia region: Fifty-eight projects, totaling $4.5 billion, were approved—a $772 million increase over the previous year.

Adjustment lending amounted to 24 percent of Bank commitments, up from the previous year's 12 percent. The fiscal 1995 adjustment totals include $1,395 million in rehabilitation-import loans and $375 million in debt-reduction loans. If these amounts had been excluded, adjustment lending would have been 16 percent of the total. Adjustment lending was particularly low in fiscal 1994, because country conditions caused delays in adjustment operations in the Europe and Central Asia region.

The largest borrower of IBRD funds was Mexico ($2,387 million for six projects), followed by China ($2,370 million for thirteen projects, including five "blend" projects) and Russia ($1,741 million for nine projects). The three largest borrowers of IDA credits were India ($945 million for six projects, plus one "blend" project), followed by China ($630 million for three projects, plus five "blend" projects) and Viet Nam ($415 million for three projects).

TABLE 3-1. TRENDS IN IBRD AND IDA LENDING, FISCAL YEARS 1993–95

(amounts in millions of US dollars; fiscal years)

Sector	1993			1994			1995		
	IBRD	IDA	Total	IBRD	IDA	Total	IBRD	IDA	Total
Agriculture	1,918.8	1,347.9	3,266.7	2,233.3	1,674.0	3,907.3	1,153.9	1,495.4	2,649.3
Education	968.0	1,038.2	2,006.2	1,499.9	658.1	2,158.0	1,280.6	816.2	2,096.8
Energy									
Oil, gas, and coal	939.8	33.1	972.9	1,202.1	186.2	1,388.3	520.5	141.6	662.1
Power	2,093.0	520.0	2,613.0	1,368.5	—	1,368.5	1,743.5	439.0	2,182.5
Environment	11.5	54.8	66.3	640.5	17.3	657.8	444.1	40.5	484.6
Financial sector	637.0	318.1	955.1	1,093.5	411.1	1,504.6	2,435.4	129.3	2,564.7
Industry	250.0	83.5	333.5	422.7	272.2	694.9	175.0	56.2	231.2
Mining and other extractive	250.0	12.0	262.0	14.0	—	14.0	—	24.8	24.8
Multisector	2,980.0	640.2	3,620.2	606.3	815.9	1,422.2	2,295.0	870.5	3,165.5
Population, health, and nutrition	706.8	1,104.8	1,811.6	366.0	519.7	885.7	451.3	711.0	1,162.3
Public sector management	765.0	230.5	995.5	370.6	322.6	693.2	1,411.2	294.4	1,705.6
Social sector	—	—	—	130.0	20.6	150.6	596.5	51.0	647.5
Telecommunications	264.0	89.1	353.1	405.0	18.0	423.0	325.0	—	325.0
Tourism	130.0	—	130.0	20.0	—	20.0	—	—	—
Transportation	3,133.1	712.6	3,845.7	2,162.5	1,130.8	3,293.3	2,026.8	104.1	2,130.9
Urban development	1,139.0	171.2	1,310.2	837.0	442.4	1,279.4	1,263.5	186.0	1,449.5
Water supply and sewerage	758.5	395.4	1,153.9	872.0	103.2	975.2	730.3	309.2	1,039.5
Total	16,944.5	6,751.4	23,695.9	14,243.9	6,592.1	20,836.0	16,852.6	5,669.2	22,521.8

One project, for $20 million, in the West Bank and Gaza was approved. The project, financed by the $50 million Trust Fund for Gaza, is financing the immediate needs of the education and health sectors and addresses institutional development objectives in the two sectors.

Disbursements

Gross disbursements by the IBRD to countries totaled $12,672 million, an increase of 21 percent over fiscal 1994's $10,447 million amount. Disbursement performance was higher than originally expected in the Europe and Central Asia region (mostly due to adjustment operations) and in the Latin America and the Caribbean and East Asia and Pacific regions, where, although the adjustment portfolio is declining, disbursements for investment projects are accelerating. IDA disbursements amounted to $5,703 million, up $171 million from the previous year. The increase was particularly noteworthy in the South Asia region.

Disbursements, by source of supply. Projects financed by the World Bank require procurement from foreign and local sources to achieve

project goals. Disbursements are made primarily to cover specific costs for foreign procurement and some local expenditures.

The procurement rules and procedures to be followed in the execution of each project depends on individual circumstances. Three considerations generally guide the Bank's requirements: the need for economy and efficiency in the execution of a project; the Bank's interest, as a cooperative institution, in giving all eligible bidders from developing countries and developed countries an opportunity to compete in providing goods and works financed by the Bank; and the Bank's interest, as a development institution, in encouraging the development of local contractors and manufacturers in borrowing countries. In most cases, international competitive bidding is the most efficient method of procurement. The Bank prescribes conditions under which preferences may be given to domestic or regional manufacturers and, where appropriate, to domestic contractors.

Table 3-2 shows consolidated foreign and local disbursements for the IBRD and IDA through the end of fiscal 1990 and for the period fiscal

TABLE 3-2. IBRD AND IDA FOREIGN AND LOCAL DISBURSEMENTS, BY SOURCE OF SUPPLY

(amounts in millions of US dollars)

Period	IBRD and IDA							
	Foreign[a]		Local		Net advance disbursements[b]		Total amount
	Amount	%	Amount	%	Amount	%	amount
Cumulative to June 30, 1990	94,556	58	64,317	39	4,408	3	163,282
Fiscal 1991	8,877	57	6,606	42	184	1	15,667
Fiscal 1992	9,038	55	6,807	42	537	3	16,381
Fiscal 1993	9,813	56	7,887	45	-325	-2	17,375
Fiscal 1994	9,010	56	7,442	47	-473	-3	15,979
Fiscal 1995	9,094	51	8,724	49	-97	†	17,720
Cumulative to June 30, 1995	140,388	57	101,783	41	4,233	2	246,404

† *Less than 0.05 percent.*
NOTE: *Details may not add to totals because of rounding.*
a. *Amounts exclude debt-reduction disbursements of $2,160 million in FY90, $313 million in FY91, $50 million in FY92, $515 million in FY93, and $655 million in FY95.*
b. *Net advance disbursements are advances made to special accounts net of amounts recovered (amounts for which the Bank has applied evidence of expenditures to recovery of the outstanding advance).*

TABLE 3-3. IBRD AND IDA FOREIGN DISBURSEMENTS, BY SOURCE OF SUPPLY

(amounts in millions of US dollars)

| | IBRD | | | | | IDA | | | | |
| | OECD | | Non-OECD | | Total | OECD | | Non-OECD | | Total |
Period	Amount	%	Amount	%	amount	Amount	%	Amount	%	amount
Cumulative to June 30, 1990	61,053	86	9,939	14	70,992	18,979	81	4,585	19	23,564
Fiscal 1991	5,018	81	1,165	19	6,183	1,804	67	889	33	2,694
Fiscal 1992	5,116	76	1,585	24	6,701	1,541	66	796	34	2,337
Fiscal 1993	5,104	73	1,873	27	6,976	1,786	63	1,050	37	2,837
Fiscal 1994	3,995	73	1,462	27	5,457	2,209	62	1,344	38	3,553
Fiscal 1995	4,584	78	1,312	22	5,896	1,987	62	1,210	38	3,197
Cumulative to June 30, 1995	84,870	83	17,336	17	102,206	28,306	74	9,875	26	38,181

NOTE: *Disbursements for debt reduction, and net advance disbursements are excluded. Details may not add to totals because of rounding. For consistency of comparison, Mexico is included as an OECD country for all periods covered by this table. Mexico became an OECD member in May 1994.*

1991 through fiscal 1995. Advance disbursements consist of payments made into special accounts of borrowers, from which funds are paid to specific suppliers as expenditures are incurred. Because balances in these accounts cannot be attributed to any specific supplying country until expenditures have been reported to the Bank, these are shown as a separate category.

Table 3-3 provides details for foreign disbursements by OECD and non-OECD countries for the IBRD and IDA separately.

Appendix 7 shows disbursements made in fiscal 1995 by the IBRD and IDA for local procurement by current borrowing countries and disbursements made for goods, works, and services procured from them by other Bank borrowers (foreign procurement) for projects funded by the Bank.

Appendix 8 shows the amounts disbursed from the IBRD and IDA separately for foreign procurement of goods, works, and services from selected member countries in fiscal 1995 and cumulatively through fiscal 1995.

Appendix 9 shows the proportion of foreign disbursements from the IBRD and IDA for specific categories of goods and services provided by selected member countries in fiscal 1995.

Appendix 10 provides a summary listing of the amounts paid to OECD and non-OECD country suppliers in each fiscal year from 1993 to 1995 under investment projects. Amounts disbursed are compared with respect to significant categories of goods procured from foreign suppliers. The extent to which OECD and non-OECD countries participated in supplying these major categories of goods in each of the past three fiscal years is also compared.

In all these tables and appendixes, IBRD figures exclude disbursements for loans to the IFC and "B" loans. IDA figures include Special Fund and Special Facility for sub-Saharan Africa credits. Disbursements for Project Preparation Facility advances are excluded for both the IBRD and IDA.

Technical Assistance

Technical assistance is a vital ingredient in the transfer of technology and build-up of capacity among the Bank's borrowing member countries. Most technical assistance is provided through the Bank's lending operations; however, a significant volume is generated through other special programs, financed mainly by grants and trust funds.

Loan-financed technical assistance in calendar year 1994 amounted to $2.6 billion. Of this amount, $2.2 billion funded components, while $400 million was accounted for by nineteen freestanding projects.

Fifty-two percent of technical assistance components were intended for capacity building (including training). The remainder went for implementation support (41 percent) and policy support (7 percent).

The Latin America and the Caribbean region used the most technical assistance ($695 million), followed by East Asia and Pacific ($591 million) and Europe and Central Asia ($246 million).

Indonesia was the single largest user of technical assistance ($300 million), followed by Mexico ($293 million) and Russia ($213 million).

The Bank's Project Preparation Facility provides advance funding to borrowers to prepare projects that may be financed by the Bank. In 1994, the Bank made 118 advances under the facility for a total of $80 million. Fifty-eight percent of the advances, accounting for 45 percent of the total volume, went to the Africa region.

In December 1994, the executive directors agreed to raise the facility's commitment authority from $220 million to $250 million.

The Institutional Development Fund provides grants to member countries to undertake innovative actions in institutional development/ capacity building. In 1994, the Bank awarded ninety such grants, amounting to $22.8 million, to fifty-four countries.

Technical assistance "quality at entry." During the past year, the Bank undertook an assessment of the quality at entry of those technical assistance operations that had been approved in fiscal 1994.

The assessment was mostly positive, although shortcomings were also noted.

Significant improvement was found in incorporating lessons of experience from completed (and some ongoing) operations. Further, project design was found to be less complex in the newer projects, and improvements were noted in projects' readiness to be implemented.

Notable progress had also taken place with regard to the use of performance indicators for judging implementation progress (a Bankwide

exercise is under way to help staff in developing performance indicators for all operations, including technical assistance). More work is needed in the specific area of monitoring outcomes rather than inputs. Considerable variation was found in the quality of supervision planning, thereby raising a question about prompt and effective intervention with respect to lagging projects. The assessment also found that while strong efforts were being made to enhance borrower involvement in project objectives and design, many operations did not provide clear evidence of borrower commitment.

The Bank and the United Nations Development Programme (UNDP). The year showed a continued, sharp decline of new funding by the UNDP for Bank-executed projects. This decline will likely continue, as the UNDP's executive board now prefers national execution.

The Bank and the UNDP held several meetings during the year on ways to enhance their collaboration in areas such as technical cooperation, aid coordination, the environment, and capacity building. Together with the Development Assistance Committee (DAC) of the Organisation for Economic Co-operation and Development (OECD), the Bank and the UNDP organized a high-level seminar, at which it was decided to establish a network to follow up on specific issues of technical cooperation. It was also agreed that the three institutions would jointly publish a semiannual journal whose target audience is practitioners and researchers in the field of international technical cooperation. The first issue of "International Journal of Technical Cooperation" is scheduled for the summer of 1995.

Cofinancing

During fiscal 1995, the vice presidency for Cofinancing and Financial Advisory Services (CFS) continued to play a catalytic role in facilitating the flow of financial resources to developing countries by carrying out various activities related to cofinancing, project finance and guarantees, private sector development, and technical assistance financing.

These activities consisted of operational support and technical assistance financing to the Bank's country departments and to borrowing

TABLE 3-4. WORLD BANK COFINANCING OPERATIONS, BY REGION, FISCAL YEARS 1994–95

(amounts in millions of US dollars)

Region and year	Projects cofinanced No.	Projects cofinanced Amount	Official[a] No.	Official[a] Amount	Export credit No.	Export credit Amount	Private Total Private No.	Private Total Private Amount	Private (of which IBRD guarantees) No.	Private (of which IBRD guarantees) Amount	World Bank contribution IBRD	World Bank contribution IDA	Total project costs
Africa													
1994	35	1,594	31	1,539	—	—	8	55	—	—	8	1,649	3,700
1995	29	1,099	27	1,088	—	—	3	11	—	—	65	1,069	3,095
East Asia and Pacific													
1994	14	1,948	9	515	1	92	7	1,341	(2)	(157)	1,899	635	7,262
1995	11	1,691	9	913	2	348	5	430	(1)	(64)	1,336	184	5,962
South Asia													
1994	9	1,584	9	1,259	1	300	1	25	—	—	474	949	8,876
1995	6	998	6	417	1	50	1	531	(1)	(240)	466	349	2,905
Europe and Central Asia													
1994	25	1,280	22	901	3	174	5	205	—	—	2,253	45	4,965
1995	37	839	35	607	—	—	4	232	—	—	2,482	424	4,870
Latin America and the Caribbean													
1994	25	1,513	22	1,377	1	2	5	133	—	—	1,740	265	5,545
1995	22	3,028	21	3,007	—	—	2	21	—	—	2,773	221	7,490
Middle East and North Africa													
1994	9	785	8	654	1	23	2	109	—	—	561	100	3,216
1995	9	593	9	593	—	—	—	—	—	—	559	53	1,761
Total													
1994	117	8,704	101	6,245	7	591	28	1,868	(2)	(157)	6,934	3,642	33,563
1995	114	8,248	107	6,626	3	398	15	1,225	(2)	(304)	7,681	2,302	26,082

— Zero.

NOTE: *The number of operations shown under different sources add up to a figure exceeding the total number of cofinanced projects because a number of projects were cofinanced from more than one source. Cofinancing data are reported by the fiscal year in which the project is presented to the Bank's executive board. Details may not add to totals because of rounding.*

a. *These figures include cofinancing with untied loans from the Export-Import Bank of Japan.*

member countries. CFS also coordinated cofinancing efforts among donor governments, official development aid agencies, and export credit agencies.[1]

The volume of cofinancing anticipated in support of World Bank-assisted operations in fiscal 1995 declined marginally to $8.2 billion from the $8.7 billion that had been mobilized in the previous year (*see Table 3-4*). Not reflected in the cofinancing volumes, however, is the better

understanding between the Bank and donors that emerges through cofinancing operations in respect of country and sector objectives and strategies. Ultimately, this improves the overall efficiency and effectiveness of aid flows and strengthens the Bank's partnerships with some of its most important supporters.

1. CFS activities related to private sector development, including the mainstreaming of guarantees, are described on page 30 of this *Annual Report*.

Official cofinancing flows of $6.6 billion increased by $381 million and still accounted for the largest source of anticipated cofinancing support. The volume of export credits and private cofinancing fell from levels realized in fiscal 1994.[2] The South Asia and Europe and Central Asia regions both realized an increase in the flow of private sector financing. In terms of lending instruments, investment loans attracted the largest volume of cofinancing support, followed by structural adjustment and financial intermediation loans.

Japan continued to be the major source of bilateral cofinancing. The cofinancing activities of its Overseas Economic Cooperation Fund (OECF) and Export-Import Bank (JExIm) accounted for the largest percentage of bilateral support to all Bank-assisted operations, reaching a total of $1.2 billion for seventeen projects approved during the year, or 46 percent of all bilateral cofinancing. To facilitate and expedite the processing of smaller cofinancing operations (cofinancing amounts below $50 million), the Bank and the JExIm agreed on a streamlined set of processing procedures. During the year, two operations were cofinanced following the streamlined procedures. Six more projects were identified as potential candidates for the near future. A similar agreement with the OECF is under discussion.

Other large bilateral cofinancing support came from Germany ($289 million equivalent), France ($264 million equivalent), the United Kingdom ($184 million equivalent), and the United States ($148 million).

Total cofinancing expected from multilateral financial institutions amounted to $3.9 billion. The Inter-American Development Bank, with $2.5 billion of planned cofinancing, continued to be the largest multilateral cofinancier and accounted for 63 percent of the total. Other substantive cofinancing support came from the Asian Development Bank, the European Investment Bank, and the European Bank for Reconstruction and Development.

As in previous years, the power sector attracted the largest amount of cofinancing ($1.5 billion as compared with $2.1 billion in fiscal 1994), followed by multisector operations ($1.1

billion as compared with $437 million in the previous year) and financial intermediation loans ($987 million, compared with $416 million in fiscal 1994).

During fiscal 1995, the Bank made a special effort to update existing cofinancing framework agreements to simplify processing procedures. It also sought to improve the consultation process with its major cofinancing partners. The main objective of this exercise was to make the consultation process more efficient by better matching the cofinancing requirements of Bank-assisted projects with the cofinancing interests and capacities of donors. During the year, the Bank held eighteen formal cofinancing consultations with representatives of fifteen donor agencies.

Since fiscal 1988, donors have been supporting the Bank-led Special Program of Assistance (SPA), which mobilizes quick-disbursing balance-of-payments support for economic reform programs in the low-income, debt-distressed countries of sub-Saharan Africa. To date, under phase three of the program, seventeen donors have pledged $6.7 billion in support of economic reform programs.[3]

To improve the effectiveness of technical assistance activities financed with trust-fund resources, the Bank introduced some important policy changes during the year. They included:

• To give recipients full ownership of activities financed with trust funds, recipient implementation of country-specific technical assistance will become the norm over a two- to three-year period.

• To return to the principle that trust-fund resources are not to be used to cover expenses that have been funded traditionally by the Bank's administrative budget, such resources

2. Cofinancing figures, which represent planned cofinancing—not actual commitments by cofinanciers—are captured at the time of presentation to the executive directors of each IBRD and IDA operation. The amounts of official cofinancing, in most cases, are firm commitments by that stage; export credits and private cofinancing, however, are generally only estimates, since such cofinancing is actually arranged as required for project implementation and gets firmed up a year or two after board approval.

3. For details, see page 55.

will no longer be used to finance core Bank activities.

• To facilitate the use of trust funds, negotiations will be carried out with donors to simplify the procedures for their use, including untying and loosening the restrictions on the use of trust funds to the extent possible.

During the year, CFS carried out detailed discussions with major donors on the Bank's efforts to improve the management of trust funds. Donors expressed broad support for the revised policies.

Despite constraints on national aid budgets, donors continued to increase their funding in support of technical assistance trust-fund programs. During the year, the two main programs, the Policy and Human Resource Development (PHRD) Fund—financed by Japan—and the Consultant Trust Funds (CTF)—provided by many donors—expanded their activities.

The PHRD program provided grant assistance to a broad range of project-related activities, with special emphasis on project preparation. In fiscal 1995, the fund approved 270 grants amounting to $177 million, as compared with 223 grants for $141 million in the previous year, for the preparation of projects that are expected to be financed by the Bank. As a part of an effort to intensify the monitoring of PHRD-funded activities, CFS issued the first annual report on the activities of the fund.

The CTF program, which consists of forty-seven consultant trust funds supported by twenty-six donors, financed consultancy services to support the Bank's operational and technical assistance work. During the year, the program financed a total of $64 million in new allocations, a 22 percent increase over fiscal 1994. The increase resulted mainly from a higher demand for consultancy services in the transitional economies, particularly in Europe and Central Asia. Major donors demonstrated their support for the program by replenishing depleted trust funds and by providing additional specific contributions for specific operations requested by the Bank and its borrowing member countries.

The CFS vice presidency also continued to maintain contacts with export credit agencies during the year, pursuing closer coordination with these agencies and with the Berne Union to develop greater participation in Bank projects. Efforts are continuing to improve coordination with export credit agencies, with special emphasis on project-finance transactions.

Portfolio Performance and Management

Early in fiscal year 1994, the executive directors of the World Bank endorsed a detailed plan of action designed to make the Bank more effective in obtaining results on the ground in borrowing countries.

The various initiatives set in motion to improve portfolio performance represented an important shift in the Bank's business practices—from what was perceived to be an excessive preoccupation with lending targets and volumes to an overriding concern with the development results in the field of Bank-supported operations.

A review of the first year's experience in implementing those initiatives found that significant progress had been made. It also concluded that progress had been made in strengthening the country focus of the Bank's development assistance and that steps had been taken to enhance the quality of the projects as they entered into the portfolio.

The review cautioned, however, that further work needed to be done to improve and sustain the Bank's internal environment so that it emphasizes and reinforces development impact. Creating an environment more supportive of effective country-portfolio management is one of the more important aspects of the portfolio-improvement program.

More recently, the "Annual Report on Portfolio Performance (ARPP)" for fiscal 1994—discussed by the executive directors in April 1995—found that "problem" projects constituted 15.2 percent of the total Bankwide portfolio of 1,762 operations under implementation in 134 countries, slightly higher than the 13.9 percent registered in the year before.

Performance was assessed for the first time using an enhanced rating methodology that emphasizes the likelihood of achieving development objectives (DO) as the key performance criterion, with implementation progress (IP) serving as a secondary criterion. This improved rating methodology was developed to increase the realism and transparency of performance ratings, as well as the quality and intensity of the review process. The methodology used until the current year had been strongly oriented towards physical and financial inputs, and although a rating on the likelihood of achieving development objectives was also assigned, it was subsumed under the rating for overall implementation status. However, the change in rating methodology increased the difficulty in coming up with a trend analysis. In principle, the changes should lead to more projects being rated as unsatisfactory or highly unsatisfactory than otherwise would be the case. In practice, however, it is not possible to disentangle this effect from that of other factors.

The review found that of the 134 country portfolios, those in only twenty-one countries, including thirteen countries in nonaccrual or civil conflict, had a very low likelihood of achieving project DOs, while seventy-two had a high likelihood of achieving development objectives.

According to the report, the Bank further intensified its efforts to promote a strong implementation culture during the year under review. Supervision intensity per project increased by 8 percent, and all six operational regions are now assigning high priority to implementation and obtaining results on the ground.

At the regional level, a number of steps were taken to enhance quality at entry of new operations. They included (a) requiring up-front actions that are critical to project success before the project is presented to the board; (b) avoiding excessive complexity in the design of new operations; (c) strengthening borrower ownership and beneficiary participation; and (d) using pilots to test new approaches and determine what projects should be followed-up on a larger scale.

The regions also continued to strengthen portfolio-management practices through various measures, including involving borrowers more closely in every aspect of portfolio management

and using mid term-review and supervision-mission findings to pursue mid course corrections (project restructurings, for example) to increase the likelihood that projects will achieve their DOs.

An independent assessment of experience with the Bank's main portfolio-management tools—country-portfolio performance reviews, mid term reviews of operations in progress, and project restructuring—was provided by the Operations Evaluation Department's second annual review of the ARPP. It recommended that the Bank pay particular attention to the extent of coverage and targeting of such tools. It also recommended that future reviews by operational staff of regional and country portfolios enhance their strategic focus and include monitorable goals for improving portfolio management and performance.

The OED review found that operational staff had made good progress in installing the more transparent system for rating operational performance, while piloting further enhancements. Although the new system had quite pronounced effects in some regions, its aggregate effect on the realism of performance ratings still appeared quite small; a substantial gap remained between ratings of projects under implementation and ratings of the same projects at their completion. Following deliberations by the executive directors' Committee on Development Effectiveness, a streamlined management process, reflecting OED recommendations, has been put in place to address the problem.

At the conclusion in fiscal 1994 of the Bankwide review of projects involving involuntary resettlement, the Bank's management agreed to continue monitoring the status of the resettlement portfolio through the preparation of a special annex in the fiscal 1995 ARPP. The annex placed special emphasis on new projects with resettlement added during fiscal 1994, on new initiatives being taken with borrowers and within the Bank to improve capacity and performance on resettlement, and on the status of implementation of the entire resettlement portfolio during fiscal 1994.

It found that all the new fiscal 1994 projects met the basic planning requirements for resettlement. Specialist supervision was at a high level. Bank country departments, especially those with the largest resettlement portfolios, began to elaborate strategic approaches to the issues involved. More dialogue on borrower policy was held. Training courses were expanded in several borrower countries.

Considerable progress was made at the "front end" of projects, the annex concluded. It noted that implementation still presents significant challenges and that, because implementation is the borrower's responsibility, resettlement policy dialogue, in-country capacity building, and creative financing of resettlement will remain the critical points for improved implementation.

Operations Evaluation

Operations evaluation at the World Bank has a threefold mandate: to measure how far and how effectively the Bank's activities are achieving their desired results; to draw and disseminate lessons for application in policies, operations, and processes; and to help Bank units and member countries to improve their own evaluation capabilities.

The Bank's independent evaluation unit, the OED, reports to the Bank's executive directors through the director general, operations evaluation (DGO). The OED rates the development effectiveness of the Bank's activities according to their (a) relevance to specific country- and sectoral assistance strategies and to the Bank's overall goals; (b) efficacy in meeting planned objectives; and (c) efficiency in using resources. Its work program evolves in response to changes in the development agenda and the concerns of the Bank. Results and recommendations are reported to the executive directors and fed back into the design and implementation of policies and lending operations.

Comprehensiveness and rigor. All lending operations are evaluated on completion by the regional offices responsible for them; borrower agencies contribute to these completion reports. The OED reviews all completion reports and produces performance audits for a representative sample of completed operations. Every completed lending operation is rated for its overall outcome, sustainability, impact on the borrower's institutional development, borrower performance, and Bank performance. The OED also evaluates country-assistance programs and the Bank's policies and processes. Evaluation findings are maintained in a development-performance data base, built up over twenty years, which now covers more than 4,000 operations.

In fiscal 1995 OED reviewed 275 completion reports and audited 123 completed operations. The cumulative total of Bank operations subjected to *ex post* evaluation reached 3,888 at the end of the fiscal year.

In impact evaluations, the OED, assisted by agencies in borrower countries, analyzes projects five to eight years after the close of loan disbursements. These evaluations assess the economic worth of projects and the long-term effects—intended and unintended—on people and the environment. The OED produced eighteen impact evaluations in fiscal 1995.

Portfolio management. The OED continued to strengthen its activities in support of improved portfolio management, outlined in last year's *Annual Report* of the World Bank. New initiatives in fiscal 1995 included:

• Country-assistance reviews. To support the Bank's focus on the country as the unit of account for the design and management of its assistance, the OED began a series of country-assistance reviews. These reviews assess the relevance and efficacy of the Bank's overall country-assistance strategy and the effectiveness of the various instruments of assistance. They make recommendations for future policies and actions.

• "Quality at entry": Economic Analysis Task Force. The 1992 Task Force on Portfolio Management pointed out that the Bank tended to be overoptimistic about projects at the appraisal stage. Following up, a joint task force of the OED and the Operations Policy Department helped to design an action program to improve the economic analysis of projects.

Evaluation studies. The OED's evaluation studies examine Bank processes and broader development issues, including policies and experience in countries, regions, and sectors. In fiscal 1995, OED sent ten studies to the board. Topics included experience with irrigation; poverty assessments; industrial restructuring; lending for electric power in Africa; conditionality in lending for forestry; and the social impact of adjustment.

Disclosure and outreach. Growing public concern with development effectiveness has led to demands for the evaluation function to be more transparent. In November 1994 the Bank's executive directors further expanded the Bank's disclosure policy to include country and sector-evaluation studies and impact-evaluation reports.

Responding to a request from the executive directors' Committee on Development Effectiveness, the OED began expanding its publications program. In fiscal 1995 it published *Evaluation Results for 1993* and five book-length studies. For decisionmakers and development practitioners, it published three "Lessons & Practices" and twenty editions of "Précis."

The OED gave seminars within and outside the Bank to discuss evaluation design and results, and issues raised by evaluation findings for the management of ongoing programs. Evaluation and the work of the OED were systematically featured in training programs for new Bank staff.

The OED organized the first international conference on development evaluation, with contributions by distinguished evaluators, academics, and development practitioners from a broad span of countries and types of organizations. The papers are being published in a professional journal.

The OED participated as an observer in meetings of the DAC Expert Group, and evaluation staff attended workshops and seminars with evaluators from other international organizations and donor countries.

Support for evaluation in borrower countries. The Bank's executive directors and management adopted recommendations by a Bankwide Task Force on Evaluation Capacity Development in the public sector of borrowing countries. For the Bank, the recommendations entail taking a more proactive approach to supporting evaluation-capacity development, regarding evaluation-capacity development as an integral part of the Bank's country portfolio-management work and of its support for public sector-management reform.

The OED responded to requests for advice on evaluation capacity development from Argentina, China, Colombia, Indonesia, Morocco, Sri Lanka, Tunisia, and Zimbabwe.

Implementation of the Bank's Disclosure Policy

In August 1993, the Bank took a number of steps to increase the range and depth of information available to the public. The revisions to the more restrictive policies of the past were undertaken in the belief that the sharing of information is essential for effective and sustainable development. Sharing stimulates debate and broadens understanding of development issues and facilitates coordination among the many parties involved in development. It also serves to strengthen public support for efforts to improve the lives of people in developing countries.

Experience with implementing the disclosure policy shows that the Bank has made substantial progress and that it is now clearly a more open organization than it had been. After initial start-up problems, Bank staff have responded well to the demands of the new policy; government officials have worked closely and constructively with operations staff to ensure its implementation, contrary to earlier predictions that borrower governments would find it difficult to adapt to the new policy; and the number of complaints from the nongovernmental organization (NGO) community about Bank unresponsiveness has lessened to such an extent that they are now very infrequent.

To meet the Bank's commitment to the principle of global accessibility to Bank information, a Public Information Center (PIC) was opened at the Bank's headquarters in January 1994, and PIC field offices were subsequently opened in the Bank's London, Paris, and Tokyo offices. Each office has a public reading room equipped with a workstation connected to the Internet. To reach clients without access to the Internet, a catalogue of available document titles is distributed by mail and is updated monthly by fax.

World Bank resident missions are an important component of the PIC network and are critical in ensuring that relevant documents are available to affected people and local organizations in borrowing countries. Each resident mission stocks a full set of publicly available documents for its country (available free of charge) and provides a point of access to any of the other information available throughout the Bank.

As of December 31, 1994, the PIC offices had received a total of almost 17,000 requests—an understatement of the true number because (a) visitor registration at a PIC is voluntary, (b) many requests are addressed to and handled directly by country departments and resident missions, and (c) data on requests serviced by resident missions are not available. During calendar 1994, a total of 1,928 documents were made available to the public. Their number included 674 Project Information Documents, which provide details on every project in the Bank's pipeline, and 601 Environmental Data Sheets, which are prepared and updated quarterly for all projects in the lending program.

The greatest demand for information came from the business community. Public agencies constituted the second largest group of requesters. Only 2 percent of visitor and telephone requests came from the NGO community, which has apparently more frequently satisfied its needs directly from the Internet, resident missions, or direct contact with country departments.

The Bank is currently intensifying its disclosure efforts by preparing a formal training module for new Bank staff that explains the rationale for the disclosure policy, its implications for operational work, and the procedures involved in carrying out the policy.

The Inspection Panel Becomes Operational

An independent Inspection Panel was established in fiscal 1994 to receive and investigate complaints that the Bank had not followed its own policies and procedures with respect to the design, appraisal, and/or implementation of a development project that it supports.

The panel complements the Bank's existing systems for quality control in project preparation and implementation. As such, it helps the Bank's executive board in its governance of the Bank and does not affect the president's accountability to the executive directors for the management of the Bank's operations. The functionally independent panel, which opened for business in the first week of September 1994, reports directly to the Bank's executive board.

On the first request presented to it—one that concerns the planned Arun III Hydroelectric Project in Nepal—the three-member panel unanimously found that apparent violations of IDA policy existed and recommended further investigation in three areas: environmental assessment, involuntary resettlement, and treatment of indigenous peoples. The Bank's executive directors subsequently authorized the panel to conduct the investigation.

The Inspection Panel completed its investigation in June 1995 and sent its report to the executive directors and to the president of the Bank on June 21. The panel's report took into account the remedial measures proposed by the Bank in the three areas where the investigation was authorized by the executive directors.

In April 1995, the panel informed the executive directors that a second request for inspection had been made. The panel subsequently rejected the request. Two additional requests for inspection—related to the Power VI Project in Tanzania and the Rondonia Natural Resources Management Project in Brazil—were registered in June 1995. After receiving a response by Bank management to the claims made in the request, the panel will make a recommendation in August 1995 to the Bank's executive directors on whether or not the claims should be investigated.

1946

March 8–18   Inaugural meeting of boards of governors of the World Bank and the International Monetary Fund is held at Savannah, Georgia. Bylaws are adopted, executive directors are elected, and Washington, D.C. is chosen as the site of the two new institutions. The Bank's subscribed capital stands at $7.67 billion.

Savannah, Georgia, March 1946; the inaugural meeting of the Bank and the International Monetary Fund

Photo: IMF archives.

May 7   The first meeting of the executive directors is held, with the director representing the United States acting as temporary chairman. He continues to do so until the election of a president.

June 18   Eugene Meyer takes office as the first president of the Bank.

June 25   The World Bank formally begins operations.

September 27–   First annual meeting of the board of governors of the World Bank is held
October 5   in Washington. The Bank has thirty-eight member nations, and its staff totals seventy-two.

1947

March 17   John J. McCloy becomes the second president of the Bank.

May 9   Executive directors approve the Bank's first loan agreement, with France, in the amount of $250 million, for reconstruction purposes. In real terms, it remains the largest loan ever made by the Bank.

July 15   The IBRD makes its first bond offer on the U.S. market in the amount of $250 million. The offering is substantially oversubscribed, and the bonds immediately sell at a premium over the public offering price.

1948

March 25   Executive directors approve the first loan agreement with a developing country—an operation in Chile, in the amount of $13.5 million for hydroelectric development.

1949

July 1   Eugene R. Black, who had been the executive director for the United States since March 1947, becomes the third president of the Bank.

Eugene Black (left), the Bank's third president, at the annual staff picnic. (Identity of the person on the right is not known.)
Photo: World Bank.

July–November   The Bank launches its first comprehensive economic survey—of Colombia's economic resources and needs—with a view to indicating the most promising lines of development, the principal obstacles in the way, and the means by which they might be surmounted.

1951

May 23   The IBRD's first public offering outside the United States is placed: a £5 million issue offered on the London market.

1952

August 13, 14 Japan and the Federal Republic of Germany become members of the Bank, bringing the Bank's membership to fifty-three.

September The first reorganization of the Bank is carried out. Three geographical Departments of Operations (Asia and Middle East; Europe, Africa, and Australasia; and Western Hemisphere) and a Department of Technical Operations are created.

1953

October 15 The first three loans to Japan, totaling $40.2 million, are approved. The loans to the Japan Development Bank are relent for power development.

At the helm of Japan's bullet train, which was partially financed with World Bank funds.
Photo: World Bank.

1955

March 11 The Economic Development Institute, serving as the Bank's staff college, is set up, with financial support from the Ford and Rockefeller Foundations. The first course is attended by fourteen officials from as many member countries.

1956

June 30 The number of Bank staff at the end of fiscal year 1956 swells to 511.

July 20 The International Finance Corporation is established as an affiliate of the Bank, with an authorized capital of $100 million.

1958

August 25–27 In the wake of a deterioration in India's balance of payments, the first meeting of the India aid consortium takes place in Washington, with attendance by representatives of the governments of Canada, Germany, Japan, the United Kingdom, and the United States.

1959

September 16 The Bank's authorized capital is increased from $10 billion to $25.3 billion.

September 29 On the occasion of the annual meetings, the United States puts forth a proposal—subsequently adopted by the board of governors—to establish the International Development Association (IDA) as an affiliate of the Bank.

1960

September 19 The Indus Waters Treaty is signed by Pakistan, India, and the World Bank in Karachi, thus opening the way to the use and development of water resources on which depends the livelihood of some 50 million people in the two countries.

September 24 IDA is established as an affiliate of the Bank. Initial subscriptions total $912 million.

September 19, 1960. The Indus Waters Treaty is signed. From left to right, Jawaharlal Nehru, prime minister of India; Ayub Khan, president of Pakistan; and Sir William Iliff of the World Bank.
Photo: World Bank.

1961

May 11 IDA extends its first development credit, totaling $9 million, to Honduras, which helps finance a program of highway development and maintenance.

June 30 By the end of fiscal year 1961, the total sales of Bank loans has passed the $1,000 million mark. In all, nearly one fifth of the Bank's loans have been sold to other investors.

1962

September 17 The first Bank financing of education is approved, as IDA extends a $5 million credit to Tunisia for school construction.

1963

January 1 George D. Woods becomes the fourth president of the Bank.

1964

June 29   The first replenishment of IDA resources becomes effective, as eighteen governments agree to provide $753 million.

1965

June 30   World Bank commitments for the fiscal year ending on June 30, 1965 exceed $1 billion for the first time.

1966

October 14   The International Centre for Settlement of Investment Disputes is established.

1968

April 1   Robert S. McNamara becomes the fifth president of the Bank.

1970

February 12   The IBRD's first borrowing from Japan (equivalent to $100 million) takes place. One month later, the IBRD borrows another $100 million equivalent from Japan.

June 16   First loan agreement for population planning, with Jamaica, is approved. The $2 million loan helps finance the development of a postpartum family-planning program.

June 30   World Bank commitments for the 1970 fiscal year exceed $2 billion for the first time.

September   An operations evaluation unit, whose responsibility it is to evaluate the contribution of World Bank Group operations to the development of member countries, is established by the president and is placed in the Programming and Budgeting Department.

1971

May 18   First loan agreement ($15 million) for pollution control (river pollution in São Paulo) is signed.

May 19   The newly founded Consultative Group on International Agricultural Research convenes in Washington. By the end of the fiscal year (June 30), the group has nineteen members.

1972

June 30   World Bank lending for the fiscal year ending June 30 crosses the $3 billion mark for the first time.

October   The second major reorganization of the Bank takes place. Five regional offices are created, incorporating seven former "area" or geographical departments and eight projects departments.

Robert
McNamara
looking at results
on the ground
during a visit to
Tunisia in 1973.
Photo by William Clark.

1974

October 24   The executive directors approve a proposal that a director general be instituted as manager of the evaluation function, and that it should have links to the executive board, as well as the president's office.

1975

December 16   The Project Preparation Facility, under which the Bank advances funds to prospective borrowers to meet gaps in project preparation and for institution building, is created.

December 23   The Intermediate Financing Facility, or "Third Window," which enables the Bank to provide finance on terms intermediate between those of the IBRD and IDA, becomes effective, when pledges of $100 million in contributions to the special Interest Subsidy Fund—enough to fund about $600 million of loans—are received.

1979

June 30   World Bank lending for the fiscal year ending June 30 crosses the $10 billion mark for the first time.

1980

January 4   The IBRD's authorized capital stock increases by $44 billion to $85 billion.

March 25   The first structural adjustment loan, to Turkey in the amount of $200 million, is approved.

May 15   The executive directors decide that the People's Republic of China represents China in the Bank.

July 1   A currency pooling scheme, designed to equalize exchange rate risks among the IBRD's borrowers, becomes operational.

1981

July 1   A.W. Clausen becomes the sixth president of the Bank.

1982

September 8   IDA donors, other than the United States, agree to provide special contributions in an amount, in general, equal to one third of their total contributions to IDA's sixth replenishment through either an "FY84 Account" or a "Special Fund." The special contributions are necessitated by legislative delays in the United States and a subsequent reduction in its appropriations for IDA-6.

1983

January 11   A new set of cofinancing instruments ("B-loan"), designed to help the Bank's borrowers increase and stabilize flows of private capital by linking part of commercial-bank flows to IBRD operations, is authorized by the executive directors.

February 22   The Special Action Program, a two-year program intended to accelerate disbursements to countries during a period of adverse external circumstances so as to ensure timely implementation of high-priority projects, is created.

1985

July 1   The Special Facility for Sub-Saharan Africa, created to support, over a three–year period, reform programs undertaken by African governments, begins its operations.

1986

July 1   Barber Conable becomes the seventh president of the Bank.

1987

May 4   The Bank is reorganized into four senior vice presidential complexes: Operations; Policy, Planning, and Research; Finance; and Administration. Within the regions, country departments are created, combining the functions formerly divided between programs and projects departments. In addition, the central Environment Department is established in the senior vice presidency for Policy, Planning, and Research.

December 4   Donors agree to establish the Special Program of Assistance to provide quick-disbursing aid to reforming low-income African countries with debt problems.

1988

April 12   The international convention establishing the Multilateral Investment Guarantee Agency takes effect.

April 27   The resolutions authorizing a general capital increase in the IBRD's authorized capital are adopted by the board of governors, bringing the IBRD's total authorized capital to $171.4 billion.

1989

August 1 The Debt-reduction Facility for IDA-only Countries, designed to ease the burden on those countries of external commercial debt, is established.

1990

January 30 The biggest-ever IBRD loan (in nominal terms)—$1,260 million—to Mexico in support of that country's debt-reduction program, is approved.

June 30 Lending for education during the fiscal year ending June 30 crosses the $1 billion mark for the first time.

July 16 *World Development Report 1990*, which outlines a strategy for reducing poverty based on experiences from developing countries around the world, is published.

November 28 The Global Environment Facility, jointly administered by the Bank, the United Nations Development Programme, and the United Nations Environment Programme, is launched.

1991

September 1 Lewis T. Preston becomes the eighth president of the Bank.

1992

May 29 Switzerland joins the Bank.

June 16 The Russian Federation becomes a member of the IBRD and IDA.

July 6–September 22 Twelve republics of the former Soviet Union become members of the IBRD.

November 3 The report of the Task Force on Portfolio Management—the "Wapenhans Report"—is transmitted to the executive directors.

1993

January 1 Three thematic vice presidencies—dealing with environment, human resources, and the private sector—are established.

September 22 The independent Inspection Panel, which receives and investigates complaints that the Bank has not followed its own policies and procedures with respect to the design, appraisal, and/or implementation of a development project that it supports, is established.

1994

January 3 The Public Information Center at the Bank's headquarters is opened.

May 3 The Bank unveils a three–year, $1.2 billion program to assist Palestinians in the West Bank and Gaza in the transition to autonomous rule.

September 8 Executive directors approve recommendations to mainstream guarantees as an operational tool of the World Bank.

1995

June 1 James D. Wolfensohn becomes the ninth president of the Bank.

AFRICA

In fiscal 1995, the Africa Region vice presidency of the Bank presented to the executive directors for discussion a document whose title, "A Continent in Transition," reflects the state of sub-Saharan Africa in the mid 1990s: one of transition from one-party systems to multiparty democracies, from centrally managed to market-oriented economies, and from economic stagnation or decline to per capita income growth in many countries *(see Box 4-1)*. Indeed, the region's gross domestic product (GDP), excluding South Africa and Nigeria, grew by 1.2 percent in 1994 and is projected to grow more than three times faster in 1995 as the steep decline of growth in countries such as Malawi and Zambia is reversed, and as countries such as Côte d'Ivoire, Ethiopia, Ghana, Kenya, Mali, Senegal, and Uganda significantly accelerate the growth of their economies. Although the recovery has been assisted by good weather conditions and an improvement in the global economic environment, it also reflects changes that augur well for the future, especially a big jump in the region's gross domestic investment.

There were variations among countries, as usual, especially linked to economic policies. Nowhere is this clearer than in the countries of the CFA zone, which signifi-

cantly realigned their common currency in early 1994. Evidence indicates that the historic decision of January 12, 1994 on realignment, along with economic reforms, has been effective in getting most economies back on the growth path. Growth of GDP turned around by 2.1 percentage points on average for the thirteen countries of the zone (excluding Comoros) in 1994, compared with 1991–93, and became positive for the first time in this decade—specifically, growth was positive in ten of the thirteen countries. Agriculture clearly responded, but so, too, did industry, which grew by 6.7 percent in Côte d'Ivoire. Although export growth accelerated, it remains relatively low, because producers still need time to respond to new opportunities. There was dramatic improvement in some activities in 1994 (Sahelian livestock, rice, canned fish, tourism, textiles, and other manufacturing); cotton production in 1994/95 is up by 50 percent in Burkina Faso and Togo and by more than 25 percent in Mali; and groundnut production is 40 percent larger than the year before in Senegal. At the same time, liquidity of banks improved. While prices rose sharply in all countries in 1994, for the zone as a whole inflation was kept below the level anticipated on the basis

of the magnitude of the devaluation.

Elsewhere, while a few countries experienced declines in real GDP (Burundi, Malawi, and Zaire, in particular), or near-stagnation (Nigeria), production was generally up. Several countries registered GDP growth of between 4 percent and 6 percent (Mauritania, Mauritius, Mozambique, Tanzania, Uganda, and Zimbabwe); for some, growth in this range was for the second, third, or fourth year in a row.

"A Continent in Transition" points out that twenty-one countries achieved positive per capita income growth during 1988–93. This trend continued and spread in 1994, especially in countries implementing economic reform programs. These countries' efforts deserve to be supported by the donor community.

Coordination and selectivity of assistance. Since 1987, Africa's partners in development have responded to African reform initiatives with quick-disbursing balance-of-payments support under the Special Program of Assistance (SPA), which constitutes the most important aid coordination and cofinancing mechanism in Africa. The third three-year phase of the SPA began in 1994. In October 1994, with the addition of Eritrea and Congo, the total number of SPA-eligible countries grew to thirty-one. To date, under

BOX 4-1. A CONTINENT IN TRANSITION

"A Continent in Transition: Sub-Saharan Africa in the Mid–1990s," asks, "What happened to the landscape of African political economy in the past five years, and what are the characteristics of the situation on the ground now? What has been learned about the development process, and how is the development agenda unfolding as Africa looks to the next decade? What are the respective roles of the partners in African development?"

The study concludes that an important part of the changing landscape is the beginning of a political transition, with significant movement towards democratization and political liberalization. This transition, although still partial and fragile, nevertheless represents a break from expectations of only five years ago. The past five years have also seen notable progress on key items of macroeconomic reform such as exchange rates and price control; progress in other areas such as fiscal balance has been slower. Although there has been relatively less progress overall on the deeper structural elements of the development agenda, successful examples can be pointed to. Twenty-one countries achieved positive per capita income growth during 1988–93. About half, representing nearly 30 percent of the region's income and nearly 40 percent of total population, attained or exceeded growth rates of between 4 percent and 5 percent annually.

Against this backdrop it is impossible to speak of sub-Saharan Africa as an undifferentiated whole. At one end are countries mired in civil strife and social unrest; at the other are countries that have made

significant progress on macroeconomic reform and that are beginning to reap the benefits. These advances, as well as examples elsewhere of innovation and progress on the structural agenda, confirm that African success stories do exist. The task now is to spread the success more widely through systematic, country-specific pursuit of the development agenda.

Elements of the agenda, in addition to maintaining macroeconomic stability, include continuing progress in education, health, and population; sustaining agriculture and the environment; reducing gender inequities; developing the private sector; building infrastructure; and supporting capacity building. Only through progress in these areas can sustainable poverty reduction—the goal of development—take place. Implementation of this structural agenda should be aided by the process of political liberalization, which facilitates open discussion and debate.

Relative success in macroeconomic reforms has been supported by donor coordination provided through the Special Program of Assistance. Without governmental and national commitment to the developmental agenda, however, larger or improved external assistance will not help. For this reason, the study concludes, there should be greater selectivity in the allocation of scarce aid resources towards governments that show such commitment. The contents of the overall envelope of resources can then be divided among debt relief, balance-of-payments support, and investment assistance based on country-specific circumstances.

SPA-3, seventeen donors have pledged $6.7 billion in balance-of-payments support to eligible countries.

Although providing resources in support of reform remains the primary purpose of the forum, SPA meetings and special working groups have been effective in coordinating policies and procedures on broader issues. Priorities under SPA-3 include integrating poverty-reduction measures into reform programs and public expenditure allocations, and strengthening local management and institutional capacity. Working groups are developing recommendations in these areas; they will also be considering ways to incorporate women's issues more systematically into economic reform programs.

The criteria of performance shaped the evolution of assistance to the CFA zone. Donors responded massively to the currency realignment. Adjustment programs in the CFA zone were assisted by more than $2.5 billion in balance-of-payments support in 1994; in addition, more than $5 billion in debt relief was provided. Multilateral institutions made the largest contribution, and the Bank's share of new funds, which went to all countries except Equatorial Guinea, was nearly 40 percent. In the calendar year following the devaluation, the Bank approved the release of thirteen tranches of ongoing adjustment operations, ten new adjustment credits, and three supplements under the "Fifth Dimension" program. The Bank's response primarily to need—as opposed to need and performance—in fiscal 1995 is illustrated by the emergency assistance provided to Burundi and Rwanda *(see Box 4-2)*.

Portfolio performance and capacity building. Portfolio performance is key to getting results on the ground. The Africa Region's portfolio performance continued to improve, whether measured by the development-objective (DO) rating, the implementation-progress (IP) rating, or the disbursement ratio. For example, the proportion of problem projects, based on the DO rating (which rates projects on the extent to which project development objectives are expected to be met), fell from 21 percent in fiscal 1992 to 19 percent in fiscal 1994. Based on the IP rating, the figure fell from 25 percent to 20 percent. The improved portfolio performance is partly the result of improvements in the political and economic environment. The improvement has also been helped by the restructuring of the portfolio, improved financial management of projects (through, for example, systematic preparation of audit reports and strengthened accounting capacity), and more effective supervision.

Such actions, which led to improved implementation of the Region's portfolio, also help to improve the effectiveness of assistance from other donors and to improve broader-level economic management in the countries concerned. For these additional reasons, the Bank has implemented a strong program of portfolio-management actions. These include the strengthening of the links between macroeconomic and sector-specific policies, programs, and activities, which is key to good project design; reaching early agreement with local stakeholders; enhancing donor dialogue leading to, among other things, common implementation arrangements; encouraging local capacity building and utilization through well-focused training (on procurement and disbursement issues, for example); and continuing emphasis on supervision.

Civil service reform is key to the successful implementation of projects, programs, and policies; it is, therefore, a priority of the Bank. Attention in this area extends beyond the narrow

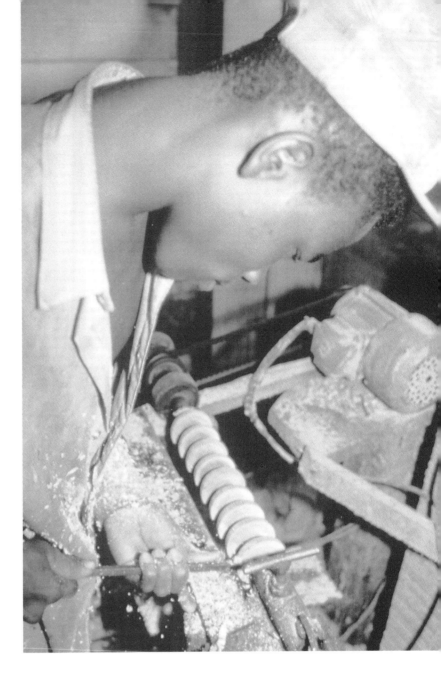

fiscal aspects and focuses, rather, on the performance of core government functions and service delivery. Reforms in this latter area are off to a good start, for example, in Malawi under the Second Institutional Development Project, which became effective in December 1994. The project aims to strengthen the capacities of the Ministry of Finance and the Department of Human Resources Management and Development. These efforts are expected to help enhance efficiency and effectiveness through improved performance of personnel and better budgetary and financial management functions.

BOX 4-2. EMERGENCY ASSISTANCE: THE CASES OF BURUNDI AND RWANDA

The tragic events of 1993 and 1994 in Burundi and Rwanda tested the creative capacity of the Bank to respond to unprecedented challenges and help reverse the damage done to these countries' economies, institutions, and social fabric.

In 1994, in the wake of the political crisis, Burundi experienced a sharp drop in food production, a breakdown in the delivery of social services, destruction of business property and public infrastructure, and the collapse of key institutions. Gross domestic product declined by 9 percent, and food production plummeted by 22 percent. Rwanda's postwar economic situation was grimmer: More than a third of the population were refugees, more than half the country's agriculture and industrial output was lost, and most Rwandan enterprises were not operational. The country's institutional memory and project-implementation capacity were severely handicapped by the disappearance and killing of personnel, destruction of files, and theft of computers and equipment. As a result, the central administrative capacity was quasi-paralyzed.

In Burundi, the Bank helped prepare and finance the Emergency Recovery Program (ERP), which addresses priority needs in health, primary and secondary education, agriculture, infrastructure, and the private sector. A donor consortium committed $53 million (including $14.6 million in IDA funds) towards the cost of the ERP. Consistent with the longer-term emphasis on equity and human-resources development, almost 70 percent of the funds have been allocated to basic health and education so as to overcome the erosion during the past two years of social standards and capacities.

In Rwanda, responding to an appeal from the United Nations, the Bank approved in August 1994 an emergency grant of $20 million, which helped finance activities of the United Nations Children's Fund, the United Nations High Commissioner for Refugees, the Food and Agriculture Organization of the U.N., and the World Health Organization. The grant money financed activities such as providing tools and seeds for returning farmers, the establishment of a seed-multiplication program, the repair of water-supply facilities, purchase of textbooks, and institutional strengthening of public health activities. The Bank subsequently helped prepare the $200 million Emergency Recovery Program, which identified the priority needs for one year in health, education, infrastructure, agriculture, and the private sector and outlined technical assistance for institutional capacity building. A $50 million IDA credit supporting the program was approved in January 1995.

Donor collaboration was instrumental in putting together rapidly the two recovery programs. At the same time, in both countries, the Bank has been restructuring its portfolio to be able to respond to new priorities and to reflect the true absorptive capacity of the countries and the activities of other donors. However, a durable solution to these countries' problems lies in actions within the countries themselves. If the people of Burundi and Rwanda do not find sufficient common ground to resolve their differences, sustainable development will not be achievable.

A special feature of the Malawi project is the reliance on considerable local participation through workshops involving a significant number of middle- and senior-level civil servants. There is also strong support for the project at the higher echelons of government. Before the project was approved by the Bank's executive board, the government of Malawi demonstrated its commitment by promulgating the Public Service Act, which contains provisions for fostering predictability, transparency, and accountability in the conduct of government business.

Broad sector approach. The broad sector approach to investment lending is a more comprehensive way of approaching lending operations in Africa. It stems from dissatisfaction with some of the results achieved by traditional investment operations financed project-by-project and donor-by-donor. The unsatisfactory results reflect insufficient government grasp and ownership of projects; inadequate allocation of recurrent resources to sustain the project; the pursuit of conflicting strategies resulting from a lack of donor coordination; and the diffusion of the limited national implementation capacity.

The broad sector approach tries to address these problems by bringing the government and donors together into a collaborative framework:

• The local stakeholders are in the driver's seat of the program from the start to ensure

TABLE 4-1. LENDING TO BORROWERS IN AFRICA, BY SECTOR, 1986–95

(millions of US dollars; fiscal years)

Sector	Annual average, 1986–90	1991	1992	1993	1994	1995
Agriculture	661.4	504.9	707.4	318.3	152.6	375.1
Energy						
Oil and gas	15.1	300.0	48.5	—	186.2	—
Power	148.5	155.0	76.0	356.0	90.0	255.3
Environment	—	—	—	—	2.6	—
Human resources						
Education	167.3	265.9	402.9	417.4	325.5	201.2
Population, health, and nutrition	109.5	432.8	100.3	131.2	161.6	311.5
Social sector	—	—	—	—	—	—
Industry and finance						
Industry	159.4	—	200.0	83.5	29.6	53.0
Financial	268.2	138.8	619.9	252.3	400.1	7.2
Infrastructure and urban development						
Telecommunications	80.5	12.8	—	89.1	—	—
Transportation	366.2	309.5	242.8	483.0	515.0	74.8
Urban development	242.4	98.3	222.6	61.2	111.4	158.0
Water supply and sewerage	124.3	256.0	297.4	67.2	74.1	248.2
Mining and other extractive	30.0	21.0	6.0	—	—	24.8
Multisector	534.3	887.0	936.7	453.6	711.0	470.9
Public sector management	79.0	12.2	113.1	104.5	48.2	104.3
Tourism	—	—	—	—	—	—
Total	2,986.1	3,394.2	3,973.6	2,817.3	2,807.9	2,284.3
Of which: IBRD	1,039.9	662.9	738.4	47.0	127.7	80.7
IDA	1,946.2	2,731.3	3,235.2	2,770.3	2,680.2	2,203.6
Number of operations	81	77	77	75	60	58

NOTE: Details may not add to totals because of rounding.
— Zero.

local ownership and sustainability. This requires a transfer of project-preparation responsibilities from donors to local stakeholders.

• The program is sectorwide in scope, covering all policies and projects, and addressing aggregate current expenditures in the sector.

• The interventions implement a coherent sector policy framework—developed in close collaboration with the country's private sector, nongovernmental organizations (NGOs), and project beneficiaries.

• Donors locate their assistance within the government's defined program, rather than promoting their own approaches.

• Efforts are made to establish common implementation arrangements for all operations within the sector.

• Long-term external technical assistance is minimized, with a focus, instead, on capacity building.

Three such operations were approved during the past eighteen months (Mozambique Second

Roads and Coastal Shipping Project, Zambia Health Sector Support Project, and Zambia Agriculture Sector Investment Program). Each incorporated features of the broad sector approach and all were carefully developed over several years. With a growing focus on impact and with an increasing understanding of this collaborative framework, the number of broad sector operations is expected to rise to about 20 percent of total lending in the next three years. Most of these operations will be in the social sectors, agriculture, and roads, because these sectors attract a multiplicity of donors in Africa and because broad government ownership is most critical if results are to be sustained.

Participatory initiatives. The Bank made strides this past fiscal year towards institutionalizing participation in order to enhance both the quality of work and the chances of getting the desired results on the ground. Participation, a broad and inclusive term, is defined as a process through which stakeholders influence and share control over the development initiatives, decisions, and resources that affect them. Participation may incorporate a wide range of techniques such as consultation (through borrower forums, for example) or joint assessments. Consultation is the form of participation that has recently been the most prominent in the Bank's Africa Region. The preparation and discussion of the strategy document, "A Continent in Transition," involved consultations in about thirty African and donor countries. Systematic borrower consultation in the form of client-feedback surveys, which assess the attitudes of borrower-government officials toward Bank services, has been undertaken in nine countries (Côte d'Ivoire, Mali, Guinea, Madagascar, Malawi, Mozambique, Uganda, Zambia, and Zimbabwe). Participatory and consultative methods are now being used increasingly in economic and sector work, especially in the preparation of poverty assessments.

On the operational side, too, the use of techniques such as participatory rural appraisals and beneficiary assessments has increased over the past two years. In Angola, for example, a beneficiary assessment on urban water and sanitation involved consultation with the primary users in urban communities to determine attitudes, preferences, and perceptions towards water and sanitation services, as well as options for community-managed water and sanitation projects.

To support such participatory activities, the Africa Region established in fiscal 1995 special Systematic Client Consultation Funds in each department. At the same time, the Africa Region vice presidency has been a major user of the Fund for Innovative Approaches in Human and Social Development, established in late fiscal 1994, which supports participation, consul-

TABLE 4-2. WORLD BANK COMMITMENTS, DISBURSEMENTS, AND NET TRANSFERS IN AFRICA, 1990–95

(millions of US dollars; fiscal years)

Item	Nigeria start 1995	Nigeria 1995	Nigeria 1990–95	Côte d'Ivoire start 1995	Côte d'Ivoire 1995	Côte d'Ivoire 1990–95	Sudan start 1995	Sudan 1995	Sudan 1990–95	Total region start 1995	Total region 1995	Total region 1990–95
Undisbursed commitments	2,053			241			1			12,200		
Commitments		—	1,954		303	1,668		—	98		2,284	19,237
Gross disbursements		273	1,919		270	1,343		—	378		2,795	16,797
Repayments		384	1,787		218	987		—	49		1,173	5,850
Net disbursements		-111	132		53	357		—	329		1,623	10,947
Interest and charges		262	1,587		160	926		—	36		819	5,040
Net transfer		-373	-1,455		-107	-569		—	293		804	5,907

NOTE: *Disbursements from the IDA Special Fund are included. The countries shown in the table are those with the largest amounts of public or publicly guaranteed long-term debt. Details may not add to totals because of rounding.*
— *Zero.*

tation, and social assessment in operations through capacity building and operational support. The Region has set fiscal 1998 as the target date for building beneficiary consultation into all its major lending and nonlending activities.

Private sector development. Improving the supply response in the wake of adjustment remains the driving force of private sector development efforts in the Africa region. During the past year, efforts continued to help client countries improve their business environment, accelerate public enterprise reform and privatization, and restructure and diversify the financial sector. In addition, efforts continue to be made to enhance private sector competitiveness through measures aimed at internal liberalization—the abolition of monopolies, the promotion of competition in domestic trade, and the rationalization of investment-incentive schemes. An example of this multipronged approach is evident in the Private Sector Adjustment and Competitiveness Credit for Senegal approved in the past fiscal year.

Attention is also being paid to increasing private sector participation and investment in infrastructure. At present, the competitiveness of African firms is undermined by the high cost and low quality of infrastructure services. Performance-based management contracts have been used to encourage private participation. A landmark project in Côte d'Ivoire, approved in fiscal 1995, supports the first privately owned and operated independent power generating plant in Africa. Early experience with private sector participation has led the government of Côte d'Ivoire to redouble its efforts to encourage additional private participation in the power sector.

In nearly every country there has been an increased emphasis on dialogue with the private sector and on supporting channels of communication between client governments and the private sector. Support to the local chamber of commerce, as planned in the Mauritania Capacity Building Project for the Development of the Private Sector, can help such organizations become better interlocutors for private sector interests. Roundtables with the business community and surveys that monitor firm-level

conditions on a continuing basis are being used to understand better the constraints faced by enterprises. In December 1994, the Africa Region vice presidency, in conjunction with the Finance and Private Sector Development vice presidency, organized a two-day seminar in Nairobi on "The Resumption of Private Sector Growth in Africa." The seminar brought together senior Bank officials and more than fifty private sector representatives from ten African countries. It confirmed the existence of large untapped potential in the African private sector, highlighted some of the problems that entrepreneurs face, and suggested ways in which the Bank could channel support to the business community more directly.

Social priorities. Human-resource development and poverty reduction, in particular, are at the forefront of the Bank's objectives in Africa. These central objectives were pursued during the year in various ways, both directly and indirectly. Many of the projects approved that support long-term growth have focused on creating the necessary environment for increased employment opportunities, improving the efficiency of markets, and redirecting the allocation of public expenditures more toward the poor. Other projects are designed to provide broadly or narrowly targeted assistance for the poor in areas that range from health to adult literacy and food security. Poverty-targeted interventions have involved diverse measures such as raising productivity in agriculture, human-resource development or improving living conditions, provision of safety nets, and better national resource management. The projects through which such objectives have been pursued have been similarly varied; the most innovative among them during the past year were the Zambia Agricultural Sector Investment Program and the Chad Population and AIDS Control Project, both of which were prepared in highly collaborative ways involving beneficiaries, official donors, and NGOs.

The best illustration of innovative, indirect, yet effective, interventions to improve social conditions has been the demobilization program in Uganda, which the government continued to implement during the year and which aims at reallocating public expenditures away from

TABLE 4-3. PROJECTS APPROVED DURING FISCAL YEAR 1995, AFRICA

Country/project name	Date of Approval	Maturities	Principal amount (millions) SDR	Principal amount (millions) US$
Benin				
Health and Population Project	May 30, 1995	2005/2035	17.90	27.80
Third Structural Adjustment Credit	May 23, 1995	2005/2035	25.80	40.00
Environmental Management Project	May 2, 1995	2005/2035	5.50	8.00
Burkina Faso				
Urban Environment Project	May 23, 1995	2005/2035	24.80	37.00
Second Urban Project (supplement)	November 10, 1994	2000/2029	6.90	10.00
Burundi				
Second Health and Population Project	May 25, 1995	2005/2035	14.30	21.30
Emergency Assistance Project	December 15, 1994	2005/2035	9.80	14.60
Cameroon				
Transport Sector Technical Assistance Project	April 11, 1995	2005/2035	6.90	10.20
Health, Fertility, and Nutrition Project	March 7, 1995	2005/2035	29.50	43.00
Economic Recovery Credit (supplement)	December 8, 1994	2004/2034	23.20	32.80
Cape Verde				
Basic Education and Training Project	January 19, 1995	2005/2034	7.80	11.50
Central African Republic				
Livestock Development and Rangeland Management Project	December 1, 1994	2005/2034	11.50	16.60
Chad				
Population and AIDS Control	March 23, 1995	2005/2034	13.90	20.40
Agricultural and Livestock Services Project	March 14, 1995	2005/2035	17.00	24.53
Social Development Action Project (supplement)	November 10, 1994	2000/2030	6.80	9.80
Second Transport Sector Project (supplement)	November 10, 1994	2003/2033	8.80	12.70
Côte d'Ivoire				
Private Sector Energy Project	June 28, 1995	2005/2035	50.60	79.66
Agricultural Export Promotion and Diversification Project	June 22, 1995	2005/2035	3.70	5.83
Municipal Support Project	April 13, 1995	2005/2035	27.20	40.00
Economic Recovery Credit (supplement)	December 8, 1994	2004/2034	55.20	77.90
Economic Recovery Credit	October 20, 1994	2004/2034	70.70	100.00
Ethiopia				
National Fertilizer Sector Project	June 13, 1995	2005/2035	82.90	120.00
Seed Systems Development Project	June 13, 1995	2005/2035	15.20	22.00
Structural Adjustment Credit (supplement)	December 8, 1994	2003/2033	0.10	0.20
Gabon				
Transport Sector Technical Assistance Project	July 7, 1994	1999/2009	n.a.	5.20
Ghana				
Mining Sector Development and Environment Project	June 13, 1995	2005/2035	7.90	12.30
Private Sector Adjustment Credit	May 9, 1995	2005/2034	46.90	70.00
Fisheries Sub-sector Capacity Building Project	May 2, 1995	2005/2034	6.20	9.00
Vocational Skills and Informal Sector Support Project	March 28, 1995	2005/2034	6.60	9.60
Thermal Power Project	February 16, 1995	2005/2034	124.10	175.60
Agricultural Sector Adjustment Credit (supplement)	December 8, 1994	2002/2031	3.60	5.00
Private Sector Development Project	December 6, 1994	2005/2034	9.00	13.00
Guinea				
Equity and School Improvement Project	May 9, 1995	2005/2035	28.50	42.50
Financial Sector Operation	October 18, 1994	2005/2034	16.30	23.00
Guinea-Bissau				
Transport and Urban Infrastructure Project	June 22, 1995	2005/2035	14.00	22.00
Kenya				
Sexually Transmitted Infections Project	March 14, 1995	2005/2035	27.70	40.00
Institutional Development and Civil Service Reform Project	December 20, 1994	2005/2034	17.20	25.35

Country/project name	Date of Approval	Maturities	Principal amount (millions) SDR	Principal amount (millions) US$
Madagascar				
Agricultural Extension Program Support Project	May 23, 1995	2005/2035	16.20	25.20
Second Irrigation Rehabilitation Project	July 12, 1994	2004/2034	15.00	21.20
Malawi				
National Water Development Project	June 28, 1995	2005/2035	50.30	79.20
Railways Restructuring Project	March 28, 1995	2005/2034	11.20	16.16
Entrepreneurship Development and Drought Recovery Program (supplement)	December 8, 1994	2002/2032	3.20	4.60
Enterpreneurship Development and Drought Recovery Program (supplement)	November 3, 1994	2002/2032	27.60	40.00
Mali				
Agricultural Trading and Processing Promotion Pilot Project	June 1, 1995	2005/2035	3.90	6.00
Education Sector Adjustment Credit	January 5, 1995	2005/2034	34.30	50.00
Public Works and Capacity Building Project (supplement)	November 10, 1994	2002/2032	6.90	10.00
Mauritania				
Private Sector Development Program	May 23, 1995	2005/2035	19.30	30.00
Capacity Building Project for the Development of the Private Sector	May 23, 1995	2005/2035	4.70	7.20
General Education V Project	April 18, 1995	2005/2034	23.80	35.00
Mauritius				
Port Development and Environment Protection Project	June 20, 1995	2001/2010	n.a.	7.10
Port Development and Environment Projection Project	June 20, 1995	2001/2010	n.a.	23.40
Higher Technical Education Project	March 23, 1995	2000/2010	n.a.	16.00
Niger				
Pilot Private Irrigation Promotion Project	April 18, 1995	2005/2035	4.60	6.80
Public Works and Employment Project (supplement)	November 10, 1994	2001/2031	6.90	10.00
Rwanda				
Emergency Recovery Project	January 31, 1995	2005/2034	34.30	50.00
Senegal				
Water Sector Project	June 29, 1995	2005/2035	63.50	100.00
Private Sector Capacity Building Project	June 29, 1995	2005/2035	8.00	12.50
Agricultural Sector Adjustment Credit	June 6, 1995	2005/2035	29.00	45.00
Community Nutrition Project	May 16, 1995	2005/2035	11.70	18.20
Private Sector Adjustment and Competitiveness Credit	February 16, 1995	2005/2034	27.60	40.00
Economic Recovery Credit (supplement)	December 8, 1994	2004/2034	2.30	3.20
Sierra Leone				
Urban Water Supply Project	April 11, 1995	2005/2034	24.50	36.00
Structural Adjustment Credit (supplement)	December 8, 1994	2004/2033	0.20	0.30
Swaziland				
Urban Development Project	November 15, 1994	2000/2015	n.a.	29.00
Tanzania				
Mineral Sector Development Technical Assistance Project	July 28, 1994	2004/2034	8.90	12.50
Togo				
Education Rehabilitation Project	June 28, 1995	2005/2035	23.30	36.60
Uganda				
Institutional Capacity Building Project	June 1, 1995	2005/2035	25.00	36.40
District Health Services Pilot and Demonstration Project	February 7, 1995	2005/2034	30.90	45.00
Second Structural Adjustment Credit (supplement)	December 8, 1994	2004/2034	0.40	0.60
Zambia				
Second Social Recovery Project	June 28, 1995	2005/2035	19.10	30.00
Urban Restructuring and Water Supply Project	May 16, 1995	2005/2035	21.30	33.00
Agricultural Sector Investment Program	March 30, 1995	2005/2034	41.20	60.00
Economic and Social Adjustment Credit (supplement)	December 8, 1994	2004/2034	9.70	13.70
Health Sector Support Project	November 15, 1994	2005/2034	38.70	56.00
			1,491.60	2,284.30

n.a. = not applicable (IBRD loan).

NOTE: Details may not add to totals because of rounding.

military interests in favor of the social sectors. The program was prompted by a public expenditure review in 1992 that revealed an expenditure pattern in which defense spending amounted to about 40 percent of the annual recurrent budget, crowding out investments in the social sectors. Given the need to design, finance, and implement a large-scale reduction in military force, the government requested that the Bank become the lead agency in putting together and mobilizing resources for such a program. As time was of the essence, the Bank, at the request of the government, restructured an ongoing IDA credit to include a component for assisting the socioeconomic reintegration of demobilized soldiers and their dependents into a productive civilian life. The program was targeted at about 50,000 veterans and their dependents (about a 50 percent reduction in force) over a three-year period.

The program provides veterans with a fresh set of civilian clothing; transportation to their home districts, a transitional safety net of cash and in-kind payments (agricultural tools, building materials for a house, for example) over a six-month readjustment period; job training; and enhanced health benefits, especially for the disabled and chronically ill. Primary school fees are also paid for veterans' children for one year. The average cost of this package is about $1,000 per veteran.

Under the program, to date, about 33,000 veterans and more than 100,000 dependents have been successfully integrated into their home communities. About $35 million has been mobilized through a Bank-coordinated, multidonor effort to achieve this result. A final-phase demobilization of 12,500 veterans is under implementation and is expected to be completed by December 1995. As a direct result of the program, over the 1992–94 period, defense expenditure was reduced from 38 percent to 22 percent of overall recurrent expenditure, making room for substantial increases in social expenditures.

EAST ASIA AND PACIFIC

The East Asia and Pacific region again recorded the most rapid aggregate growth rate among regions in the world: 9.6 percent in 1994, up slightly from the 9.4 percent posted in 1993. Nearly all countries in the region participated. For example, growth in China eased slightly to 11.8 percent, compared with 13.9 percent in 1993, as the government experienced some success in cooling the economy, and the Philippines recorded a satisfying increase in its growth rate to 5.1 percent. Other countries in the region were able to maintain growth in the 5 percent-to-8 percent range, with the exception of the Pacific islands and Mongolia. In the Pacific islands, aggregate growth was close to 2 percent—an improvement over the recent past; Mongolia, which succeeded in reversing past declines, also registered growth of about 2 percent.

Impressive as this overall picture is, it is important to recognize that a large development agenda remains. The region is diverse: It contains the largest and the smallest Bank member countries, as well as countries that number among the Bank's most prosperous and poorest borrowers. The maturing middle-income countries, with an established reputation for economic performance, constitute only 7.2 percent of the population, and their share in Bank operations is declining. The Republic of Korea received its last two loans from the Bank in fiscal year 1995, and it is graduat-ing—following the precedents of Australia (1962), Japan (1967), New Zealand (1972), and Singapore (1975). The vast majority of the people in developing East Asia, some 1.3 billion, live in low-income member countries, including the six economies in transition (Cambodia, China, the Lao People's Democratic Republic, Mongolia, Myanmar, and Viet Nam). In addition, such large borrowers as Indonesia and the Philippines have annual per capita incomes of under $1,000, and, despite rapid progress, continue to face difficult development problems. At the other end of the spectrum, the small Pacific island member states are struggling to attain higher growth rates and participate in the dynamic economic expansion of the Pacific Rim. The primary challenge facing all these countries is, of course, reducing poverty. The economies in transition face particular problems in moving to a market-oriented system based on more private-sector activity. The region is still largely rural and will undergo rapid urbanization in the coming decades, adding to the already large backlog of demand for infrastructure. Moreover, the region's growth has placed a heavy burden on its natural resources and environmental quality, which will require major remedial and preventive action.

A look at the record. The East Asian countries have been quite effective in translating their high rates of growth into a reduction of poverty. The number of people living in absolute poverty has declined to about 180 million (11 percent of the total population), down from an estimated 330 million in 1980. This represents about 17 percent of the poor in all developing countries. In addition to the income figures, other social indicators in the region have shown remarkable improvement: Life expectancy has risen to 68 years (compared with 64 years for all developing countries), primary education is essentially universal, and secondary enrollments are 53 percent (compared with 45 percent), while infant mortality is only 39 per 1,000 (compared with 65 per 1,000 for all developing countries). There is, of course, significant variation among individual countries.

The bulk of the resources needed to sustain this performance has been generated domestically. Savings rates have been above 30 percent of gross domestic product (GDP) for most countries, and rates are rising toward that level in the others. Much investment has been made in education and training, even in the low-income countries. Furthermore, these countries are following outward-looking development strategies. Strong export growth has been a mainstay of their rapid expansion, including countries whose economies are in transition. The past year has witnessed a further liberalization of trade throughout the re-

TABLE 4-4. LENDING TO BORROWERS IN EAST ASIA AND PACIFIC, BY SECTOR, 1986–95

(millions of us dollars; fiscal years)

Sector	Annual average, 1986–90	1991	1992	1993	1994	1995
Agriculture	666.9	1,374.7	826.7	1,089.3	1,735.4	818.6
Energy						
Oil and gas	49.2	—	100.0	225.0	266.0	245.0
Power	662.2	275.0	1,745.9	760.0	1,048.5	1,383.0
Environment	—	—	—	50.0	216.5	110.0
Human resources						
Education	284.9	592.0	474.1	478.9	436.6	526.5
Population, health, and nutrition	55.8	164.0	129.6	200.4	160.0	242.2
Social sector	—	—	—	—	9.7	20.0
Industry and finance						
Industry	197.2	361.7	82.7	250.0	40.0	175.0
Financial	341.9	439.3	—	457.0	100.0	—
Infrastructure and urban development						
Telecommunications	84.6	—	375.0	134.0	250.0	325.0
Transportation	728.1	323.6	1,182.5	1,132.2	1,340.0	960.0
Urban development	261.4	543.1	168.0	110.0	349.0	208.5
Water supply and sewerage	112.3	177.8	275.0	310.0	—	75.0
Multisector	348.0	250.0	70.0	200.0	82.7	167.0
Public sector management	6.1	62.0	17.0	173.0	—	438.0
Tourism	—	—	—	—	—	—
Total	3,798.6	4,563.2	5,446.5	5,569.8	6,034.4	5,693.8
Of which: IBRD	3,189.7	3,471.0	4,386.9	4,404.8	4,623.8	4,592.6
IDA	608.8	1,092.2	1,059.6	1,165.0	1,410.6	1,101.2
Number of operations	38	39	45	45	43	42

NOTE: Details may not add to totals because of rounding.
— Zero.

gion. East Asian countries' integration into world markets is remarkable. These developing countries currently account for over one third of developing country trade (10 percent of total world trade). It is estimated that over one third of the increment to world trade between now and the end of the decade will be generated from developing East Asia.

Integration into world markets, along with strong economic performance and stable policy, has made East Asia the predominant destination of private international capital flows, both directly and in portfolio investment. The region received an estimated $90 billion in foreign capital flows in 1994, of which $82 billion was from private sources and $43 billion was direct investment. Rising interest rates in the United States dampened international investment flows in 1994, compared with the previous year, but

East Asian countries were able to maintain their access to markets better than most. Furthermore, they have been able to use the foreign savings effectively: Recipients of large flows have raised domestic investment rates by several percentage points of GDP as they absorbed the foreign capital. The combination of effective use of foreign investment, sound macroeconomic policies, and high export growth was an important reason why these economies were largely spared from the disruptions in currency markets and investment flows that have been affecting developing countries since the end of 1994.

Challenges ahead. Despite outstanding growth performance in recent years, reducing poverty is still the most critical issue facing the low-income countries. In addition to the 180 million living in absolute poverty, 280 million more live just above the poverty line, with incomes barely one third above that of the poorest, and almost 400 million more people get by on incomes no more than double that of the poverty line. Analysis of poverty issues and recommendations on poverty reduction are core elements of Bank work in these countries: A major poverty analysis, in cooperation with the government of Viet Nam, was completed in 1994; a similar study (and a subsequent conference held to discuss its findings) in China was followed by that government's first comprehensive plan to fight poverty (the 7-8 Plan);[1] a large part of the Bank's agriculture and almost all of its social sector operations in China have shifted to the poorer provinces; and the poverty study for Indonesia, completed in fiscal 1994, has led to greater poverty focus in projects in that country.

Most of the low-income countries in the region are economies in transition. Success in sustaining high rates of growth depends critically on their completing the necessary legal, budgetary, and governance reforms that market economies require. While these countries have been open to change and have undertaken substantial reforms already, the process is far from complete. China unified its exchange rate in January 1994 and moved to open its capital market further. The Bank is currently working with the government on state-owned enterprise and financial sector reform. A structural adjustment credit was prepared and approved for Viet Nam

1. So called because its target is to eliminate poverty among the 80 million people China considers poor in seven years (by the year 2000).

in fiscal 1995, and an emergency rehabilitation credit was approved for Cambodia to assist in its transition.

The surging demand for infrastructure in the region is related both to its rapid rate of growth and its accelerating urbanization. Nearly all the countries in the region are experiencing bottlenecks, and investment demands for infrastructure have been estimated at $1.5 trillion between now and the end of the decade. The Bank is increasing its financing of vital infrastructure—transport, power, water, sanitation, and telecommunications—in East Asia, which rose to $2.7 billion in fiscal 1995. The share of Bank commitments in support of infrastructure investments is expected to continue its climb, but the demand is greater than public sources are likely to be able to meet, and more private financing must be encouraged. The Philippines has led the way by sponsoring more than thirty BOT (build-operate-transfer) investments in power supply, effectively using private financing to solve its most pressing infrastructure bottleneck.[2] China, Indonesia, Malaysia, and Thailand are also encouraging private financing of infrastructure, and other countries in the region are investigating the potential. The Bank has advised countries on the necessary regulatory and legal structure for promoting such investments while protecting public interests. Several billions of dollars of private equity funds have been raised for infrastructure investment in the region.

Protecting the environment and assuring the effective use of natural resources is increasingly being recognized by the authorities in these countries as vital to sustaining their continued prosperity. In the past two years, the Bank has completed or initiated comprehensive environmental studies in most of the countries. Governments have begun to take stronger actions on both natural resources conservation and environmental pollution. Controlling industrial pollution is an area that has received widespread attention. The high investment rates and rapid growth in the region imply that most of the industry that will be in place twenty years from now hasn't been built yet. Priority is being placed on ensuring that new installations

are properly located and use clean technology. Regional approaches are also being considered, for example, to develop coordinated policies on logging and offshore fishing in the Pacific islands.

The Bank's activities. The remaining development agenda is more than enough to severely tax any likely amount of resources available from the Bank or other international institutions. High domestic savings in these countries will properly and necessarily provide the bulk of the resources for development, and that will be supplemented by foreign investment. The Bank's contribution is, nevertheless, significant. Commitments in fiscal 1995 were $5.7 billion, leading to gross disbursements of $4.5 billion and net disbursements of $1.6 billion; net transfers, taking account of interest as well as principal repayments, were a negative $634 million *(see Table 4-5)*. Within these overall figures, it is important to note major shifts in the allocation of resources. The mature borrowers, Korea, Malaysia, and Thailand, are net repayers, and their share of new lending from the Bank is stable or declining. They do, however, continue to rely on the Bank for special studies and projects in innovative areas. Some countries, most recently Indonesia, have taken advantage of favorable reserve positions to prepay some of their Bank loans. These factors partially mask the large positive net transfers going to the low-income countries of the region. Net transfers to China, for example, amounted to some $1.4 billion.

The Bank is becoming more focused and selective in its activities, concentrating on areas of high priority agreed with its clients. These correspond to the priorities noted earlier, with varying emphasis by country according to specific situations. In the more mature economies, economic and sector work (ESW) tasks have been developed in close cooperation with the clients to address specific topics—the environment, poverty/income-distribution issues, and

2. Typically in a BOT, a private party (or consortium) agrees to finance, construct, operate, and maintain a facility for a specified period (supplying power, in this case, to the national distribution grid) and then transfer the facility to a government or other public authority.

TABLE 4-5. WORLD BANK COMMITMENTS, DISBURSEMENTS, AND NET TRANSFERS IN EAST ASIA AND PACIFIC, 1990–95

(millions of US dollars; fiscal years)

Item	China start 1995	China 1995	China 1990–95	Indonesia start 1995	Indonesia 1995	Indonesia 1990–95	Philippines start 1995	Philippines 1995	Philippines 1990–95	Total region start 1995	Total region 1995	Total region 1990–95
Undisbursed commitments	8,956			5,047			1,911			18,260		
Commitments		3,000	13,937		1,417	8,632		18	3,432		5,694	31,026
Gross disbursements		2,214	9,325		1,144	7,053		398	3,022		4,536	23,424
Repayments		353	1,337		1,313	4,645		388	1,968		2,972	14,279
Net disbursements		1,861	7,988		-169	2,408		10	1,054		1,565	9,145
Interest and charges		459	1,839		935	4,973		369	1,939		2,199	11,776
Net transfer		1,402	6,149		-1,104	-2,565		-359	-885		-634	-2,631

NOTE: *Disbursements from the IDA Special Fund are included. The countries shown in the table are those with the largest amounts of public or publicly guaranteed long-term debt. Details may not add to totals because of rounding.*

social security reform in Thailand; transport issues in Korea; the labor market in Malaysia.

Elsewhere, the Bank is concentrating on priority areas where it has greater comparative advantage. In Indonesia, it has reduced its activities in traditional irrigation and power projects and shifted more toward improving the quality of human-resource development, urban management, and development in the (poorer) outer islands. In the Philippines, the Bank has helped the government attract private financing for power and other traditional infrastructure and is shifting its support to activities that support development in rural areas and help protect the environment. Bank support for industry projects in China has been reduced, and more attention is being directed in its operations to incorporating environmental issues and addressing urban problems. China has made effective use of IDA resources to advance its poverty-reduction program and has drawn on IDA resources for human-resource development. The Bank's program in the Indochinese states has concentrated on issues of transition and of facilitating aid flows from interested donors. The latter issue has been supported through donor meetings chaired by the Bank in Viet Nam, aid groups supported by the Bank in Cambodia and Lao PDR, and through extensive technical assistance. In Viet Nam, the lending program, aided

by a substantial body of ESW and a close dialogue with the government, has expanded rapidly since lending activities resumed in fiscal 1994. The Bank's operations there give priority to rural devlopment, human-resource activities, and the rehabilitation of infrastructure. The Bank also chairs consultative groups for Indonesia, Mongolia, Papua New Guinea, and the Philippines.

In all countries a major objective of Bank activity has been to facilitate greater private involvement in the development process. Given the wide diversity of countries, this has taken different forms in different countries. But the overwhelming lesson from the successful countries in the region is that harnessing the energies of the private sector can add greatly to the prospects for growth, and, if managed properly, as has generally been the case in East Asia, can also reduce poverty. High domestic private savings rates are a key factor when they are accompanied by sound and stable domestic policy. But beyond this, there is ample evidence that the establishment of appropriate legal and regulatory systems, particularly in economies in transition, is vital to promoting strong domestic private sectors and attracting stable foreign investment. The regional vice presidency has made the development or strengthening of market infrastructure a central point of its activities.

TABLE 4-6. PROJECTS APPROVED DURING FISCAL YEAR 1995, EAST ASIA AND PACIFIC

Country/project name	Date of Approval	Maturities	Principal amount (millions) SDR	Principal amount (millions) US$
Cambodia				
Social Fund Project	June 8, 1995	2005/2035	13.40	20.00
Technical Assistance Project	December 6, 1994	2005/2034	11.60	17.00
China				
Iodine Deficiency Disorders Control Project[a]	June 28, 1995	2001/2015	n.a.	7.00
Iodine Deficiency Disorders Control Project[a]	June 28, 1995	2005/2030	12.70	20.00
Inland Waterways Project	June 20, 1995	2001/2015	n.a.	210.00
Southwest Poverty Reduction Project[a]	June 15, 1995	2005/2030	128.60	200.00
Southwest Poverty Reduction Project[a]	June 15, 1995	2001/2015	n.a.	47.50
Seventh Railway Project	June 1, 1995	2001/2015	n.a.	400.00
Yangtze Basin Water Resources Project[a]	April 25, 1995	2005/2030	74.80	110.00
Yangtze Basin Water Resources Project[a]	April 25, 1995	2001/2015	n.a.	100.00
Fiscal Technical Assistance Project[a]	April 25, 1995	2005/2030	16.80	25.00
Fiscal Technical Assistance Project[a]	April 25, 1995	2001/2015	n.a.	25.00
Sichuan Power Transmission Project	February 28, 1995	2000/2015	n.a.	270.00
Technology Development Project	February 28, 1995	2000/2015	n.a.	200.00
Zhejiang Power Development Project	February 28, 1995	2000/2015	n.a.	400.00
Economic Law Reform Project	October 18, 1994	2005/2029	6.90	10.00
Comprehensive Maternal and Child Health Project	October 18, 1994	2005/2029	61.90	90.00
Basic Education in Poor and Minority Areas Project	September 6, 1994	2005/2029	69.20	100.00
Shenyang Industrial Reform Project	September 6, 1994	2000/2014	n.a.	175.00
Xinjiang Highway Project	August 30, 1994	2000/2014	n.a.	150.00
Liaoning Environment Project	July 26, 1994	2000/2014	n.a.	110.00
Enterprise Housing and Social Security Reform Project[a]	July 5, 1994	2000/2014	n.a.	275.00
Enterprise Housing and Social Security Reform Project[a]	July 5, 1994	2000/2029	53.10	75.00
Indonesia				
Second Technical Assistance Project for Public and Private Provision of Infrastructure	June 22, 1995	2001/2015	n.a.	28.00
Telecommunications Sector Modernization Project	June 15, 1995	2001/2015	n.a.	325.00
Fourth Health Project	June 15, 1995	2001/2015	n.a.	88.00
Book and Reading Development Project	May 23, 1995	2001/2015	n.a.	132.50
Village Infrastructure Project for Java	May 23, 1995	2001/2015	n.a.	72.50
Second Agricultural Research Management Project	May 16, 1995	2001/2015	n.a.	63.00
Kalimantan Urban Development Project	March 21, 1995	2000/2015	n.a.	136.00
Second Rural Electrification Project	February 28, 1995	2000/2015	n.a.	398.00
Second Professional Human Resources Development Project	December 15, 1994	2000/2015	n.a.	69.00
Second Accountancy Development Project	September 22, 1994	2001/2014	n.a.	25.00
Land Administration Project	September 15, 1994	2000/2014	n.a.	80.00
Korea, Republic of				
Waste Disposal Project	December 20, 1994	2000/2009	n.a.	75.00
Pusan Urban Transport Management Project	December 20, 1994	2000/2009	n.a.	100.00
Ports Development and Environmental Improvement Project	September 15, 1994	2000/2009	n.a.	100.00
Lao People's Democratic Republic				
Health System Reform and Malaria Control Project	January 5, 1995	2005/2035	12.90	19.20
Philippines				
Women's Health and Safe Motherhood Project	March 9, 1995	2000/2015	n.a.	18.00
Thailand				
Clean Fuels and Environmental Improvement Project	May 23, 1995	2001/2012	n.a.	90.00
Lam Takhong Pump Storage Project	May 9, 1995	2001/2012	n.a.	100.00
Third Land Titling Project	September 22, 1994	2000/2011	n.a.	118.10
Distribution System Reinforcement Project	September 22, 1994	2000/2011	n.a.	50.00
Second Gas Transmission Project	September 22, 1994	1999/2011	n.a.	155.00
Viet Nam				
Urban Restructuring and Water Supply Project	May 16, 1995	2005/2035	110.60	165.00
Irrigation Rehabilitation Project	April 25, 1995	2005/2035	67.00	100.00
Structural Adjustment Credit	October 25, 1994	2005/2034	103.50	150.00
			743.00	5,693.80

n.a. = not applicable (IBRD loan).

a. "Blend" loan/credit.

Provision of economic infrastructure is also vital to private sector development, and that has figured prominently in the Bank's lending activities. Although the Bank does not lend directly to the private sector, it is exploring ways to help governments promote necessary longer-term financing for privately financed infrastructure.

Dissemination of the results and recommendations of the Bank's ESW is as important as the results themselves, and the Bank is being more active in assuring the wide distribution of its work in order to enlarge the work's impact. A regional study of trade and investment was widely discussed with policymakers in all major trading countries prior to the November 1994 Asia Pacific Economic Cooperation meeting in Jakarta. The Regional Environmental Strategy has also been widely disseminated. A third regional study of the Pacific island members was completed, and its conclusions were discussed at a regional ministers' meeting and elsewhere throughout the area. Individual country work has also been reaching a wider audience. Some 6,000 copies of the economic report on Viet Nam (in English and Vietnamese) have been made widely available to the public, both inside the country and abroad. This has contributed to a fruitful dialogue within the country on the liberalization process. Reports have been translated and distributed in other countries, as well.

Improved portfolio performance. Project effectiveness is a function of both quality at entry—well-designed projects—and careful supervision. The Bank has adopted measures to improve its project performance above current levels by strengthening the project-preparation process and by enhancing supervision. The region's overall success rating on projects remains above average—95 percent of projects under implementation are currently rated satisfactory with respect to their likelihood of achieving their development objectives, and 87 percent of projects exiting supervision in fiscal 1994 were found to be satisfactory. Studies by the Bank's Operations Evaluation Department of completed projects approved since 1980 show that 81 percent of those in the East Asia and Pacific region met their development objectives and are sustainable.

Improving the quality of life is the central development objective for the countries of South Asia. Despite considerable economic potential, relatively high rates of growth through the 1980s, and slow but steady economic recovery in recent years, countries in the South Asia region are still characterized by widespread poverty and unacceptably low standards of living. One fifth of the world's population lives in South Asia, but it is home to nearly half of the world's poor—between 400 million and 500 million people.

Per capita gross national product (GNP) in the region ranges from a low of $200 in Nepal to a high of $900 in the Maldives; with the notable exception of Sri Lanka and several states in India, living conditions are harsh. Only in Africa is life expectancy lower. One out of every ten children born dies before the age of one. Poor health and high rates of malnutrition are accompanied by low levels of literacy—as of 1990, only 45 percent of South Asian men and 31 percent of women could read and write. Recent estimates suggest that nearly half of all children do not even complete primary school.

The development strategy of the countries in the region has traditionally been inward oriented, and the public sector has been given a large role in the economy. But increasing pressures for faster progress on growth and poverty reduction have led to an era of reform. South Asian countries are dismantling restrictions on domestic and foreign private investment, removing trade restrictions, and reducing tariffs. Although they have also adopted privatization programs, progress has generally been slow except in Pakistan, where, after some initial delay, a major privatization program is under way (including industrial enterprises, banks, and energy and telecommunications companies). Financial markets are being liberalized across the region, providing greater scope for private participation and market determination of interest rates and credit allocation. There has also been a substantial relaxation of exchange and capital controls. For example Bangladesh, India, Pakistan, and Sri Lanka removed remaining exchange restrictions on current account transactions in 1994, while Nepal had done so earlier.

International financial markets have reacted favorably to these reforms. In 1994, portfolio equity inflows increased significantly, amounting to about one fifth the total flows to all developing countries. This new-found access to international capital markets marks a major change in the South Asia economic environment. But inflows, particularly of foreign direct investment (FDI), continue to be hampered by bureaucratic regulation and low labor-market flexibility. Flows of FDI in 1994 are estimated at about $1 billion, less than one tenth the amount of all private inflows to developing countries. Nevertheless, total private capital inflows currently amount to 2 percent of GDP, and, if used to finance incremental high-return investment, they could raise growth rates by at least 0.5 percent annually. However, in the near-term, inflows have tended to appreciate real exchange rates, mainly by fueling inflation, for example in India and Sri Lanka.

Challenges for the future. Reducing poverty, improving living conditions, and sustaining economic growth are critical development issues facing countries throughout the region. The region's growth record was good during the 1980s, and there is convincing evidence that high growth rates raised per capita consumption at all income levels and caused levels of poverty to fall. However, while growth rates were high, they were not sustainable, and, in many parts of the region, rising per capita consumption levels were not accompanied by commensurate improvements in social indicators. To ensure continued economic and social progress, countries of the region—whether they be small, island economies like the Maldives or semi-industrial giants like India—must address five major challenges:

• They must stay the course on macroeconomic reforms.

• Economic reforms, aimed at higher growth and greater economic resilience, must be extended and deepened.

• Coverage of crucial infrastructure services must be expanded.

• Measurable steps to reduce poverty and improve living conditions to further develop the human-resource base are essential.

• Natural resources must be managed so that the region's development path is environmentally sustainable.

Economic growth and the private sector. The broad consensus in development thinking —borne by the successes and failures of past decades—is that countries do better, both in generating growth and reducing poverty, with more market-friendly policies and outward-looking strategies. Economywide, this means starting with macroeconomic stability and developing a leaner and more efficient public sector.

Private sector development is essential for generating and maintaining economic growth.

TABLE 4-7. LENDING TO BORROWERS IN SOUTH ASIA, BY SECTOR, 1986–95

(millions of us dollars; fiscal years)

Sector	Annual average, 1986–90	1991	1992	1993	1994	1995
Agriculture	864.3	773.0	346.1	480.7	387.8	551.3
Energy						
Oil and gas	218.6	735.2	330.0	—	—	120.8
Power	999.2	200.0	730.0	960.0	230.0	250.0
Environment	—	—	—	—	14.7	168.0
Human resources						
Education	221.5	307.1	145.6	339.0	220.0	423.7
Population, health, and nutrition	104.1	388.5	377.5	827.0	233.1	257.9
Social sector	—	—	—	—	—	—
Industry and finance						
Industry	198.7	528.0	—	—	250.3	3.2
Financial	419.8	123.5	28.4	65.8	—	916.0
Infrastructure and urban development						
Telecommunications	89.0	57.0	55.0	—	—	—
Transportation	294.9	178.9	306.0	120.0	491.3	—
Urban development	220.5	—	—	—	246.0	39.0
Water supply and sewerage	115.4	306.6	—	208.2	—	275.8
Mining and other extractive	68.0	—	—	12.0	—	—
Multisector	120.8	7.0	680.2	403.5	—	—
Public sector management	—	—	—	—	296.8	—
Tourism	—	—	—	—	—	—
Total	3,934.7	3,604.8	2,998.8	3,416.2	2,370.0	3,005.7
Of which: IBRD	2,376.7	1,540.1	1,348.0	1,145.0	474.0	1,584.8
IDA	1,558.1	2,064.7	1,650.8	2,271.2	1,896.0	1,420.9
Number of operations	30	30	24	26	19	18

NOTE: Details may not add to totals because of rounding.
— Zero.

The region has made progress in promoting the private sector in three areas: (a) reforming fiscal and financial incentives and the regulatory and legal environments to improve the environment for private sector development; (b) privatizing those public sector activities that are more efficiently carried out by private sector; and (c) opening sectors to private investment that had previously been reserved for the public sector. The Bank has taken steps to improve its support to private sector development. For example, starting in 1994, it broadened its efforts to help India in mobilizing global resources from private sources. The Aid India Consortium was replaced by the India Development Forum, which included discussions with both official donors and, for the first time, private sector representatives. A similar approach was followed for the 1995 Pakistan and Sri Lanka Aid Consortiums.

The Bank is discussing with all countries in the region the need to stay the course on the macro policy front and to continue accelerating trade and financial sector reforms. It is also establishing closer links with the private sector and developing a better assistance strategy by undertaking private sector assessments. These assessments aim to identify the obstacles that private firms believe are blocking expansion. Assessments have been completed for India and Sri Lanka. An assessment is currently being prepared for Pakistan.

Two lending operations that support financial sector reforms were approved during the past year. The Bank's largest-ever loan to India, for $700 million in support of the Financial Sector Development Project, is assisting in the modernization of that country's banking system. Reforms supported by the loan will make it possible for India to move forward with a more diversified and competitive financial sector. The reforms support the central government's financial sector reform agenda through recapitalizing and restructuring state-owned banks and allowing banks to raise capital from the market. These reforms are expected to strengthen India's banking system and contribute to the development of capital and money markets. The $216 million Financial Sector Deepening and Intermediation Project in Pakistan will strengthen the regulatory framework under which banks operate and expand the long-term supply of credit to private enterprises.

Sectoral policies and reforms are also crucial. For example, infrastructural bottlenecks—particularly in roads, power, ports, and telecommunications—slow private sector expansion. Agricultural reforms are also important; this sector is a key source of income for the rural poor in South Asia.

The Bank's efforts to help meet the region's massive infrastructure requirements have focused on developing mechanisms to improve efficiency and expand private sector participation in the funding and management of basic infrastructure. Progress to date has been limited to utilities (power, telecommunications, and gas) and transport. During the past year, a $250 million operation was approved to assist the government of Pakistan increase the private sector's role in the development, ownership, and operation of power and related infrastructure by providing long-term financing through a replenishment of the Private Sector Energy Development Fund for subprojects that are either under implementation or are shortly to be launched. In India, efficiency, accountability, and competition are being encouraged through greater private sector participation in the power sector. Efforts are also under way to improve the efficiency of transport operations in India (railways, roads, and ports) by introducing commercial principles, more efficient pricing policies,

and easier entry for the private sector. In Bangladesh, a $120.8 million IDA credit is assisting the government in implementing further reforms to improve the enabling environment for private participation in the natural gas sector.

Addressing the needs of the poor. Economic growth alone is not sufficient to address the needs of South Asia's poor. Around the world, on average, increases in per capita income levels have been accompanied by improvements in standards of living of the poor; but the relationship is not inevitable. Evidence suggests that the pattern of public spending, and, in particular, spending on basic services—education, health, nutrition, and family planning—and safety net programs has an important effect on living standards. Furthermore, this effect is distinct from that of increases in private income levels and concomitant reductions in poverty.

As a part of ongoing reforms, most countries in the region have taken steps to reorient public spending to better address the needs of the poor. Bank-led public expenditure and investment reviews are discussed annually with the governments of Pakistan and Sri Lanka, and a review of education spending was completed this past fiscal year for Bangladesh.

Bank support for human-resource development in South Asia has expanded rapidly since the late 1980s. For example, in the period

TABLE 4-8. WORLD BANK COMMITMENTS, DISBURSEMENTS, AND NET TRANSFERS IN SOUTH ASIA, 1990–95

(millions of US dollars; fiscal years)

Item	India start 1995	India 1995	India 1990–95	Pakistan start 1995	Pakistan 1995	Pakistan 1990–95	Bangladesh start 1995	Bangladesh 1995	Bangladesh 1990–95	Total region start 1995	Total region 1995	Total region 1990–95
Undisbursed commitments	9,084			2,908			1,662			14,769		
Commitments		2,064	11,851		706	3,703		184	2,205		3,006	18,900
Gross disbursements		1,783	11,576		691	3,503		287	2,010		2,939	18,223
Repayments		1,062	4,632		235	920		42	152		1,359	5,807
Net disbursements		721	6,943		456	2,583		246	1,858		1,580	12,416
Interest and charges		904	4,737		233	1,108		44	218		1,203	6,183
Net transfer		-183	2,206		223	1,475		202	1,640		377	6,233

NOTE: *Disbursements from the IDA Special Fund are included. The countries shown in the table are those with the largest amounts of public or publicly guaranteed long-term debt. Details may not add to totals because of rounding.*

1986–90, lending for education, health and nutrition, and family planning accounted for 8 percent of the total portfolio. In fiscal 1995, it accounted for 23 percent of the portfolio. The Bank's strategy for the social sectors has three elements: (a) improving coverage and quality of services; (b) improving efficiency and cost effectiveness; and (c) developing innovative approaches to expand community participation to ensure service improvements. There has been a shift away from focusing solely on the public provision of services and—as in other sectors— a rethinking of the role of public and private sectors. The Bank is working closely with member governments to identify areas where there is a need for more public sector involvement, areas that are better left to private providers, and ways to encourage stronger partnerships between governments, the private sector, and nongovernmental organizations (NGOs).

The South Asia region is host to some of the world's best-known NGO groups; the diverse programs supported by them have great potential for helping to reduce poverty and improve living conditions in the region. In some Bank-assisted projects, NGOs play a role in the delivery of services—for example, in the $59.8 million Integrated Nutrition Project in Bangladesh (approved in fiscal 1995), the Cataract Blindness Control Project in India (approved in fiscal 1994), and the Rural Water Supply and Sanitation Fund Project in Nepal (under preparation in fiscal 1995).

Ensuring sustainable development. The region's current development strategies hold the promise of sustained, poverty-reducing economic growth. This growth, superimposed on a rapidly growing and urbanizing population, will put more pressure on air, water, and land resources. Problems are already apparent: In many areas, there are increased levels of air and water pollution, contamination by toxic wastes, soil erosion, land degradation, and deforestation. In addition, the environment is adversely affected in many countries by the presence of incentive regimes that encourage bad environmental practices—intensive use of high-polluting energy, inefficient use of surface water and groundwater,

underinvestment in sanitation and waste management, and inadequate protection of soils and forests.

Promoting sustainable agricultural growth is crucial for South Asia. Although traditionally the slowest growing sector, agriculture currently accounts for 32 percent of South Asia's GDP and employs more than 50 percent of the labor force. Agriculture is a key source of income for South Asia's poor. A substantial share of Bank lending is directed toward agriculture, with the aim of increasing output levels, particularly for smallholders. Much of the ongoing dialogue with member countries has focused on ways to increase private investment in the sector and to reduce the role of government in the supply and distribution of agricultural inputs. A number of critical issues—such as reducing fertilizer subsidies in India and Nepal, for example—have been addressed in recent public expenditure reviews. A substantial amount of economic and sector work in agriculture is either ongoing or has recently been completed for Bangladesh, India, Nepal, and Pakistan.

Within the agriculture sector, research and extension has a high payoff in terms of increased yields and higher profits. Research and extension is the focus of the $59.5 million Agriculture Human Resources Development Project in India. The project seeks to improve the quality and relevance of higher agricultural education and in-service training programs and strengthen the capacity of participating states to develop and manage human resources.

The lack of water is a key constraint to a more rapid expansion of agricultural output in many parts of South Asia. The Bank is providing support for overall water-resources management and for expansion and improvement of irrigation infrastructure (canals and tubewells, for instance). A strategy paper for the irrigation and drainage sector in Pakistan was completed during the past year; it calls for market forces to play a larger role in the sector. Recognition of individual water-property rights was identified as crucial for improving the efficiency of Pakistan's water-distribution system. An enhanced role for local farmers' groups and broader community participation was also en-

TABLE 4-9. PROJECTS APPROVED DURING FISCAL YEAR 1995, SOUTH ASIA

Country/project name	Date of Approval	Maturities	Principal amount (millions)	
			SDR	US$
Bangladesh				
Integrated Nutrition Project	May 30, 1995	2005/2035	40.10	59.80
Gas Infrastructure Development Project	May 9, 1995	2005/2034	83.40	120.80
Jute Sector Adjustment Credit (supplement)	December 8, 1994	2004/2034	2.30	3.20
India				
Tamil Nadu Water Resources Consolidation Project	June 20, 1995	2005/2030	181.90	282.90
Second Madras Water Supply Project	June 20, 1995	2001/2015	n.a.	275.80
Assam Rural Infrastructure and Agricultural Services Project	May 25, 1995	2005/2030	81.00	126.00
Agricultural Human Resources Development Project	March 30, 1995	2005/2030	40.50	59.50
Madhya Pradesh Forestry Project	March 30, 1995	2005/2030	39.40	58.00
Capital Restructuring Loan Agreement	March 23, 1995	2000/2015	n.a.	350.00
Modernization and Institutional Development Loan Agreement	March 23, 1995	1998/2005	n.a.	150.00
Backstop Facility Loan Agreement	March 23, 1995	2003/2009	n.a.	200.00
Andhra Pradesh First Referral Health System Project	December 1, 1994	2005/2029	90.70	133.00
District Primary Education Project	November 22, 1994	2005/2029	180.00	260.30
Industrial Pollution Prevention Project[a]	July 26, 1994	2000/2014	n.a.	93.00
Industrial Pollution Prevention Project[a]	July 26, 1994	2000/2014	n.a.	50.00
Industrial Pollution Prevention Project[a]	July 26, 1994	2004/2029	17.70	25.00
Maldives				
Second Education and Training Project	April 11, 1995	2005/2035	9.30	13.40
Pakistan				
Punjab Forest Sector Development Project	June 20, 1995	2005/2030	16.00	24.87
Population Welfare Program Project	March 14, 1995	2005/2030	45.00	65.10
North West Frontier Province Primary Education Program	March 14, 1995	2005/2030	104.00	150.00
Second Private Sector Energy Development Project	November 29, 1994	2000/2015	n.a.	250.00
Financial Sector Deepening and Intermediation Project	November 15, 1994	2000/2015	n.a.	216.00
Sri Lanka				
Colombo Environmental Improvement Project	June 29, 1995	2005/2035	24.80	39.00
			956.00	3,005.70

n.a. = not applicable (IBRD loan).

NOTE: Details may not add to totals because of rounding.

a. "Blend" loan/credit.

couraged. The Balochistan Community Irrigation Project, currently under preparation, adheres to the sector strategy articulated in the paper. Community management and maintenance of local irrigation infrastructure are fundamental parts of the project. Local participation is also important in a series of state-level water-resources projects under preparation in India (one such project—the $282.9 million Tamil Nadu Water Resources Consolidation Project in India—was approved during the year). The projects are designed to improve planning and allocation for all water uses, and for agriculture, the largest user of water, enhanced efficiency of use.

Protecting the natural resources of the region is a complex and long-term process. Governments face difficult policy dilemmas as they search for ways to accelerate growth and still ensure environmental sustainability. Some progress has been made in recent years in addressing these issues. National environmental action plans (NEAPs) have been completed in all countries of the region, and follow-up work is in progress. Parallel to the NEAP process, explicit steps are being taken to strengthen environmental management. The Bank is assisting in this process. In India, for example, IBRD and IDA funds are supporting the strengthening of four state pollution-control boards, with the aim of enhancing their technical capability to monitor and enforce pollution regulations. Funds will also be onlent to highly polluting industries to encourage them to adopt cleaner technologies.

Improving portfolio performance. Intensive work has been carried out in recent years to reassess potential project impact on the basis of the past and present record of project implementation, institutional capacity, and the political will to undertake policy actions essential for project sustainability. As a result, components of several projects have been reoriented, and efforts continued during fiscal 1995 to turn around problem projects, as well as to further improve performance, sustainability, and development impact through project restructuring.

Project proposals are now consistently screened with a view to ensuring that their design is simple and that major policy reforms are in place. The use of pilot projects has been extended, supervision plans make explicit provision for mid term reviews, and an increased borrower role in supervision is being actively pursued. Portfolio-management practices have been strengthened by increasing the organizational support for sectoral supervision, enhancing the role of resident missions, and, more generally, by seeking to foster an implementation culture among managers and staff. As a result of all these measures, the number of problem projects in the region has fallen steadily since fiscal 1991.

To achieve enduring improvements in project implementation, certain governance-related issues—accounting, audit, and procurement, for example—are being addressed in several countries. Successful completion of this work is expected to improve the enabling environment for a greater private sector role in economic activities.

The recent output performance in the Europe and Central Asia (ECA) region shows that countries that advanced early and more rapidly on the road toward stabilization and structural reform—Albania, Estonia, and Poland, for example—are experiencing a recovery of output. Positive rates of growth were registered for countries in transition throughout Central Europe and in the Baltic states; the process has been helped by the end of recession and the subsequent recovery of import demand from Western Europe. Where reform has been delayed, output decline has been extremely sharp; during 1994, for example, official GDP fell some 20 percent in Belarus and Ukraine.

The containment of central bank credit to finance the budget and directed credit to state enterprises has been crucial for stabilization. But this has not been easy—particularly in the newly independent states of the former Soviet Union (FSU). As the tax base shrinks (in the Russian Federation, tax revenues fell by about 10 percent between 1992 and 1994, and the pressure to continue subsidies remains) governments face difficult choices. In terms of their fiscal repercussions, sector policies, such as recapitalization of banks, pension and social transfer policies, and public investment programs, have to be carefully weighed. In such situations it becomes

critical to put together modern tax systems with a large base covering the emerging private sector and to redirect public expenditures to the highest priority areas. Thus, it is crucial to move from subsidizing enterprises to subsidizing the most vulnerable citizens, that is, from protecting enterprises to protecting the poorest households.

Sustaining output recovery in Central Europe will require accelerating privatization (and provision of postprivatization investment financing), reforming the banking sector, improving access of privatized firms to term financing, and increasing the financial discipline of those enterprises that remain in the public sector. This is particularly true for Bulgaria and Romania. In Hungary and Poland, where important reforms were originally made in these areas, efforts to deepen the process must be renewed.

Some positive developments are taking place on the policy front in many of the newly independent states of the FSU. Latecomers to the reform process, such as Ukraine and Uzbekistan, have now devised major programs of stabilization, price liberalization, and privatization. The end of conflict in Armenia, Azerbaijan, and Georgia has allowed those countries to focus on economic reform and structural change. In Russia, a new program of stabilization—reflecting an emerging consensus among the execu-

tive and legislative branches of the government and the central bank—was put into place during the first half of 1995, incorporating strict ceilings on credit expansion and aiming at a sharp reduction in inflation by the end of the year. This program is accompanied by further liberalization measures in the energy sector, particularly oil exports.

Activities of the Bank. The volume of lending to the countries of the ECA region increased from $3.7 billion in fiscal 1994 to $4.5 billion in fiscal 1995, and the number of operations increased from forty-two to fifty-eight. Some $1,741 million, or 39 percent of the total, was committed to nine projects in Russia. First-time borrowers included Azerbaijan, Georgia, and Turkmenistan. Gross disbursements increased as well, up from $1,980 million in fiscal 1994 to $2,677 million. Bank support to the region spans sectors and lending instruments, and intensive economic work and policy dialogue complement lending activities.

The Bank has sharply stepped up its assistance to a number of countries that have recently put together comprehensive programs of reform. Rehabilitation loans, supporting overall economic liberalization and privatization, were approved for Armenia, Georgia, Ukraine, and Uzbekistan. In each case these rehabilitation loans were accompanied by investment loans to help stem the deterioration of key infrastructure, including energy and agricultural irrigation.

A second generation of adjustment operations is supporting the continuation of sectorwide reforms in Kazakhstan, Kyrgyz Republic, Moldova, and Russia. In Russia, the $600 million Second Rehabilitation Loan is supporting key measures to liberalize the energy sector—particularly energy exports—and the implemen-

tation of a more transparent and competitive allocation of scarce pipeline rights. During the year financial and enterprise adjustment operations were approved for Albania and the former Yugoslav Republic of Macedonia. These operations are designed to further privatization efforts and financial sector reforms and to enhance financial discipline in enterprises that remain in the public sector. Debt-reduction

TABLE 4-10. LENDING TO BORROWERS IN EUROPE AND CENTRAL ASIA, BY SECTOR, 1986–95

(millions of US dollars; fiscal years)

Sector	Annual average, 1986–90	1991	1992	1993	1994	1995
Agriculture	241.6	100.0	155.0	525.4	582.9	157.0
Energy						
Oil and gas	28.0	520.0	246.0	703.0	856.1	285.3
Power	234.6	600.0	270.0	—	—	132.7
Environment	3.6	—	—	—	—	123.0
Human resources						
Education	59.3	250.0	—	67.0	59.6	40.0
Population, health, and nutrition	15.0	—	280.0	91.0	—	220.4
Social sector	—	—	—	—	10.9	127.5
Industry and finance						
Industry	253.9	100.0	60.0	—	375.0	—
Financial	275.7	710.0	—	55.0	280.0	232.0
Infrastructure and urban development						
Telecommunications	14.0	270.0	—	30.0	153.0	—
Transportation	233.9	300.0	—	378.0	352.0	486.0
Urban development	29.0	—	200.0	285.0	171.0	418.0
Water supply and sewerage	132.0	—	32.0	129.5	109.6	161.0
Multisector	120.0	1,017.0	691.1	1,245.0	566.3	2,049.0
Public sector management	—	—	209.2	335.0	210.0	66.9
Tourism	—	—	—	—	—	—
Total	1,640.6	3,867.0	2,143.3	3,843.9	3,726.4	4,498.8
Of which: IBRD	1,640.6	3,867.0	2,102.2	3,739.5	3,533.3	3,953.8
IDA	—	—	41.1	104.4	193.1	545.0
Number of operations	12	19	14	30	42	58

NOTE: *Details may not add to totals because of rounding.*
— *Zero.*

operations in Bulgaria and Poland will help those countries regain access to international financial markets.

Supporting the emergence of the private sector. Through its assistance the Bank is supporting ownership changes, improvements in the legal and economic environment for private sector growth, and increased access of the private sector to credit. How to remove business constraints is a topic in all the country economic memoranda produced for the countries of the region. Separate private sector assessments (PSAs), based on interviews with entrepreneurs, have been completed for Hungary and Lithuania; these document business constraints as seen by the private sector and assess the potential for infrastructure privatization at the central and local levels.

Programs of mass privatization are also being assisted through the Bank's adjustment operations. Rapid privatization is essential; it needs, however, to be accompanied by shifts in enterprise governance and a strengthening of creditors' rights. The Bank's technical assistance program, therefore, is helping to shape legal changes aimed at clarifying ownership and creditors' rights and implementing systems for the subsequent trading of shares.

Impediments to the emergence of new private enterprises remain an issue in some countries, particularly for newcomers to the reform program. Through its adjustment operations, the Bank is backing policies that replace state orders with competitive procurement (limited to the states' own needs), break up trading and transport monopolies, and improve private sector access to commercial real estate.

In an effort to increase the volume of credit available to the emerging private sector, the Bank is assisting in resolving the portfolio problems of state banks and limiting allocations of additional credit to large loss-making state enterprises. In countries with more independent banks and a stronger prudential framework (Poland, for instance), the creditor banks themselves participate in such workouts with the debtor enterprises. In countries where banks lack the relevant capacity, the preferred approach is to isolate the large loss-makers from regular bank credit. Budgetary support is made available only if these money-losing firms downsize and restructure. Assistance in this area has been central to the adjustment operations approved during the year for Kazakhstan and the former Yugoslav Republic of Macedonia.

Because the process of unfreezing bank lending (largely tied up in rolling over nonperforming loans) and redirecting credit to the private sector will take some time, the Bank, in the interim, is providing resources directly to private firms. Credit lines were approved in fiscal 1995 in the three Baltic states; these were components of innovative operations that included equity cofinancing from a capital fund created by the Swedish government and technical assistance funded by several international donors. A postprivatization and credit program was approved for Kyrgyz Republic, and an innovative pre-export guarantee project was approved for Moldova.

Poverty and the protection of social services. During fiscal 1995, the Bank accelerated its analytical work on poverty issues so as to identify better operational priorities. Comprehensive poverty assessments were completed for Kyrgyz Republic, Poland, and Russia, and work in other countries is well under way. The poverty assessments reveal an increase in poverty, stemming from an overall decline in income and employment, combined with a worsening in-come distribution. The majority of poor households are working poor or have unemployed members. In some countries, poverty is shallow, with households bunched around the poverty line. In others, there is greater depth of poverty but evidence of movement of many households in and out of severe poverty. These findings suggest that growth of output and employment is at the center of the solution.

At the same time, it is critical that steps be taken to prevent leaving groups behind. Social transfers and safety nets, while costly in many countries, failed to mitigate the increase in inequality and protect the most vulnerable groups, including families with many children and elderly nonworking pensioners. Structural unemployment has increased. Measures to make government programs and policies more effective in this area were addressed by several operations during the past year:

• Adjustment operations in Georgia, Kazakhstan, the former Yugoslav Republic of Macedonia, Moldova, and Ukraine are supporting measures to better target and assure the sustainability of transfers (particularly pensions);

• the Second Rehabilitation Loan for Russia supports measures to ensure that the country's unemployment fund focuses its resources on

TABLE 4-11. WORLD BANK COMMITMENTS, DISBURSEMENTS, AND NET TRANSFERS IN EUROPE AND CENTRAL ASIA, 1990–95

(millions of US dollars; fiscal years)

Item	Russia start 1995	Russia 1995	Russia 1990–95	Turkey start 1995	Turkey 1995	Turkey 1990–95	Poland start 1995	Poland 1995	Poland 1990–95	Total region start 1995	Total region 1995	Total region 1990–95
Undisbursed commitments	2,303			2,370			2,302			10,710		
Commitments		1,741	4,631		250	2,469		215	3,872		4,499	20,270
Gross disbursements		142	729		288	2,372		585	1,789		2,677	10,343
Repayments		—	—		866	4,280		—	—		1,205	7,388
Net disbursements		142	729		-579	-1,908		585	1,789		1,472	2,954
Interest and charges		48	74		414	2,808		107	252		905	5,019
Net transfer		94	655		-993	-4,716		478	1,537		567	-2,065

NOTE: *Disbursements from the IDA Special Fund are included. The countries shown in the table are those with the largest amounts of public or publicly guaranteed long-term debt. Details may not add to totals because of rounding.*
— *Zero.*

BOX 4-3. CONFRONTING THE HEALTH-CARE CRISIS

Two challenges in particular confront the health-care system in the ECA region: immediate shortages of supplies and services, especially in the countries of the former Soviet Union, and the need to introduce structural change. In Russia, for example, per capita consumption of pharmaceuticals fell by half from 1989 to 1993, while the availability of cardiovascular drugs declined by a third; in the Kyrgyz Republic, the shortage of pharmaceuticals is so acute that routine surgery has almost ceased; and in Georgia, patients need to bring their own drugs, linens, and lamps for surgical interventions.

The Bank's health portfolio in the region is growing: Four health projects are already under implementation, and during fiscal 1995, health projects were approved for Albania, Croatia, and Estonia.[1] In Albania, the focus is on the rehabilitation of services, while in Estonia, the emphasis is on support for health-promotion and disease-prevention programs. Responding quickly in Croatia, the Bank approved a project within six months of identification addressing critical shortages of basic equipment for the emergency medical system, intensive care units, and perinatal care units in selected hospitals.

The Bank is also supporting the transfer of critical social assets from restructuring enterprises (which used to provide many social services, especially in the former Soviet Union, but which now face hardened budget constraints) to local governments.

In the first project of its kind, this divestiture process is being supported in Kazakhstan, where the rehabilitation of critical health and early childhood facilities in five cities is being funded, along with funding for incremental costs on a declining basis, as a prelude to a national strategy. The Privatization Implementation Assistance Project in Russia, approved in fiscal 1993, was amended to include a component to improve the nutrition of preschoolers who attend kindergartens that have been transferred from state-owned enterprises to municipal governments.

Health projects are also addressing needed structural changes. These include strengthening primary health care services (with a particular emphasis on maternal and child health) and developing public health interventions to encourage effective promotion of healthy lifestyles and integrated delivery of primary health care (as, for example, in the health project approved for Estonia).

1. A Second Health Project, for $150 million, was also approved for Turkey. Turkey's health-care needs, however, are quite distinct from those of other ECA countries. Global health indicators in Turkey have improved to a point where many are now comparable with those of other countries with a similar per capita income. In Turkey, the burden of disease reflects regional disparities in, for instance, the health and status of women, education of parents, the prevalence of malnutrition, and in the availability of clean water.

unemployment-compensation payments rather than on financing transfers to enterprises to sustain output; and

• loans were approved for Kyrgyz Republic, the former Yugoslav Republic of Macedonia, and Romania to assist in the redesign of more targeted transfer programs and the provision of employment and retraining services to equip workers for change.

A pressing problem throughout much of the region is to avoid the collapse of key social services previously provided by enterprises now in the process of downsizing or closure. Transferring these services to the care of local governments is essential. In Russia, a $90 million technical assistance project, approved in fiscal 1993, supporting mass privatization was restructured during the past year to permit a portion of the remaining funds to be used to support the

transfer of kindergartens operated by state-owned enterprises (SOEs) to local governments. In the first project of its kind the transfer of social services from SOEs to local governments in five cities in Kazakhstan is being assisted; the project is financing the rehabilitation, as well as the incremental recurrent costs, of critical health and preschool facilities transferred from the SOEs. Severing the link between social services and employment also facilitates mobility of workers.

The quality of basic health services in much of the region has been deteriorating alarmingly. In response to this crisis the Bank committed funds to help finance four basic health projects during the year; another five are under preparation *(see Box 4-3)*. Most have components to strengthen maternal and child health care, public health, and emergency care. In addition, the

TABLE 4-12. PROJECTS APPROVED DURING FISCAL YEAR 1995, EUROPE AND CENTRAL ASIA

Country/project name	Date of Approval	Maturities	Principal amount (millions)	
			SDR	US$
Albania				
Rural Roads Project	May 25, 1995	2005/2034	10.10	15.00
Rural Development Project	February 14, 1995	2005/2034	4.10	6.00
Power Loss Reduction Project	January 24, 1995	2005/2034	3.40	5.00
Health Services Rehabilitation Project	November 8, 1994	2005/2034	8.60	12.40
Irrigation Rehabilitation Project	September 6, 1994	2005/2034	7.10	10.00
Enterprise and Financial Sector Adjustment Credit	August 2, 1994	2005/2034	10.60	15.00
Tax Administration Modernization Project	July 26, 1994	2005/2034	2.83	4.00
Armenia				
Rehabilitation Project	February 28, 1995	2005/2030	41.50	60.00
Power Maintenance Project	December 8, 1994	2005/2029	9.40	13.70
Irrigation Rehabilitation Project	December 8, 1994	2005/2029	29.40	43.00
Azerbaijan				
Greater Baku Water Supply Rehabilitation Project	June 28, 1995	2005/2030	38.80	61.00
Petroleum Technical Assistance Project	April 20, 1995	2005/2029	14.30	20.80
Bulgaria				
Debt and Debt Service Reduction Program	September 22, 1994	2000/2014	n.a.	125.00
Croatia				
Highway Sector Project	April 20, 1995	1999/2012	n.a.	80.00
Health Project	February 14, 1995	2000/2011	n.a.	40.00
Estonia				
Haapsalu and Matsalu Bays Environment Project	April 20, 1995	2000/2010	n.a.	2.00
Health Project	January 19, 1995	2000/2010	n.a.	18.00
Financial Institutions Development Project	October 18, 1994	2000/2010	n.a.	10.00
Georgia				
Rehabilitation Credit	March 30, 1995	2005/2030	51.00	75.00
Municipal Infrastructure Rehabilitation Project	November 8, 1994	2004/2029	12.50	18.00
Institution Building Project	July 5, 1994	2004/2029	7.30	10.10
Hungary				
Budapest Urban Transport Project	June 15, 1995	2000/2010	n.a.	38.00
Kazakhstan				
Structural Adjustment Loan	June 8, 1995	2001/2012	n.a.	180.00
Social Protection Project	May 30, 1995	2001/2012	n.a.	41.10
Financial and Enterprises Development Project	April 18, 1995	2001/2012	n.a.	62.00
Kyrgyz Republic				
Agricultural Privatization and Enterprise Adjustment Credit	June 28, 1995	2005/2030	28.60	45.00
Private Enterprise Support Project	May 4, 1995	2005/2030	10.10	15.00
Social Safety Net Project	July 5, 1994	2004/2029	12.00	17.00
Latvia				
Jelgava District Heating Rehabilitation Project	May 23, 1995	2000/2012	n.a.	14.00
Liepaja Environment Project	December 6, 1994	2000/2012	n.a.	4.00
Enterprise and Financial Sector Restructuring Project	September 20, 1994	2000/2011	n.a.	20.00
Enterprise and Financial Sector Restructuring Project	September 20, 1994	2000/2011	n.a.	10.00
Enterprise and Financial Sector Restructuring Project	September 20, 1994	2000/2011	n.a.	5.00

Kazakhstan Social Protection Project contains a significant health component.

Infrastructure and the environment. In many countries of the region, infrastructure investments have fallen to dangerously low levels. The Bank is addressing the problem in a variety of ways: It supports rehabilitation or maintenance of infrastructure that is complementary to private sector growth; through sector work, it is assisting governments in prioritizing public investment, particularly in the Baltic countries and in Russia; and it is

Country/project name	Date of Approval	Maturities	Principal amount (millions)	
			SDR	US$
Lithuania				
Enterprise and Financial Sector Assistance Project	April 13, 1995	2005/2005	n.a.	17.50
Enterprise and Financial Sector Assistance Project	April 13, 1995	2005/2015	n.a.	4.50
Enterprise and Financial Sector Assistance Project	April 13, 1995	2005/2005	n.a.	3.00
Klaipeda Environment Project	December 8, 1994	2000/2015	n.a.	7.00
Macedonia, former Yugoslav Republic of				
Social Reform and Technical Assistance Project	May 16, 1995	2000/2030	9.00	14.00
Financial and Enterprise Sector Adjustment Credit	May 16, 1995	2005/2030	54.70	85.00
Transit Facilitation Project	April 18, 1995	2000/2015	n.a.	24.00
Moldova				
Pre-Export Guarantee Facility	March 9, 1995	2005/2015	n.a.	30.00
Structural Adjustment Project	December 8, 1994	2000/2005	n.a.	60.00
Poland				
Katowice Heat Supply and Conservation Project	November 17, 1994	2000/2011	n.a.	45.00
Debt and Debt Service Reduction Loan and Related Measures to Support the Debt Reduction Program	October 25, 1994	2000/2012	n.a.	170.00
Romania				
Employment and Social Protection Project	March 7, 1995	2000/2015	n.a.	55.40
Russian Federation				
Second Rehabilitation Loan	June 6, 1995	2000/2012	n.a.	600.00
Urban Transport Project	May 16, 1995	2000/2012	n.a.	329.00
Gas Distribution Reconstruction and Energy Efficiency Project	May 2, 1995	2000/2012	n.a.	106.50
Emergency Oil Spill Recovery and Mitigation Project	April 25, 1995	2000/2012	n.a.	99.00
Tax Administration Modernization Project	March 9, 1995	2000/2012	n.a.	16.80
Housing Project	March 7, 1995	2000/2012	n.a.	400.00
Portfolio Development Project	February 16, 1995	2000/2012	n.a.	40.00
Management and Financial Training Project	December 15, 1994	2000/2011	n.a.	40.00
Environmental Management Project	November 8, 1994	2000/2011	n.a.	110.00
Turkey				
Antalya Water Supply and Sanitation Project	May 25, 1995	2000/2012	n.a.	100.00
Second Health Project	September 22, 1994	2000/2011	n.a.	150.00
Turkmenistan				
Institution Building/Technical Assistance Project	September 15, 1994	2000/2014	n.a.	25.00
Ukraine				
Seed Development Project	May 23, 1995	2001/2012	n.a.	32.00
Hydropower Rehabilitation and System Control Project	April 11, 1995	2000/2012	n.a.	114.00
Rehabilitation Loan	December 22, 1994	2000/2012	n.a.	500.00
Uzbekistan				
Cotton Sub-sector Improvement Project	May 25, 1995	2000/2015	n.a.	66.00
Rehabilitation Loan	March 28, 1995	2000/2015	n.a.	160.00
			365.40	4,498.80

n.a. = not applicable (IBRD loan).

NOTE: *Details may not add to totals because of rounding.*

actively exploring possibilities of attracting foreign direct investment for infrastructure projects through its newly mainstreamed program of guarantee instruments.

Almost a third of the projects approved during the past year provided financing for key infrastructure projects. Highway projects were approved for Croatia and the former Yugoslav Republic of Macedonia—crucial for them to keep their trade links with the rest of Europe. A $400 million housing project in Russia is supporting a liberalization of urban land markets

BOX 4-4. EMERGENCY RESPONSE: DEALING WITH THE OIL SPILL IN KOMI

In 1994, one of the world's largest oil spills took place in the Komi Republic in northern Russia as a result of failures from the regional Kharyaga-Usinsk pipeline, about 1,000 miles northeast of Moscow, near the Arctic circle.

The authorities constructed temporary dams and dikes to contain the spill in the autumn, but these measures were not fully effective. More than 730,000 barrels of oil—triple the amount released during the Exxon Valdez oil spill—were estimated to be trapped in the frozen bogs and creek beds.

Assistance was urgently requested from the Bank in late January 1995 to mitigate the problem after the Russian government and the pipeline operator were unable to mobilize the needed resources. The timing was crucial: To prevent further contamination of the downstream rivers (the Kolva, Usa, and Pechora) and the Barents sea, the construction of new containment structures and the reinforcement of existing structures had to begin well before the spring thaw, which usually starts in early May. The Bank agreed to prepare an emergency loan—if the government immediately financed containment and clean-up activities by an international contractor and Russian subcontractors until Bank funds were available.

In addition to financing containment infrastructure, the $140 million project, approved three months after the original request was made by the Russian government, will continue the clean-up in an environmentally appropriate way. It will also minimize, to the extent possible, given the difficult site conditions, damage to the affected areas; provide assistance to affected people in coordination with a local nongovernmental organization; support safe pipeline operations in the near term and evaluate the need in the future for a replacement pipeline-investment project; and identify and implement other measures to mitigate against future oil spills.

In addition to $99 million in IBRD funds, the project is being financed by the European Bank for Reconstruction and Development ($25 million) and the pipeline operator ($16 million). Canada and the United States financed the provision of key consultant services to support project preparation.

Given the time constraints and the complexity of the operation, there is a high risk that the project will not completely prevent substantial environmental damage. However, partial success is better than inaction, as even limited clean-up and containment far outweigh the negative consequences—the wholesale release of the oil into the river systems—which would have occured if actions had been delayed until the following winter. As of the end of June 1995, the containment structures had been successfully strengthened, and there had been virtually no release of oil into the rivers.

and the auctioning of public land, as well as providing credit for private land developers. Municipal infrastructure funds, including those for water projects, were approved for Azerbaijan, Georgia, and Turkey, in addition to urban transport projects for Hungary and Russia. To facilitate energy conservation and the adjustment to higher energy prices, the Bank supported both district heating investments—in Latvia and Poland—and power-improvement projects—in Albania, Armenia, and Ukraine. Projects supporting key agricultural infrastructure, particularly irrigation, were approved for Albania, Armenia, Ukraine, and Uzbekistan.

The Bank continued to provide leadership in investing in environmental improvements and in promoting regional environmental programs. The Bank's first environmental loan to Russia,

the $110 million Environmental Management Project, for instance, is strengthening environmental policy, improving hazardous waste and water-quality management, and promoting pollution-abatement projects. Since many resource-recovery and industrial pollution-abatement projects require small investments and have short payback periods, a new funding mechanism has been created specifically for this operation. It uses funds from the Bank and other donors, together with those from local sources, to lend to enterprises to finance projects such as copper recovery from dust and waste tailings, as well as hydrocarbon-vapor and oil recovery.

Another area of environmental focus is coordinated investments to protect water resources.

Projects were approved in Estonia, Latvia, and Lithuania to protect their shared Baltic coast. The three projects are designed to reduce the discharge of partially treated, as well as untreated, wastewater to the Baltic sea; restore water quality near recreational beaches; improve water supply and sanitation services; and promote environmentally sustainable management and the development of the shared coastal zone and protected areas. The Bank is also playing a key role in regional initiatives involving two other seas. The Black Sea Environmental Programme has developed an "urgent investment portfolio" for Bulgaria, Georgia, Russia, and Ukraine. The Bank approved its first loan under the program when it approved financing for two wastewater-treatment facilities in the Georgian coastal cities of Batumi and Poti. In Central Asia, the Bank is working with the five countries of the Aral sea basin—Kazakhstan, Kyrgyz Republic, Tajikistan, Turkmenistan, and Uzbekistan—to advance the first phase implementation of a nineteen-project program that balances environmental, economic, and social objectives. In fiscal 1995, the Bank also completed the Strategic Action Plan aimed at improving the quality and availability of water in the Danube basin and at reducing the negative impact of human activities on its ecosystem, as well as on that of the Black sea.

The Bank also responded to an environmental emergency during the year—the oil pipeline spill in Russia's Komi Republic, which threatens the marine systems of the Kolva river and beyond into the Usa and Pechora rivers—by approving a $99 million emergency project to mitigate the spill's effects *(see Box 4-4)*.

Governments continued to be assisted in developing national environmental action plans (NEAPS) and environmental strategies; during the past year, the governments of Kyrgyz Republic and Moldova became the eleventh and twelfth in the region to request Bank assistance in preparing a NEAP or an environmental strategy. The Bank remains ready to support other countries in the region that wish to undertake such activities.

Portfolio management. The number of operations under supervision continued to increase during fiscal 1995. On June 30, 187 projects were under supervision as compared with 150 on the same day in 1994. To deal with the growing portfolio, an intensified dialogue is being maintained with member-country governments on implementation issues. Yearly or biennial in-country portfolio reviews with most member governments are now organized to identify country-specific implementation issues and to agree on measures to deal with them. Reviews were held in Albania, Bulgaria, Russia, and Turkey and are planned for early fiscal 1996 in Kazakhstan, Kyrgyz Republic, Poland, and Russia.

A strategy to give the Bank's resident missions a prominent role in the routine supervision of projects is being put in place to take advantage of their better knowledge of local conditions. In Russia, a permanent working group, comprising government officials and resident mission staff, has been set up to coordinate Bank work, including project supervision, to ensure that implementation proceeds without delays. The functions of the Budapest Regional Office were also redefined to give it regional responsibility for supervising human-resources projects.

As measured by standard indicators, calendar 1994 was largely a good year for the Latin America and the Caribbean (LAC) region.

The rate of growth of regional gross domestic product (GDP) increased, reaching its highest level in years (4.2 percent), and per capita income gained back ground lost in the 1980s; inflation continued to fall (most dramatically in Brazil); poverty declined slightly in some of the larger countries; the prospects for accelerating hemispheric integration received a boost at the Miami Summit of the Americas; the electoral process resulted in smooth transitions of government in many countries; and Haiti returned to the international fold.

At the same time, however, points of vulnerability lay below this progress in the shape of low domestic savings rates, high current account deficits, and sometimes precarious fiscal balances. What had been a positive year turned more somber when the Mexican peso began its collapse on December 20.

The crisis unfolded by the devaluation of Mexico's peso uncovered the remaining high vulnerability of many countries to external shocks. The crisis also reinforced the importance of some key policies. First, it hit very hard many of the countries that, at the time, had relatively weak fiscal positions, thereby heightening the importance of strengthening the fiscal accounts in the early stages of reform programs. The crisis also heightened the importance of policies that will generate an increase in domestic savings. Among such policies, the development of a sound financial sector remains a goal that many countries in the region have yet to realize.

The Mexican crisis offers— or more accurately, reaffirms— seven fundamental lessons for the countries of the LAC region and for other nations embarked on adjustment and reform programs:

• In view of the dangers posed by a decline in savings during the reform process, reformers should move very fast to create an environment that encourages savings. During recent years, savings-rate declines have been compounded by two factors. First, far-reaching reforms have opened more investment opportunities than domestic savings can finance. Second, in some cases, the initial stages of reform have been accompanied by declining domestic savings. Both these factors have led to an increasing reliance by the region on voluntary foreign savings and an increase in current account deficits.

• The composition of capital flows—portfolio versus longer-term direct investment funds—is extremely important. Short-term flows are very sensitive to short-term changes in interest rates and other political and macro- economic variables. Longer-term direct investment funds, however, are less volatile and do not respond in the same way to possibly ephemeral short-term speculative factors. Encouraging long-term investment—as Argentina and Chile have done—has been a success. Increasing the share of long-term investment funds is not easy, however.

• Significant care is needed in managing stabilization programs based on fixed nominal exchange rates. Although such programs can be effective in reducing inflation, experience has also shown that they tend to generate real exchange-rate appreciation and a resulting decline in external competitiveness. This is particularly true in countries in which contracts and other components of production costs are subject to some inertia. This tendency can be offset by rapid productivity increases and by the implementation of reforms aimed at reducing domestic distortions. Countries that rely on fixed exchange rates should implement fiscal and monetary frameworks that allow them to react promptly to signs of external disequilibrium.

• Productivity gains are a fundamentally important determinant of the way the overall external sector develops. Productivity growth is at the heart of export expansion and, thus, contributes to keeping the current account in balance. Countries that experience productivity gains early on in their reform and adjustment programs—before real exchange-rate appreciation takes place—will generally be in a better position to handle external disturbances.

• A healthy banking system is particularly important in open economies subject to external shocks. Banks should be able to withstand changes in financial conditions, including temporary increases in interest rates and changes in the flow of foreign funds. If this is not the case, the banking system can become the Achilles heel of the economy. This means that a modern regulatory and supervisory system should be developed early on in the reform process.

• Improving income distribution and reducing poverty cannot be left to the trickle-down effects of economic growth. Government policies—in particular, fiscal programs and the ways in which tax administrations are run—and programs are critical. As Mexico is discovering, stabilization programs have a better chance of succeeding if social stability can be secured with the help of essential safety nets.

• In redefining the role of the state, it is important not to forget that a strong state is a prerequisite for a robust economy. The state should draw its strength not through ownership of assets, management of public institutions, and the conduct of commerce, but through building powerful institutions that promote competition, protect the consumer, and provide the framework within which the response of all economic agents can be predicted with reasonable accuracy.

In support of the objective of increasing savings, the Bank is stepping up its involvement in savings-enhancing initiatives. In particular, it continues to work with member countries in reforming and strengthening the financial sector and capital markets and in devising related pension-system reforms. There is strong cross-country evidence suggesting that these reforms will increase domestic savings, helping to achieve manageable current account positions.

To encourage investment and long-term capital inflows, the Bank is supporting policy reforms—including the design of regulatory frameworks, privatization, the strengthening of supervisory

systems, and the modernization of the judiciary system. These reforms, in turn, have an impact on productivity.

To further increase productivity, the Bank is supporting the modernization reforms undertaken by a large number of countries. The Bank is also supporting a second generation of reforms affecting fiscal federal relations and markets and provincial finances—in Argentina, for example—that will further improve productivity.

The Bank's work in helping strengthen the financial and banking sectors of member countries takes a two-pronged approach: On the one hand, policy dialogue and economic and sector work have continuously emphasized the need to implement modern prudential regulations; on the other hand, a number of operations have focused on the restructuring of the banking sector. Mexico's Financial Sector Restructuring Program and the Provincial Bank Privatization Loan in Argentina are products of an effective dialogue that enabled the two countries, with assistance from the Bank and others, to strengthen their financial sector management and contain the crisis in confidence of private investors. In the case of Mexico, the need to assist financial sector reforms had been anticipated even before the peso crisis with the approval in January 1995 of the Financial Sector Technical Assistance Project.

The Bank's activities, fiscal 1995. The LAC region's short- and medium-term development agenda poses major challenges to the Bank in how best to apply its limited resources in support of suitably focused country-assistance programs. The Mexican peso crisis underlined the volatility of private capital flows to the region and required the Bank to focus on fostering macroeconomic stability as a prerequisite for sustained and equitable growth.

While the Bank continues to encourage higher domestic savings, the uncertainty of private capital flows reinforced the demand for long-term official finance. The immediate impact of the peso crisis on the Bank's programs included demand for crucial technical assistance and significant amounts of financial assistance to support essential social programs to cushion

higher than in the previous year, with large increases occurring in Argentina, Chile, Ecuador, and Peru. Net disbursements and transfers remained negative, however, for the region as a whole and for most of the region's major borrowers.

Many of the smaller countries of the region continue to seek Bank assistance to adjust and modernize their economies in the face of market and trade-relationship changes.

During the year, for example, Ecuador received assistance through a structural adjustment loan, two related technical assistance loans to improve its fiscal and public sector management, and funds to support the implementation of a debt agreement with its commercial creditors. Bolivia received support to modernize its public sector management through a project to reform the judiciary system. And, together with the help of others, the Bank responded quickly to the special needs of Haiti through an Emergency Economic Recovery Credit and an operation for highway maintenance and rehabilitation. To bring greater cohesion among donor agencies, the Bank has increased its coordination with bilateral and multilateral donors involved in the region's development. Consultative group and aid-coordination meetings were chaired by the Bank for Bolivia, Guatemala, and Haiti, and another, for El Salvador, was cochaired with the Inter-American Development Bank (IDB). As a further step towards sharing more aid-coordination activities in the region, the Bank participated in a consultative group meeting for Nicaragua chaired by the IDB at the Bank's Paris office. It also participated in meetings of the Steering Committee of the Consultative Group for Cooperation in Economic Development (CGED), at which work programs were designed and current development issues were reviewed. More generally, work program and cofinancing arrangements were strengthened with the IDB, and overlapping activities were reduced, allowing the Bank to be more selective in its country-assistance strategies. Close cooperation continued with the Caribbean Development Bank, with the two institutions jointly organizing an

the impact of adjustment. (Specifically, in the case of Mexico, the crisis modified the Bank's operational strategy; some projects with medium-term goals were postponed to provide space in the pipeline for newly emerging operations.) In the medium term, a continued strong demand for external capital for investment in human resources and infrastructure is anticipated.

As a consequence, the Bank's financial commitments to the countries of the region—$6.1 billion in fiscal year 1995—were significantly greater than had been planned. Gross disbursements of $4.2 billion were also significantly

Export Development seminar, which led to the identification of investment needs in member countries.

An important aspect of the Bank's involvement with its clients, and with the larger development community, is its program of economic and sector analysis. Such work takes a variety of forms.

Informal policy analysis is frequently undertaken at the request of governments who want the Bank's advice or who want to learn of experience in other countries. More formal reports (also reviewed by client governments) are designed to inform the Bank's executive board (and consultative group members) of country performance in areas such as medium-term growth strategies and prospects, poverty reduction, and private sector development. During the past year, the regional vice presidency conducted a thorough overhaul, designed to lower

TABLE 4-13. LENDING TO BORROWERS IN LATIN AMERICA AND THE CARIBBEAN, BY SECTOR, 1986–95

(millions of US dollars; fiscal years)

Sector	Annual average, 1986–90	1991	1992	1993	1994	1995
Agriculture	1,114.5	941.5	1,569.6	390.0	446.9	515.7
Energy						
Oil and gas	65.9	260.0	110.1	44.9	—	11.0
Power	659.9	—	11.0	372.0	—	161.5
Environment	—	—	—	16.3	418.0	28.6
Human resources						
Education	64.6	595.3	786.1	588.7	1,083.3	747.1
Population, health, and nutrition	140.6	337.3	47.5	374.0	331.0	94.6
Social sector	5.6	—	—	—	130.0	500.0
Industry and finance						
Industry	240.1	—	—	—	—	—
Financial	1,037.9	844.5	877.0	125.0	604.5	1,409.5
Infrastructure and urban development						
Telecommunications	13.4	—	—	—	—	—
Transportation	490.8	218.0	564.2	1,697.5	595.0	371.0
Urban development	390.6	260.0	490.0	170.0	402.0	575.0
Water supply and sewerage	157.3	485.0	250.0	439.0	521.5	221.5
Mining and other extractive	11.4	200.0	—	250.0	14.0	—
Multisector	817.3	422.3	593.8	1,318.1	62.2	328.6
Public sector management	188.9	672.8	362.2	383.0	118.3	1,096.4
Tourism	—	—	—	—	20.0	—
Total	5,398.8	5,236.7	5,661.5	6,168.5	4,746.7	6,060.5
Of which: IBRD	5,255.6	5,067.2	5,256.5	5,851.8	4,434.5	5,715.3
IDA	143.2	169.5	405.0	316.7	312.2	345.2
Number of operations	44	44	45	50	48	52

NOTE: Details may not add to totals because of rounding.
— Zero.

costs, increase responsiveness, and improve dissemination, of its economic and sector work program. It also began to integrate more fully its analytic work within the context of overall country-assistance strategies, while stressing certain regional themes such as trade integration, mobilization of domestic savings, and the modernization of state functions.

The diversity of topics and formats of economic and sector analysis can be illustrated with a few examples.

In response to the accelerated policy dialogue that surfaced following the election of Brazil's President Cardoso, a country economic memorandum reviewed the government's stabilization program and highlighted structural reform policies that would be needed to consolidate the program's initial success. In addition, a series of notes for the incoming government outlined issues and recommended priority policy actions. Similarly, a series of policy notes was provided to Mexican authorities to help them address various policy issues. A poverty assessment, conducted jointly with the Colombian government, was concluded, with the main effort at local dissemination being undertaken by Colombian authorities. In Honduras, the Bank undertook a comprehensive public expenditure review in collaboration with the IDB. Overall,

the Bank continued its program of poverty analysis, which is increasingly moving from mapping poverty to a more detailed examination of the links between poverty and national and sectoral policies.

In the Caribbean, the Bank is increasingly taking a regional approach to economic and sector work. A series of papers on European policy toward Carribean bananas was produced, as well as reports—dealing with economic policies in the Organization of Eastern Caribbean States, environmental issues, and private sector development—for the CGCED. Further regional reports—on the public sector, poverty issues, and export services—are under way in preparation for the 1996 CGCED meeting.

In accordance with its decision to be more selective in its activities in the region, the human-resources and infrastructure sectors have been identified as priorities for support. Support for infrastructure is based on a report completed by the Bank that highlights the neglect of infrastructure in Latin American countries and the need for new investments—estimated at $60 billion annually—to stimulate growth, and delineates the roles that should be played by the public and private sectors. It is expected that human-resources and infrastructure operations will account for about 25 percent and 45 per-

TABLE 4-14. WORLD BANK COMMITMENTS, DISBURSEMENTS, AND NET TRANSFERS IN LATIN AMERICA AND THE CARIBBEAN, 1990–95

(millions of US dollars; fiscal years)

Item	Brazil start 1995	Brazil 1995	Brazil 1990–95	Mexico start 1995	Mexico 1995	Mexico 1990–95	Argentina start 1995	Argentina 1995	Argentina 1990–95	Total region start 1995	Total region 1995	Total region 1990–95
Undisbursed commitments	5,363			4,246			1,806			17,761		
Commitments		552	5,829		2,387	11,050		1,425	5,046		6,061	33,839
Gross disbursements		881	4,280		1,113	9,776		831	3,620		4,182	26,489
Repayments		1,385	7,524		1,223	5,811		285	1,976		4,450	24,164
Net disbursements		-504	-3,244		-110	3,965		547	1,644		-268	2,325
Interest and charges		515	3,692		959	5,116		291	1,380		2,703	16,414
Net transfer		-1,019	-6,936		-1,069	-1,151		256	264		-2,971	-14,089

NOTE: *Disbursements from the IDA Special Fund are included. The countries shown in the table are those with the largest amounts of public or publicly guaranteed long-term debt. Details may not add to totals because of rounding.*

cent, respectively, of total lending for the next three years. Rural poverty alleviation will also continue to be a major focus in selected countries or in regional programs within countries.

Several of the Bank's fiscal 1995 human-resources operations were designed in response to the challenge posed by the low quality of education in the region. The problem of low quality is most serious in basic education, with international comparators showing that public school achievement in the LAC region to be far lower than in East Asian countries, for example. The Technical Education and Training Modernization Project in Mexico features the introduction of trade-certification standards, while the Program of Essential Social Services, also in Mexico, provides a safety net to maintain key services to cushion the impact of the significant adjustment that was made in public expenditures in the wake of the peso crisis. And the Education Reform Project in Bolivia is supporting the first phase of a long-term reform process whose sustainability will depend on continued firm commitment and strong leadership from the government over several administrations with respect to both institutional and financial policy measures, as well as sustained support from the international community. The project is receiving support from the IDB, Germany, the Netherlands, and Sweden, as well as from the Bank.

Because the LAC region will require huge annual investments to rehabilitate and expand its physical infrastructure, the Bank is identifying ways to support private sector investment in priority infrastructure. The Lima Water Rehabilitation and Management Project is a good example of the role that the Bank can play in the privatization of infrastructure functions. The Bank, as part of its efforts to mainstream environmental management, has also integrated environmental requirements into the design of infrastructure projects. An innovative example of integration in the fiscal 1995 portfolio of projects was the Solid Waste Management Project that benefits the four member states of the Organization of Eastern Caribbean States—Dominica, St. Kitts and Nevis, St. Lucia, and St. Vincent and the Grenadines. The project includes a component financed by the Global Environment Facility to manage the disposal of waste materials from ships to protect the marine environment.

Portfolio management and dissemination of information. At the beginning of the fiscal year 326 projects in twenty-nine countries, with commitments of $31.8 billion (of which about half was undisbursed), were under implementation. Brazil and Mexico together accounted for one third of the total number of projects and for more than half of total commitments. Projects in the agriculture and transport sectors were the most numerous. Projects in the education, health, public sector management, and transportation sectors have all increased as a percentage of the portfolio, reflecting shifts in lending strategies in recent years.

As a follow-up to the 1992 report of the Bank's Task Force on Portfolio Management, the region has developed an integrated approach to managing its portfolio. This includes not only steps to improve project quality at entry, but full or partial cancellation of slow-disbursing projects. Steps to improve project quality at entry range from promoting social assessments and participation in project design and implementation, through simplifying the policy objectives associated with projects by linking investments to early resolution of a few essential policy actions, to parallel dialogue and assistance for broader and longer-term policy change. Capacity-building programs for indigenous people, designed to help them identify their needs and development priorities, have been pioneered, using proceeds from the Institutional Development Fund. These training programs have been launched in Bolivia, Chile, Colombia, Costa Rica, Ecuador, Guatemala, Mexico, and Nicaragua.

Resources devoted to implementation continued to rise. Developing borrower capacity to implement Bank-financed projects has been supported by an increase in the number of staff and consultants based in field offices. Training seminars for borrower staff on procurement—a chronic bottleneck to timely project implementation—were held in eight countries; more than 150 officials in each of the past two fiscal years have attended the seminars. The Bank gave considerable attention to disseminating the lessons

TABLE 4-15. PROJECTS APPROVED DURING FISCAL YEAR 1995, LATIN AMERICA AND THE CARIBBEAN

Country/project name	Date of Approval	Maturities	Principal amount (millions) SDR	Principal amount (millions) US$
Argentina				
Second Provincial Development Project	May 4, 1995	2000/2010	n.a.	225.00
Provincial Bank Privatization Loan	May 4, 1995	2001/2010	n.a.	500.00
Second Municipal Development Project	March 23, 1995	2000/2010	n.a.	210.00
Provincial Reform Loan	January 24, 1995	2000/2010	n.a.	300.00
Decentralization and Improvement of Secondary Education Project	September 15, 1994	2000/2009	n.a.	190.00
Belize				
Second Power Development Project	July 5, 1994	2000/2011	n.a.	11.50
Brazil				
Recife Metropolitan Transport Decentralization Project	June 29, 1995	2001/2010	n.a.	102.00
Belo Horizonte Metropolitan Transport Decentralization Project	June 29, 1995	2001/2010	n.a.	99.00
Rural Poverty Alleviation Project - Bahía	June 29, 1995	2001/2010	n.a.	105.00
Rural Poverty Alleviation Project - Ceará	June 29, 1995	2001/2010	n.a.	70.00
Rural Poverty Alleviation Project - Sergipe	June 29, 1995	2001/2010	n.a.	36.00
Urban Development and Water Resource Management Project	September 6, 1994	2000/2009	n.a.	140.00
Bolivia				
Judicial Reform Project	April 13, 1995	2005/2035	7.60	11.00
Structural Adjustment Credit (supplement)	December 8, 1994	2001/2031	6.10	8.60
Education Reform Project	August 5, 1994	2004/2034	28.80	40.00
Regulatory Reform and Capitalization Technical Assistance Project	July 26, 1994	2004/2034	10.50	14.70
National Land Administration Project	June 13, 1995	2005/2035	13.70	20.40
Chile				
Secondary Education Quality Improvement Project	May 9, 1995	2001/2010	n.a.	35.00
Third Road Sector Project	December 22, 1994	2000/2010	n.a.	120.00
Colombia				
Agricultural Technology Development Project	April 20, 1995	1999/2012	n.a.	51.00
Energy Sector Technical Assistance Project	December 15, 1994	1999/2012	n.a.	11.00
Dominica				
Solid Waste Management[a]	May 4, 1995	2001/2012	n.a.	0.60
Solid Waste Management[a]	May 4, 1995	2005/2030	0.50	0.60
Dominican Republic				
Irrigated Land and Watershed Management Project	May 2, 1995	2000/2015	n.a.	28.00
Ecuador				
Modernization of the State Technical Assistance Project	December 13, 1994	2000/2015	n.a.	20.00
Public Enterprise Reform Technical Assistance Project	December 13, 1994	2000/2015	n.a.	12.00
Debt and Debt Service Reduction Loan	December 13, 1994	2000/2015	n.a.	80.00
Structural Adjustment Loan	December 13, 1994	2000/2015	n.a.	200.00
Guatemala				
Integrated Financial Management Project	May 30, 1995	2001/2015	n.a.	9.40
Guyana				
Private Sector Development Adjustment Credit	June 20, 1995	2005/2035	10.00	15.50
Private Sector Development Adjustment Credit (supplement)	June 20, 1995	2005/2035	2.00	3.10
Financial Sector and Business Environment Project	December 15, 1994	2005/2034	2.40	3.50

Country/project name	Date of Approval	Maturities	Principal amount (millions)	
			SDR	US$
Haiti				
Road Maintenance and Rehabilitation Project	March 23, 1995	2005/2035	34.60	50.00
Emergency Economic Recovery Credit	December 20, 1994	2005/2034	26.80	40.00
Honduras				
Basic Education Project	March 28, 1995	2005/2035	20.40	30.00
Environmental Development Project	March 28, 1995	2005/2035	7.40	10.80
Agricultural Sector Adjustment Credit (supplement)	December 8, 1994	2003/2033	18.60	26.30
Mexico				
Financial Sector Restructuring Program	June 22, 1995	1999/2010	n.a.	1,000.00
Financial Sector Technical Assistance Project (supplement)	June 22, 1995	2000/2010	n.a.	13.80
Program of Essential Social Services	June 22, 1995	2000/2010	n.a.	500.00
Financial Sector Technical Assistance Project	January 24, 1995	2000/2010	n.a.	23.60
Technical Education and Training Modernization Project	October 27, 1994	2000/2010	n.a.	265.00
Second Decentralization and Regional Development Project	September 13, 1994	2000/2009	n.a.	500.00
Rainfed Areas Development Project	July 12, 1994	2000/2009	n.a.	85.00
Nicaragua				
Basic Education Project	March 16, 1995	2005/2035	23.10	34.00
Institutional Development Project	March 16, 1995	2005/2035	15.70	23.00
Economic Recovery Credit II (supplement)	December 8, 1994	2004/2034	4.40	6.30
Panama				
Rural Health Project	February 7, 1995	2000/2012	n.a.	25.00
Paraguay				
Asunción Sewerage Project	February 14, 1995	2000/2011	n.a.	46.50
Private Sector Development Project	July 5, 1994	1999/2011	n.a.	25.00
Private Sector Development Project	July 5, 1994	1999/2011	n.a.	25.00
Peru				
Primary Education Quality Project	December 15, 1994	2000/2012	n.a.	146.40
Electricity Privatization Adjustment Loan	November 22, 1994	2000/2014	n.a.	150.00
Lima Water Rehabilitation and Management Project	November 22, 1994	2000/2014	n.a.	150.00
St. Kitts and Nevis				
Solid Waste Management Project	May 4, 1995	2001/2010	n.a.	2.13
St. Lucia				
Solid Waste Management Project[a]	May 4, 1995	2001/2010	n.a.	2.28
Solid Waste Management Project[a]	May 4, 1995	2005/2030	1.60	2.30
Basic Education Reform Project[a]	January 24, 1995	2000/2009	n.a.	3.36
Basic Education Reform Project[a]	January 24, 1995	2005/2029	2.30	3.36
St. Vincent and the Grenadines				
Solid Waste Management Project[a]	May 4, 1995	2000/2012	n.a.	1.81
Solid Waste Management Project[a]	May 4, 1995	2005/2030	1.30	1.80
Trinidad and Tobago				
Environmental Management Project	March 30, 1995	1998/2010	n.a.	6.25
Water Sector Institutional Strengthening Project	August 2, 1994	2000/2009	n.a.	25.00
Uruguay				
Health Sector Development Project	March 21, 1995	2000/2010	n.a.	15.60
Venezuela				
INPARQUES (National Institute of Parks) Project	June 13, 1995	2000/2010	n.a.	55.00
Agricultural Extension Project	March 28, 1995	2000/2010	n.a.	39.00
Health Services Reform Project	December 13, 1994	2000/2010	n.a.	54.00
			237.80	6,060.49

n.a. = not applicable (IBRD loan).

Note: Details may not add to totals because of rounding.

a. "Blend" loan/credit.

of its operations, the results of economic and sector analysis, and examples of best practice through seminars and workshops for officials from the region. Most were jointly sponsored with bilateral donors and international organizations. Of particular interest was a Health Sector Reform seminar that was held in San José, Costa Rica, in February 1995, which was attended by all the health ministers of Central American countries, as well as representatives from the Pan American Health Organization and other aid agencies.

Finally, a major innovation during the past year was the convening of the first annual Bank-sponsored conference on development issues (held in Rio de Janeiro in June 1995 for policymakers and development practitioners from the public and private sectors), which focused on key development challenges facing the region. Topics covered in the meeting included political economy, savings and growth, trade and economic integration, income inequality and sustainable development, education and growth, and the impact of capital flows.

Aggregate growth of gross domestic product (GDP) in those economies of the Middle East and North Africa (MENA) region in which the Bank is most active[3] was just under 4.2 percent in 1994—a substantial improvement over the 2.25 percent achieved in 1993. As in previous years, however, performance varied widely from country to country. Yemen—beset by severe macroeconomic difficulties and civil war—actually grew more slowly than in 1993, while growth in Morocco reached 14 percent, dramatically rising from drought-related stagnation in 1993.

Challenges and opportunities. The MENA region faces substantial development challenges. Slow overall GDP growth during the 1980s and early 1990s, combined with the region's high rate of population growth (close to 3 percent a year), led to an actual decline in aggregate per capita income. Both poverty and unemployment rates remain unacceptably high. About 65 million people, or 25 percent of the region's population, are living in poverty. Unemployment averages about 20 percent, and youth unemployment is often much higher (as much as 50 percent in Algeria, for example). Although the countries of the region have traditionally invested heavily in education and health care, and despite great progress in quantitative expansion of schools and health facilities over the past three decades, the quality and availability of basic human services still need substantial improvement. Meanwhile, rapid population growth has meant that simply maintaining services has strained available resources.

The region has substantial assets, however, including a high degree of cultural identity, a long tradition of trade and entrepreneurship—fostered in part by its advantageous location between Europe, Africa and western Asia—and a relatively well-trained labor force. While arable land and fresh water are in increasingly limited supply, several countries are richly endowed with oil.

A major obstacle to development in the past has been the region's uncertain political situation, which has preoccupied policymakers, diverted domestic resources away from growth-enhancing investments, and deterred foreign private investors from participation in the economies of the Maghreb and the Mashreq. The recent advances in the Middle East Peace Process present an opportunity for the countries of the region to use the reduction of tensions to frame and implement new strategies for restoring soundly based prosperity for their peoples.

At the first Middle East and North Africa Economic Summit, held in Casablanca at the end of October 1994, the Bank proposed a three-pronged strategy that synthesized both expressed client priorities—and how to support them—and country-assistance strategy discussions in the Bank's executive board.

• First, growth must be rapid, so as to make up for past lost ground and lay the foundations for long-term prosperity.

• Second, growth must be widely shared throughout national populations so as to broaden opportunities across all segments of society and make the most of the human capital on which the resource-poor, population-rich countries of the region must depend for their development.

• Third, growth must be environmentally sustainable, both to address the existing environmental problems facing the region and to ensure that future growth will not be eroded by spiralling environmental penalties.

In addition, the Bank suggested that growth prospects would be enhanced by the development of productive transnational partnerships, both among countries in the region and between MENA countries and external partners. The development agenda for action by MENA countries is formidable. The Bank's contribution to realizing it during the past fiscal year included a lending program of nearly $1 billion, which

3. Algeria, Egypt, Iran, Jordan, Lebanon, Morocco, Tunisia, the West Bank and Gaza, and Yemen.

was based on selective assistance in priority areas indicated by the three-pronged strategy, together with a substantial program of analytical and advisory work directed at supporting the policy framework necessary to ensure rapid, shared, and sustainable growth.

Promoting rapid growth. Promoting rapid growth is the core requirement for reducing poverty and raising living standards in the region. Rapid growth, in turn, will depend critically on moving away from past public sector-oriented development strategies and adopting a "new paradigm" for prosperity, based on unleashing the energies of the private sector as the engine of growth. But private sector development is a complex task, involving a wide range of policy actions, ranging from macroeconomic stabilization and reduction of constraints on in-

TABLE 4-16. LENDING TO BORROWERS IN MIDDLE EAST AND NORTH AFRICA, BY SECTOR, 1986–95

(millions of us dollars; fiscal years)

Sector	Annual average, 1986–90	1991	1992	1993	1994	1995
Agriculture	328.6	13.2	299.2	463.0	601.7	231.6
Energy						
Oil and gas	3.5	84.0	160.0	—	80.0	—
Power	107.9	114.0	220.0	165.0	—	—
Environment	—	—	—	—	6.0	55.0
Human resources						
Education	119.0	241.4	75.0	115.2	33.0	158.3
Population, health, and nutrition	27.4	245.0	26.8	188.0	—	35.7
Social sector	—	—	—	—	—	—
Industry and finance						
Industry	28.7	365.0	—	—	—	—
Financial	123.2	235.0	—	—	120.0	—
Infrastructure and urban development						
Telecommunications	32.2	—	—	100.0	20.0	—
Transportation	113.0	162.0	—	35.0	—	239.1
Urban development	48.0	250.0	110.0	684.0	—	51.0
Water supply and sewerage	111.1	—	57.0	—	270.0	58.0
Mining and other extractive	11.2	—	—	—	—	—
Multisector	208.0	310.0	525.0	—	—	150.0
Public sector management	35.8	—	9.0	—	19.9	—
Tourism	—	—	—	130.0	—	—
Total	1,297.6	2,019.6	1,482.0	1,880.2	1,150.6	978.7
Of which: IBRD	1,245.8	1,784.0	1,324.0	1,756.4	1,050.6	925.4
IDA	51.8	235.6	158.0	123.8	100.0	53.3
Number of operations	20	20	17	19	16	14

NOTE: Details may not add to totals because of rounding.
— Zero.

ternational trade and investment to rationalization of the role of the public sector in the
economy so as to provide room for a dynamic
private sector to develop and thrive.

Most countries in the region have already
taken substantial steps toward macroeconomic
stabilization and trade and investment liberalization. Morocco and Tunisia have moved beyond this stage and into wide-ranging reforms
designed to enhance the business climate. These
reforms are already paying off in terms of private sector development and increased foreign
investment. Jordan, too, has been successful in
implementing its reform program.

Lebanon has taken steps toward stabilization
and has seen a revival of business confidence
and investment over the past two years, while
Egypt has put in place a number of measures
that underpin the second phase of its economic
reform and structural adjustment program. For
Egypt, the stabilization program has been successful in achieving its immediate goals; further
monetary and fiscal adjustment is required to
consolidate the gains made. Algeria has taken
important steps towards stabilization, but still
must do more to reduce the role of the public
sector. The special difficulties facing Iran and
Yemen have meant that their progress has been
more limited. Nevertheless, Iran is undertaking
an economic program that includes tariff reform
and privatization.

Bank support for private sector development
combines analytical and advisory work with selective lending operations to buttress it. During
the past year, Bank staff prepared private sector
assessments (PSAs) for Lebanon and Jordan. Like
their predecessors for Egypt, Morocco, and
Tunisia, these analytical reports evaluate both
the potential for, and the constraints against,
rapid private sector growth and propose policy
initiatives for consideration.

Other substantial items of analytical and advisory work during the year included a study of
export-growth determinants and prospects in
Morocco and Tunisia (a follow-up to the PSAs
for these two countries); a report on financial
policy for Lebanon, which indicated major areas
for financial sector reform to support stabilization, reconstruction, and private sector development; and a Morocco Public Sector Review,

which evaluated priority needs for public expenditure and ways to accommodate them,
while still reducing the overall weight of the
public sector in the economy so as to permit
further rapid private sector growth.

Lending designed to help promote private
sector development during the year included
support for a project that is helping Algeria to
accelerate its transition to a market economy.
The Bank-supported Economic Rehabilitation
Support Loan will encourage private sector
development (including the launching of a
privatization program), public expenditure reform, and financial sector reform. A highways

loan to Algeria; a secondary, tertiary, and rural roads operation in Morocco; and projects in Tunisia for rural roads and rural finance are also expected to facilitate private sector development, including commercial activities of poor, small-scale farmers.

Supporting shared growth. Ensuring that the fruits of growth are widely shared depends critically on creating more and better private sector jobs and incomes. But it also requires that steps be taken to provide greater equality of opportunity to all citizens, including women. Here, education is the great equalizer. Good basic schooling for all means that anyone can enter the job market with the chance to compete for new employment created by a dynamic private sector. Supporting widely shared growth also means that basic health care be available to all citizens. Finally, special attention has to be paid to the needs of the poor, not all of whose needs may be addressed by rapid growth alone.

The Bank's long-standing partnerships with MENA governments on programs to support human-resources development have enabled it to continue to respond strongly and selectively to priority client needs. Lending during the year included operations that build on existing country success stories, as in Jordan (where a $60 million IBRD loan supported the second phase of comprehensive general education reform designed to enhance quality and further expand access to basic schooling) and Tunisia (where the latest in a series of Bank-supported operations will extend the government's ambitious reform program from lower basic to upper basic and secondary schooling). Bank operations have also assisted new clients facing special needs—as in the West Bank and Gaza (where both education and health services were supported by a $20 million loan on IDA terms from the Trust Fund for Gaza) and Lebanon (where the Health Sector Rehabilitation Project will help strengthen the capacity of the Ministry of Health and rehabilitate hospitals and primary health-care centers, including centers operated by nongovernmental organizations).

Addressing poverty has remained at the forefront of country dialogue and Bank analytical work, which has included preparation of a so-

cial welfare study (for Egypt) and a poverty assessment (for Tunisia). Tunisia's stabilization and reform program, based on economic growth and consequential expansion of employment opportunities, has already led to marked reductions in poverty. As poverty becomes more localized, targeted interventions to reduce its incidence will become more important. This targeted approach is exemplified in an innovative community-development program that is currently under preparation by the government of Lebanon and the Bank. Under the program, poor rural communities will be helped to implement small-scale social infrastructure projects. The program is designed to be demand-driven and to encourage grassroots and private self-help initiatives.

Finally, supporting widely shared growth involves paying special attention to enhancing the socioeconomic position of women. A Bank document prepared for the International Conference on Population and Development in Cairo[4] emphasized not only the need to improve family health care (including family planning for those seeking it) but also the imperative of expanding opportunities for women, especially through more and better schooling for girls. Education is a necessary but not a sufficient condition for empowering women in society, however; in this connection, the government of Morocco and the Bank are currently discussing a comprehensive strategy for better integrating women in the development process as a whole.

Securing environmentally sustainable growth. The countries of the region are already facing widespread environmental pollution, loss of arable land, and, above all, freshwater scarcity and degradation of its quality. The Bank has continued to support countries' efforts to grapple with these problems, both through its analytical and advisory work and through selective lending for priority needs. During the year, Bank staff worked with the government of Iran on an environmental strategy study and with Morocco and Tunisia on water-sector reviews.

4. World Bank. 1994. "A Population Perspective on Development: The Middle East and North Africa." Middle East and North Africa Regional Office. Washington, D.C.

Drawing on the extensive work undertaken on environmental issues conducted in close cooperation with clients over more than a decade, the Bank also prepared both a comprehensive environmental strategy and action program for the MENA region and a regional water-strategy paper.

The environmental strategy, launched at the December 1994 meeting of the ministers of the League of Arab States concerned with the environment, estimates that environmental degradation is currently costing the region as much as 3 percent of regional GDP a year through adverse health effects and lost economic opportunities. It proposes an urgent program of remedial action, based on improved institutional arrangements for dealing with environmental issues, enhanced incentives for pollution reduction and more efficient use of resources, targeted investments to clear up the worst consequences of past pollution and prevent its future escalation, and measures to improve environmental awareness among citizens and policymakers alike.

The regional water-strategy paper proposes a new approach to the increasingly severe water shortage in the region, involving pricing water to reflect economic costs, an emphasis on conservation and water-saving technologies, national management of water resources and co-operative management of water resources across national boundaries where appropriate, and investigation of nonconventional supply sources such as water imports and desalination.

Both the environmental and water-strategy documents have been well received in the region, and the proposals contained in them are expected to be central to the Bank's future policy dialogue with member governments.

Lending during fiscal 1995 supported the objectives of both the environmental and water strategies. Thus both the Irrigation Improvement Project in Egypt (assisted by a $26.7 million IBRD loan and a $53.3 million IDA credit) and a $80 million loan to support agricultural sector adjustment in Jordan included measures to promote the efficient use of agricultural water. A $58 million loan to Tunisia for water supply and sewerage will help improve demand management and cost recovery, and the Solid Waste and Environmental Management Project in Lebanon (assisted by a $55 million IBRD loan) will reduce solid and hazardous waste pollution and support cost recovery for waste-disposal services.

Facilitating partnerships for development. The concept of partnership is assuming growing importance in an increasingly interdependent global business and trading environment. The

TABLE 4-17. WORLD BANK COMMITMENTS, DISBURSEMENTS, AND NET TRANSFERS IN MIDDLE EAST AND NORTH AFRICA, 1990–95

(millions of US dollars; fiscal years)

Item	Egypt start 1995	Egypt 1995	Egypt 1990–95	Algeria start 1995	Algeria 1995	Algeria 1990–95	Morocco start 1995	Morocco 1995	Morocco 1990–95	Total region start 1995	Total region 1995	Total region 1990–95
Undisbursed commitments	1,022			1,280			1,680			6,103		
Commitments		80	1,370		331	1,815		58	2,452		979	8,902
Gross disbursements		130	898		440	1,793		232	2,125		1,245	7,166
Repayments		215	1,192		237	1,043		333	1,563		1,113	5,456
Net disbursements		-84	-294		203	750		-102	562		132	1,710
Interest and charges		123	780		126	623		279	1,491		765	4,086
Net transfer		-207	-1,074		77	127		-381	-929		-633	-2,376

NOTE: *Disbursements from the IDA Special Fund are included. The countries shown in the table are those with the largest amounts of public or publicly guaranteed long-term debt. Details may not add to totals because of rounding.*

Bank stands ready to assist member countries of the region in assessing the feasibility of implementing common infrastructure projects in order to better allocate scarce available resources.

The Bank has traditionally helped to bring donors and developing member countries together through its cofinancing and aid-coordination activities, including Bank-chaired consultative groups and special fora such as the Ad Hoc Liaison Committee for the West Bank and Gaza, and through its role as cosponsor of, and active participant in, bodies that link European and MENA countries such as the Mediterranean Environmental Technical Assistance Program. It has played an active role in the Working Groups on Regional Economic Development, the Environment, and Water set up under the auspices of the Middle East Peace Process. It has also brought together experts from different countries within the region through meetings of its regional Council of Advisers and through its sponsorship of the regional Economic Research Forum.

Especially with the new emphasis across the region on private sector-led development, the impetus is likely to grow for government–private sector partnerships within countries and for increased links between government and business groups in MENA and external partners, especially in Europe.

During the past year, the Bank encouraged the establishment of high-level government–private sector links designed to accelerate private sector development in Morocco and Egypt. It also strengthened its own ties with the League of Arab States, Arab multilateral and bilateral funds, and the European Union (EU), and is discussing with the EU possible participation in the recently announced EU initiative for a Euro-Mediterranean partnership—a large-scale,

TABLE 4-18. PROJECTS APPROVED DURING FISCAL YEAR 1995, MIDDLE EAST AND NORTH AFRICA

Country/project name	Date of Approval	Maturities	Principal amount (millions) SDR	Principal amount (millions) US$
Algeria				
Sixth Highway Project	January 31, 1995	2000/2011	n.a.	130.00
Economic Rehabilitation Support Loan	January 12, 1995	2000/2011	n.a.	150.00
Emergency Reconstruction Project	December 1, 1994	2000/2011	n.a.	51.00
Egypt				
Irrigation Improvement Project[a]	December 22, 1994	2000/2014	n.a.	26.70
Irrigation Improvement Project[a]	December 22, 1994	2005/2029	35.70	53.30
Jordan				
Second Human Resources Development Investment Project	March 30, 1995	2000/2015	n.a.	60.00
Agriculture Sector Adjustment Operation	December 8, 1994	2000/2015	n.a.	80.00
Agriculture Sector Technical Support Project	December 8, 1994	2000/2015	n.a.	6.60
Lebanon				
Solid Waste Environmental Management Project	June 6, 1995	2001/2012	n.a.	55.00
Health Sector Rehabilitation Project	December 20, 1995	1999/2012	n.a.	35.70
Morocco				
Secondary, Tertiary, and Rural Roads Project	June 8, 1995	2000/2015	n.a.	57.60
Tunisia				
National Rural Finance Project	May 23, 1995	2001/2012	n.a.	65.00
Rural Roads Project	January 31, 1995	2000/2011	n.a.	51.50
Secondary Education Support Project	August 23, 1994	2000/2011	n.a.	98.30
Water Supply and Sewerage Project	July 28, 1994	2000/2011	n.a.	29.00
Water Supply and Sewerage Project	July 28, 1994	2000/2011	n.a.	29.00
			35.70	978.70

n.a. = not applicable (IBRD loan).
a. "Blend" loan/credit.

five-year program of assistance to southern and eastern Mediterranean rim countries. In addition, the Bank has responded to the transnational initiative jointly proposed by Jordan and Israel for the integrated development of the Jordan rift valley. Bank staff worked with Jordanian and Israeli teams on a preliminary report outlining the scope of the development program, and the Bank is helping to finance the program's preparatory planning stage.

Improving internal organization, procedures, and business practices. Internally, the Bank's regional management and staff worked during the year to further enhance responsiveness to client needs. A broad-based approach to meeting those needs, involving a judicious blend of financing and analytical work selectively targeted to critical issues, is being complemented by organizational and procedural improvements designed to enhance the quality and timeliness of both lending and analytical activities. The region's strategic focus has been sharpened through organizational change involving consolidation of Country Department operational units into four thematic divisions—for country-assistance strategy, private sector development and infrastructure, human resources, and natural resources. Even stronger emphasis than hitherto has been placed on country-assistance strategy documents and comprehensive country portfolio-performance reviews in response to country priorities. Cost effectiveness and results orientation are being promoted by greater delegation of authority, both within headquarters staff and to field offices, with the latter expanded to include resident missions in Yemen and Gaza.

In line with the recommendations of the Task Force on Portfolio Management (November 1992), the region is continuing to strengthen the portfolio-management and supervision function, to encourage task manager problem-solving in the field during supervision missions, and to increase local participation in supervision tasks wherever appropriate. Regional management and staff have worked intensively on ways to streamline the processing of all tasks and products, with the aim of reducing processing stages and production time while still rigorously maintaining product quality. The regional vice presidency has also been a leader in developing new training programs designed to enhance staff capacity and upgrade technical skills. Taken together, these initiatives should pay substantial dividends in terms of further improvements in the quality of the Bank's products and their responsiveness to client needs.

AGRICULTURE

§‡ Albania	IDA—$10 million. More than 50,000 poor farm families are expected to benefit from a project that seeks to increase agricultural production by raising farm productivity through the rapid rehabilitation of existing irrigation and drainage infrastructure. Total cost: $44.1 million.
§‡ Albania	IDA—$6 million. Small farm and off-farm activities will be promoted, basic rural infrastructure repaired, and employment created for the rural population. Total cost: $12 million.
‡ Armenia	IDA—$43 million. The level of irrigated agriculture production for food security will be maintained and water-resource management improved through the rehabilitation of irrigation infrastructure and the streamlining of the water-management system. Total cost: $57.2 million.
Benin	IDA—$8 million. Funds will be provided to help finance projects and programs generated in line with recommendations of the country's national environmental action plan. Total cost: $9.3 million.
Bolivia	IDA—$20.4 million. The government's efforts to strengthen land-administration institutions, improve land management, and provide land to landless peasants will be supported. Total cost: $27.2 million.
§‡ Brazil	IBRD—$211 million. The quality of life for some 2.7 million people in the rural areas of Bahia, Ceará, and Sergipe will be improved by providing better access to water supply and other basic social and economic infrastructure and by increasing their production, incomes, and employment. Total cost: $351.7 million.
§‡ Central African Republic	IDA—$16.6 million. Some 25,000 low-income households are to benefit from a project that seeks to raise livestock productivity by expanding animal-health services. Total cost: $32.5 million.
§‡ Chad	IDA—$24.5 million. A program to enhance the supply response of the agriculture and livestock sectors is expected to bring more productive and sustainable technology to 550,000 producers—primarily smallholder farmers—and increase family incomes and well-being. Total cost: $25.6 million.
§‡ China	IBRD—$47.5 million; IDA—$200 million. Absolute poverty in thirty-five of the very poorest counties in the southwest will be reduced by increasing the incomes and productivity and improving the health and educational status of about 2.8 million upland smallholders. Total cost: $486.4 million.
‡ China	IBRD—$100 million; IDA—$110 million. Some 5 million people in Hubei and Hunan provinces will benefit directly from a project that will finance high-priority water-control investments. Total cost: $551.9 million.

Note: Data used in this section have been compiled from documentation provided at the time of project approval. Projects marked by (§) are included in the Program of Targeted Interventions, and those marked by (†) are poverty-focused adjustment operations. Projects marked by (‡) include the participation of primary stakeholders.

§‡ Colombia	IBRD—$51 million. A four-year program of technology development and adaptation (emphasizing investment and research with potential to benefit small farmers) and institutional development will be financed. Total cost: $84 million.
Côte d'Ivoire	IDA—$5.8 million. Actions designed to diversify and expand private agricultural exports will be supported. Total cost: $16.4 million.
§‡ Dominican Republic	IBRD—$28 million. Productivity, employment, and incomes on about 5,000 small farms should increase through investments in irrigation infrastructure and improved support services. Total cost: $43.2 million.
§‡ Egypt	IBRD—$26.7 million; IDA—$53.3 million. Incomes of about 95,000 mostly poor farm households should increase as a result of the provision of timely and adequate amounts of irrigation water to three irrigation command areas. Total cost: $182.3 million.
Ethiopia	IDA—$120 million. Support for policy reforms that create an enabling environment for the growth of a competitive fertilizer sector will contribute to accelerated and sustainable growth in agricultural production and productivity. Total cost: $230.4 million.
‡ Ethiopia	IDA—$22 million. The development of the informal and formal seed sectors, institutional strengthening, and human-resource development will be supported. Total cost: $31.8 million.
‡ Ghana	IDA—$9 million. The long-term sustainability of the fisheries subsector will be established, thereby maximizing its contribution to the economy. Total cost: $10.5 million.
Ghana	IDA—$5 million. Funds from IDA reflows will be provided to supplement the agriculture-sector adjustment credit approved in fiscal 1992.
‡ Honduras	IDA—$26.3 million. Funds from IDA reflows will be provided to supplement the agriculture-sector adjustment credit approved in fiscal 1994.
‡ India	IDA—$282.9 million. A statewide program to improve the productivity and sustainability of Tamil Nadu's irrigation sector will be supported. Total cost: $491 million.
§‡ India	IDA—$126 million. Agricultural extension services will be strengthened and employment opportunities offered to some 300,000 poor rural people in Assam state, thereby contributing to agricultural growth and income generation. Total cost: $146.6 million.
India	IDA—$59.5 million. Changes in the way the central government and the states develop and employ human resources in efforts to modernize the agricultural sector and achieve greater sectoral productivity will be introduced. Total cost: $74.2 million.
§‡ India	IDA—$58 million. The first stage of a long-term development strategy of the forestry sector in Madhya Pradesh—whose main beneficiaries will be tribal peoples and forest-fringe villagers—will be supported. Total cost: $67.3 million.
§ Indonesia	IBRD—$80 million. Efficient and equitable land markets will be fostered and social conflicts over land alleviated through acceleration of nonforest land titling and registration. Lower-income groups will be the main beneficiaries. Total cost: $140.1 million.

‡ Indonesia	IBRD—$63 million. Regional agricultural research and development will be strengthened, ensuring the location-specificity of technology and emphasizing the development of market-oriented technology packages. Total cost: $101.8 million.
Jordan	IBRD—$80 million. The transition to a more sustainable and efficient use of resources, particularly water, will be supported, and markets will be freed up to enable the private sector to invest, produce, and trade in line with the country's comparative advantage in agriculture.
Jordan	IBRD—$6.6 million. The government will be assisted in implementing its agriculture-adjustment program. Total cost: $13.3 million.
§‡ Madagascar	IDA—$25.2 million. The first four years of a long-term extension program to improve agricultural advisory services in the country's twenty-eight extension districts will be supported. Total cost: $36.6 million.
§‡ Madagascar	IDA—$21.2 million. The incomes of about 40,000 small-scale farm families are expected to rise as a result of a project that will increase agricultural output and improve production and productivity on irrigation schemes. Total cost: $25.7 million.
‡ Mali	IDA—$6 million. Key sectoral constraints to private investment in agricultural marketing and processing will be addressed. Total cost: $6.9 million.
‡ Mexico	IBRD—$85 million. Agricultural productivity will increase in selected rainfed areas through a program of rural investments, the transfer of agricultural technology through private sector extension, and institutional development. Total cost: $225.6 million.
§ Niger	IDA—$6.8 million. A pilot project will test the private provision of services to small-scale irrigation farmers and promote the adoption of low-cost technologies that meet small-farmer requirements and capabilities. Total cost: $7.5 million.
§‡ Pakistan	IDA—$24.9 million. By improving the performance of the forestry sector in Punjab, rural production (mainly in farm forestry and livestock) will be increased, as will employment and income for smallholders. Total cost: $33.8 million.
Senegal	IDA—$45 million. The government's resumed program of agriculture adjustment following the January 1994 devaluation of the CFA franc will be supported.
§ Thailand	IBRD—$118.1 million. Secure land tenure will be granted to an estimated 1.1 million predominantly rural families from among the poorest segments of the population. Total cost: $206.8 million.
§ Tunisia	IBRD—$65 million. Credit will be made available through the National Agricultural Bank (BNA) for onfarm processing and marketing investments, fisheries, and other rural investments. Total cost: $420 million.
Ukraine	IBRD—$32 million. The national seed-system's capacity to produce high-quality seed efficiently will be improved. Total cost: $63.3 million.
Uzbekistan	IBRD—$66 million. The cotton subsector will be modernized by supporting selective interventions to open it up to the world market and build the basis for efficiency improvements. Total cost: $84.6 million.

‡ Venezuela	IBRD—$55 million. The management of national parks and other protected areas will be strengthened, and public environmental research, training, and education intensified. Total cost: $95.9 million.
§‡ Venezuela	IBRD—$39 million. A new decentralized public agricultural extension service to serve the needs of poor farmers who are now without adequate extension services will be established. Total cost: $79 million.
§‡ Viet Nam	IDA—$100 million. More than 300,000 farm families in low-income regions will benefit directly from a project that aims to increase agricultural production through the rehabilitation and completion of seven irrigation schemes. Total cost: $135.7 million.
§‡ Zambia	IDA—$60 million. An investment program will support the agricultural sector's objectives of improving household food security, promoting better use of natural resources, generating incomes and employment, and increasing export earnings. Total cost: $350 million.

EDUCATION

Argentina	IBRD—$190 million. Student learning in seven selected provinces will be increased by financing investments designed to increase the quality and efficiency of secondary education. Total cost: $268.7 million.
§‡ Bolivia	IDA—$40 million. The first step in a long-term process of reform and quality improvement to strengthen the quality, efficiency, and equity of basic education will be supported. Total cost: $178.9 million.
§ Cape Verde	IDA—$11.5 million. A basic education and training project aims to achieve universal primary education by 1999, increase the skill levels and productivity of the labor force, and enhance institutional capacity. Total cost: $15.8 million.
‡ Chile	IBRD—$35 million. The internal and external efficiency, quality, and equity of all the 1,600 publicly financed secondary schools in the country will be improved.
China	IBRD—$200 million. Reforms in technology policy and institutions will be supported so as to promote the development of clean, productivity-enhancing technologies for China's industries. Total cost: $402 million.
§‡ China	IDA—$100 million. About 5 million poor schoolchildren will benefit from a project to expand basic education, especially in remote areas inhabited by minority nationalities. Interventions to improve school attendance by girls are included. Total cost: $177 million.
§‡ Ghana	IDA—$9.6 million. A demand-driven reorientation of the vocational skill-training system and improvements in informal sector productivity in selected occupational areas are expected to benefit informal sector workers, including the poorest urban dwellers. Total cost: $12.4 million.
§‡ Guinea	IDA—$42.5 million. A project to increase primary school enrollment and completion rates, improve teaching and student learning, and strengthen education-system management will target girls and poor households in rural areas. Total cost: $53 million.
§‡ Honduras	IDA—$30 million. The national policy of equitable access to educational opportunities will be supported by channeling resources especially to rural and indigenous areas. Total cost: $53.1 million.

| §‡ India | IDA—$260.3 million. Access to primary education will be improved, more than 1.5 million children will complete primary education by reducing dropout rates, and the instruction of, and learning achievement among, some 14 million children will be upgraded. Total cost: $310.5 million. |

§ Indonesia — IBRD—$132.5 million. About 250 million textbooks will be provided to primary and junior secondary students, with priority given to poor children. In addition, textbook production will be transferred from the government to the private sector. Total cost: $355.2 million.

Indonesia — IBRD—$69 million. The quality of professional, managerial, and science and technology staff in key government ministries and agencies will be upgraded. Total cost: $95 million.

Indonesia — IBRD—$25 million. The government's strategy to modernize government accounting-information systems will be further supported. Total cost: $33.9 million.

Jordan — IBRD—$60 million. A Second Human Resources Development Investment Project seeks to further the improvement of educational quality, building on the accomplishments of its predecessor. Total cost: $186.7 million.

Maldives — IDA—$13.4 million. Primary and secondary education quality will be improved, the shortage of teachers (especially in the atolls) reduced, atoll primary teacher skills upgraded, and secondary education will be made more widely available in the atolls. Total cost: $17.9 million.

†‡ Mali — IDA—$50 million. Balance-of-payment support will be provided in conjunction with the promotion of urgently needed education reforms.

§‡ Mauritania — IDA—$35 million. A project to increase primary enrollment in underserved regions, increase girls' enrollment, expand lower-secondary education capacity, and improve education quality and planning will be supported. Total cost: $42.6 million.

Mauritius — IBRD—$16 million. The government's program for higher and polytechnic education, aimed at producing the manpower needed to support a more competitive economy, will be supported. Total cost: $26.5 million.

‡ Mexico — IBRD—$265 million. The quality of technical education and training will be improved so that it meets the needs of the productive sector. Total cost: $412 million.

§‡ Nicaragua — IDA—$34 million. Efforts of the government to achieve a better quality of primary education and greater efficiency of the school system will be supported. Total cost: $39.3 million.

§‡ Pakistan — IDA—$150 million. Support will be provided to North-West Frontier Province's primary education program, which seeks to improve access, equity, and efficiency, while enhancing the quality of the learning environment. Total cost: $813.1 million.

§‡ Peru — IBRD—$146.4 million. The quality of primary education will be raised by rehabilitating dilapidated classrooms in poor, rural areas and by distributing teaching materials and training teachers on their use. Total cost: $298.6 million.

Russia		IBRD—$40 million. The quality and supply of skills needed to support the transition to a market economy will be increased, and priority market-oriented training programs will be developed. Total cost: $51.4 million.
	St. Lucia	IBRD—$3.4 million; IDA—$3.3 million. Reforms to basic education—aimed at increasing educational efficiency and effectiveness and at enhancing equity of access—will be supported. Total cost: $12.8 million.
§‡	Togo	IDA—$36.6 million. School quality will be improved through school construction and rehabilitation, textbook provision, and the introduction of school-based experiments in teaching and learning processes. Total cost: $46.6 million.
§	Tunisia	IBRD—$98.3 million. Basic and secondary education quality will be raised and access increased so as to accommodate the projected increase in school enrollments. Total cost: $184.3 million.

ENVIRONMENT

	China	IBRD—$110 million. The main water resources in Liaoning province will be protected to allow their sustained economic and safe use for drinking, industrial, and agricultural purposes. Total cost: $350.8 million.
‡	Estonia	IBRD—$2 million. Pollution in Haapsalu bay and in the Matsalu bay catchment area will be reduced through support for the decentralization of environmental management responsibilities. Total cost: $8.4 million.
‡	Honduras	IDA—$10.8 million. The institutional framework required for successful environmental management and implementation of needed investments at the local level will be developed. Total cost: $12.5 million.
	India	IBRD—$143 million; IDA—$25 million. Four state pollution-control boards will be strengthened, and efforts by individual firms to abate pollution will be supported. Total cost: $330 million.
‡	Latvia	IBRD—$4 million. In the context of the country's legal obligations to protect the Baltic sea from ecological degradation, water and wastewater services in Liepaja will be improved. Total cost: $21.2 million.
	Lebanon	IBRD—$55 million. Unsanitary dumping of solid waste will be eliminated, and methods of waste collection and disposal improved. Total cost: $135 million.
	Lithuania	IBRD—$7 million. In the context of the country's legal obligations to protect the Baltic sea from ecological degradation, water and wastewater services in Klaipeda will be improved. Total cost: $23.1 million.
	Organization of Eastern Caribbean States countries	IBRD—$6.8 million; IDA—$4.7 million. Public health risks will be reduced and the environmental integrity of the four island states of the Organization of Eastern Caribbean States will be protected by improving solid waste-management facilities and facilitating compliance of measures restricting dumping of ship-generated solid waste into the international and territorial waters of the wider Caribbean sea. Regional opportunities for reduction, recycling, reuse, and recovery of waste will also be identified. Total cost: $50.5 million.

	Russia	IBRD—$110 million. Environmental management institutions at the federal level and in three demonstration regions will be strengthened, and pollution-abatement projects developed and undertaken. Total cost: $194.8 million.
	Trinidad and Tobago	IBRD—$6.3 million. The institutional capacity to plan and implement sound environmental management will be built. Total cost: $10.5 million.

FINANCIAL SECTOR

	Argentina	IBRD—$300 million. The government's effort to promote fiscal reform in its provinces will be supported.
	Estonia	IBRD—$10 million. The implementation of reforms in the financial and enterprise sectors will be supported. Total cost: $31.8 million.
	Guyana	IDA—$15.5 million. The environment for the private entrepreneur will be improved and the direct role of the state in economic activities reduced.
‡	Guyana	IDA—$3.5 million. Sustainable institution-building mechanisms supporting the financial and private sectors will be implemented. Total cost: $4 million.
	Guyana	IDA—$3.1 million. IDA reflows will be made available to help finance the Private Sector Development Adjustment Credit, approved in the amount of $15.5 million (see above).
	India	IBRD—$700 million. Greater market orientation, allocative efficiency, technical competence, and competition will be fostered in India's financial system, thus contributing to meeting the long-term financing needs of the country's investors. Total cost: $1,534.1 million.
	Kazakhstan	IBRD—$62 million. Fundamental restructuring in the enterprise and financial sectors will be accelerated and deepened.
	Kyrgyz Republic	IDA—$15 million. Private enterprises will be assisted through provision of technical assistance and, through a newly established financial intermediary, foreign exchange for investment and incremental working capital. Total cost: $20.3 million.
	Latvia	IBRD—$35 million. Reforms in the enterprise and financial sectors will be accelerated. Total cost: $114 million.
	Lithuania	IBRD—$25 million. Credit will be channelled through selected participating banks to help finance investment and related permanent working capital needs of private and privatized enterprises. Total cost: $50.3 million.
†	Macedonia, former Yugoslav Republic of	IDA—$85 million. Implementation of major reforms in the enterprise and banking sectors will be supported. Moreover, the ability of the social safety net program to provide more equitable protection against poverty will be strengthened.
	Mauritania	IDA—$7.2 million. Activities in support of the government's private sector development program, including those encouraging investor interest in the private sector and financial sector strengthening, will be financed. Total cost: $7.9 million.

Mexico	IBRD—$1,000 million. The government's program for restructuring of the financial sector will be supported.
Mexico	IBRD—$23.6 million. Technical assistance will be provided to improve financial-system soundness, support pension-system development, and strengthen public investment evaluation and budgeting. Total cost: $31.4 million.
Mexico	IBRD—$13.8 million. Supplemental funds will be provided to help finance the Financial Sector Technical Assistance Project (see above).
Pakistan	IBRD—$216 million. A set of long-term policy and institutional development objectives for the financial sector will be implemented. Total cost: $1,016 million.
Paraguay	IBRD—$50 million. The private sector will be stimulated to play an enhanced role in fostering economic growth. Total cost: $90 million.

INDUSTRY

Bangladesh	IDA—$3.2 million. Funds from IDA reflows will be provided to supplement the jute sector-adjustment credit approved in fiscal 1994.
China	IBRD—$175 million. Shenyang's industrial base will be reformed and reorganized through the creation of a modern, corporate-led sector, with substantial private participation. Total cost: $363.2 million.
Ghana	IDA—$13 million. Efforts to restructure, reform, and commercialize the country's technical research and development establishment along competitive and demand-driven principles will be supported. Total cost: $15.6 million.
Senegal	IDA—$40 million. A program of policy reforms—necessary for establishing an environment conducive to supply-response and self-sustained growth of the private sector—will be supported.

MINING/OTHER EXTRACTIVE

| § Ghana | IDA—$12.3 million. Sustainable mining sector development will be supported through the strengthening of mining sector institutions and assistance to small-scale mining enterprises. Total cost: $13.7 million. |
| ‡ Tanzania | IDA—$12.5 million. The development of mining by the private sector in an environmentally sustainable manner will be supported. Total cost: $13.9 million. |

MULTISECTOR

| Albania | IDA—$4 million. Procedures in tax and customs administration, as well as a value-added tax system, will be developed and implemented. Total cost: $4.4 million. |
| †‡ Algeria | IBRD—$150 million. A broad program of policy reforms to accelerate the transition to a market economy will be supported. |

† Armenia	IDA—$60 million. The government's structural reform program, designed to break inflationary expectations, promote sustained economic growth, and improve living standards of the poor, will be supported.
† Benin	IDA—$40 million. Management of public resources and the delivery of basic social services will be improved.
Bolivia	IDA—$8.6 million. Funds from IDA reflows will be provided to supplement the structural adjustment credit approved in fiscal 1992.
Bulgaria	IBRD—$125 million. A portion of the upfront costs of the recent debt and debt-service reduction agreement on the restructuring of public external debt will be financed.
Burundi	IDA—$14.6 million. Imports needed to improve the social conditions of the population, rehabilitate infrastructure, and restore basic government functions will be financed. Total cost: $53 million.
Cambodia	IDA—$17 million. The transition to a market economy will be assisted through a program of technical assistance. Total cost: $18.7 million.
Cameroon	IDA—$32.8 million. Funds from IDA reflows will be provided to supplement the economic recovery credit approved in fiscal 1994.
Côte d'Ivoire	IDA—$100 million. The government's stabilization and structural adjustment program for the 1994-96 period will be supported.
Côte d'Ivoire	IDA—$77.9 million. Funds from IDA reflows will be provided to supplement the credit supporting the government's stabilization and structural adjustment program (see above).
Ecuador	IBRD—$200 million. The government's modernization program will be supported by solidifying recent gains toward macroeconomic stability and accelerating the country's structural adjustment process.
Ecuador	IBRD—$80 million. The implementation of a debt agreement between Ecuador and its commercial bank creditors will be supported by helping to finance the principal and interest collateral for par and discount bonds.
Ethiopia	IDA—$200,000. Funds from IDA reflows will be provided to supplement the structural adjustment credit approved in fiscal 1993.
† Georgia	IDA—$75 million. The government's economic reform program, aimed at restoring macroeconomic stability, promoting the resumption of growth, improving living standards, and maintaining a safety net, will be supported.
† Ghana	IDA—$70 million. The government's program to promote private sector growth and to reallocate public expenditures toward basic education, health, and rural infrastructure will be supported.
† Guinea	IDA—$23 million. Reforms to strengthen the monetary, regulatory, supervisory, and judicial environment; develop a bridge between the formal and informal sectors; build upon the human-resource base; and improve institutional capacity will be supported.
‡ Haiti	IDA—$40 million. Emergency imports will be financed to help reactivate the economy and give an immediate stimulus to economic growth.

†	Kazakhstan	IBRD—$180 million. The rapid and effective restructuring of the enterprise sector will be supported.
†	Kyrgyz Republic	IDA—$45 million. Agricultural productivity will be increased and marketing channels improved, thereby increasing farmers' incomes and alleviating poverty in rural areas, where the most impoverished live.
‡	Malawi	IDA—$40 million. Funds will be made available to supplement the Entrepreneurship Development and Drought Recovery Project approved in fiscal 1992.
‡	Malawi	IDA—$4.6 million. Funds from IDA reflows will be provided to supplement the Entrepreneurship Development and Drought Recovery Project approved in fiscal 1992.
†	Moldova	IBRD—$60 million. Measures needed to induce a quick response in the real economy to macroeconomic tightening and relative price movements, as well as those aimed at strengthening the safety net, will be supported.
	Moldova	IBRD—$30 million. Guarantees against the risks associated with government performance and war and civil disturbance *force majeur*—available on a first-come, first-served basis to any foreign commercial entity financing a pre-export transaction in Moldova—will be backstopped.
	Poland	IBRD—$170 million. Part of the costs expected to be incurred in connection with the implementation of a debt and debt-service reduction operation will be financed.
	Russia	IBRD—$600 million. The government's program of macroeconomic stabilization and structural reforms will be supported.
	Russia	IBRD—$40 million. Funds will be provided to prepare projects and related activities for which Bank financing has been or is expected to be requested during the next three fiscal years. Total cost: $79.5 million.
	Rwanda	IDA—$50 million. The country's emergency recovery program will be supported through the financing of high-priority imports and technical assistance.
	Senegal	IDA—$3.2 million. Funds from IDA reflows will be provided to supplement the economic recovery credit approved in fiscal 1994.
	Sierra Leone	IDA—$300,000. Funds from IDA reflows will be provided to supplement the structural adjustment credit approved in fiscal 1994.
	Uganda	IDA—$600,000. Funds from IDA reflows will be provided to supplement the second structural adjustment credit approved in fiscal 1994.
†	Ukraine	IBRD—$500 million. The government's economic reform program, designed to stabilize the economy, create the conditions for a resumption of economic growth, and provide an adequate safety net, will be supported.
†	Uzbekistan	IBRD—$160 million. The government will be assisted in the design and implementation of its structural reform program, which includes an equitable reform of the pension system.
†	Viet Nam	IDA—$150 million. The government's medium-term program of macroeconomic stabilization and structural reform, and including social issues of adjustment, will be supported.

Zambia	IDA—$13.7 million. Funds from IDA reflows will be provided to supplement the Economic and Social Adjustment Credit approved in fiscal 1994.

OIL, GAS, AND COAL

Azerbaijan	IDA—$20.8 million. Technical assistance will be provided for the restructuring of the offshore Guneshli oil field and for strengthening petroleum subsector institutions. Total cost: $22.9 million.
Bangladesh	IDA—$120.8 million. The two gas transmission subsystems in the country will be interconnected, thereby alleviating gas-supply shortages. Total cost: $161.6 million.
Colombia	IBRD—$11 million. Technical assistance will be provided to help implement legal/regulatory reforms for the energy sector and to strengthen associated public institutions. Total cost: $12.4 million.
Latvia	IBRD—$14 million. The district heating system in the city of Jelgava will be rehabilitated. Total cost: $18.2 million.
Poland	IBRD—$45 million. Funds will be provided to the Katowice District Heating Enterprise to help finance investments in energy conservation and efficiency, asset-life extension, and reduction of air pollution. Total cost: $92.9 million.
Russia	IBRD—$106.5 million. Funds will be provided to help finance investments to rehabilitate the gas-distribution network in the city of Volgograd, investments in energy-efficient equipment by gas utilities in ten cities, and related technical assistance. Total cost: $131.4 million.
Russia	IBRD—$99 million. Emergency measures will be taken to contain and clean up the enormous oil spill in the Komi Republic, which took place in 1994. Total cost: $140 million.
Thailand	IBRD—$155 million. An offshore and onshore gas pipeline, together with related facilities, will be constructed, thereby increasing the utilization of domestic natural gas resources. Total cost: $674.5 million.
Thailand	IBRD—$90 million. Air pollution attributable to petroleum fuels will be reduced through the reformulation of gasoline and diesel oil and improvements in the refinery operations of Bangchak Petroleum Public Company. Total cost: $329.1 million.

POPULATION, HEALTH, AND NUTRITION

§ Albania	IDA—$12.4 million. Steps will be taken to prevent further deterioration of basic health services in poorer regions during the country's economic transition. Total cost: $16 million.
§‡ Bangladesh	IDA—$59.8 million. The development of a national nutrition program, focusing on the undernourished (particularly poor women and children) will be initiated. Total cost: $67.3 million.
§‡ Benin	IDA—$27.8 million. The quality and efficiency of priority health services will be improved and family-planning services expanded, thereby improving the health and well-being of the country's people, particularly the most vulnerable groups. Total cost: $33.4 million.

| ‡ Burundi | IDA—$21.3 million. Health services will be rehabilitated, key sector reforms implemented, and family-planning activities strengthened, thereby improving the quality of health services, making them more accessible, and slowing population growth. Total cost: $36.9 million. |

§‡ Cameroon — IDA—$43 million. Expansion of primary health care to underserved low-income populations, development and implementation of a national population policy, and reforms of the health ministry will be supported. Total cost: $48.1 million.

§‡ Chad — IDA—$20.4 million. A project to help the government implement its population, family planning, and AIDS-control policies will disproportionately benefit the poor. Total cost: $27.2 million.

Chad — IDA—$9.8 million. Funds will be provided to supplement the Social Development Action Project approved in fiscal 1990 in the amount of $13.4 million.

§ China — IDA—$90 million. About 100 million people from among the poorest counties in eight provinces will benefit from increased access to, and improved quality and effectiveness of, maternal and child-health care. Total cost: $138.7 million.

China — IBRD—$7 million; IDA—$20 million. To reduce the incidence of iodine-deficiency disorder, salt-iodization capacity will be increased from about 3.5 million tons per year (Mtpy) to about 8.2 Mtpy through modernization of existing capacity and creation of new capacity. Total cost: $152.3 million.

§ Croatia — IBRD—$40 million. The government's health-care reform program, which concentrates on providing primary health care to underserved areas, will be supported. Total cost: $54 million.

Estonia — IBRD—$18 million. Health-promotion and disease-prevention programs will be emphasized, the efficiency and quality of health services enhanced, and sector human resources developed. Total cost: $34.5 million.

§‡ India — IDA—$133 million. The efficiency in the allocation of health resources in Andhra Pradesh will be upgraded, and the quality, effectiveness, and coverage of health services will be improved. Total cost: $159 million.

§‡ Indonesia — IBRD—$88 million. The delivery and quality of basic health care in six provinces on five islands will be improved, thus benefiting about 27 million people, most of whom are impoverished. Total cost: $134.3 million.

§‡ Kenya — IDA—$40 million. Preventive measures will be taken to reduce the risk of sexually transmitted infections, and provision of health and community care for infected persons will be increased. Institution-building measures are included. Total cost: $65.5 million.

§‡ Lao People's Democratic Republic — IDA—$19.2 million. Basic health services will be upgraded in two provinces, and a program of malaria control will be undertaken in eight of the country's seventeen provinces. Total cost: $24 million.

§ Lebanon — IBRD—$35.7 million. Health facilities will be rehabilitated, with particular attention given to improving the availability of essential public services to underserved people. Total cost: $48.1 million.

§‡ Pakistan

IDA—$65.1 million. The entire national population program, which plans to increase dramatically the coverage and quality of family-planning services, especially to rural and poor urban areas, will be supported. Total cost: $287.6 million.

§‡ Panama

IBRD—$25 million. The nutrition and health status of those living in Panama's twenty-eight poorest districts will improve, and new water-supply systems will be constructed in about 450 unserved communities. Total cost: $41.7 million.

§‡ Philippines

IBRD—$18 million. Attempts to improve the health status of women—those of reproductive age, in particular—will be supported, thereby reducing fertility, female morbidity, and maternal mortality. Total cost: $136.4 million.

§‡ Senegal

IDA—$18.2 million. The deterioration in the nutritional status of the most vulnerable groups in the poorest urban areas will be halted, and local capacity to deliver community-managed nutrition services with private sector efficiency established. Total cost: $28 million.

§‡ Turkey

IBRD—$150 million. Equity in access to essential primary health-care services will be improved in twenty-three low-income eastern provinces, and the effectiveness and efficiency of the health service-delivery system will be enhanced. Total cost: $200 million.

§‡ Uganda

IDA—$45 million. A demonstration project will test the feasibility of delivering an essential health-services package to district populations within a prudent financial policy framework for the health sector. Total cost: $75.1 million.

Uruguay

IBRD—$15.6 million. The government will be helped in setting a methodological and institutional foundation to rationalize health-sector spending. Total cost: $28 million.

§ Venezuela

IBRD—$54 million. Gains in the health status of 3 million users of government health services will be made through a strengthening of health-service delivery in four states. Total cost: $108 million.

Zambia

IDA—$56 million. The government's health-sector reform program will be supported. Total cost: $536.9 million.

§‡ Zambia

IDA—$30 million. The government's poverty-reduction program will be assisted by financing community initiatives (feeder roads, water-supply systems, and other public infrastructure) and building capacity for poverty monitoring and analysis. Total cost: $47.7 million.

POWER

Albania

IDA—$5 million. An action plan to reduce nontechnical power-system losses will be implemented. Total cost: $8.7 million.

Armenia

IDA—$13.7 million. The deterioration of selected power-generation units will be arrested and reversed, and electricity-dispatch communications and distribution systems will be strengthened and maintained. Total cost: $14.5 million.

‡ Belize

IBRD—$11.5 million. Electric power supply will be improved by integrating major load centers and providing access to economic, reliable, and clean sources of energy. Total cost: $33 million.

China	IBRD—$400 million. Rapidly expanding power demand in Zhejiang province will be met through large generation additions and associated transmission, and power-sector reforms will be promoted. Total cost: $1,789.3 million.
China	IBRD—$270 million. The construction of a 500-kv network will greatly increase critically needed power-transmission capability in Sichuan province and the southwest China power grid. Total cost: $874.4 million.
Côte d'Ivoire	IDA—$79.7 million. Finance will be provided in support of power-sector reform, power-generation expansion through a private power producer, and power-system reinforcement works. Total cost: $86.3 million.
Ghana	IDA—$175.6 million. The generating capacity required to meet electricity demand will be constructed, and improvements will be made to transmission and generation systems. Total cost: $414.3 million.
Indonesia	IBRD—$398 million. The coverage and supply of electricity to rural areas will be expanded through a time-slice investment program. Total cost: $841.3 million.
Pakistan	IBRD—$250 million. The private sector's role in the development, ownership, and operation of power and related infrastructure facilities will increase though the financing of selected subprojects. Total cost: $2,390 million.
Peru	IBRD—$150 million. The government's electricity-privatization program and related legal/regulatory and institutional reforms will be supported.
‡ Thailand	IBRD—$100 million. The Electricity Generating Authority of Thailand will be assisted in optimizing its investment decisions and in meeting peak power demand from 2000 onwards at least cost. Total cost: $475.4 million.
Thailand	IBRD—$50 million. The Provincial Electricity Authority's subtransmission network will be expanded, and its power-distribution system will be upgraded. Total cost: $375 million.
Ukraine	IBRD—$114 million. A Hydropower Rehabilitation and System Control Project seeks to improve the efficiency and availability of hydropower plants and increase efficiency in the loading of hydro- and thermal power-generation units. Total cost: $215.1 million.
Viet Nam	IDA—$165 million. The government will be assisted in its efforts to rehabilitate and expand the country's power system. Total cost: $247.9 million.

PUBLIC SECTOR MANAGEMENT

Albania	IDA—$15 million. Support will be provided for the development of a banking system, continued privatization in the industrial sector, and downsizing or liquidation of inviable state enterprises.
Argentina	IBRD—$500 million. The government will be assisted in providing an orderly framework for costs associated with the privatization/closure of weak provincial banks.
Bolivia	IDA—$14.7 million. The government's privatization program will be supported, and an overall regulatory framework for the future development of key sectors will be designed and established. Total cost: $23.3 million.

Bolivia	IDA—$11 million. The first phase of a comprehensive judicial reform program will be supported. Total cost: $12.8 million.
China	IBRD—$275 million; IDA—$75 million. A strategy to develop a market-based housing system and a robust social security system that would free enterprises of these responsibilities will be tested and further developed in four cities. Total cost: $950 million.
China	IBRD—$25 million; IDA—$25 million. Consultancies, training, studies, and equipment at the central and provincial levels will be financed to help the government implement its major reform of fiscal institutions and practices. Total cost: $105.5 million.
China	IDA—$10 million. The legal framework needed to support economic reform will be improved and strengthened. Total cost: $13.3 million.
Ecuador	IBRD—$20 million. Technical assistance will be provided to ensure that the fiscal and management objectives embodied in the government's modernization strategy are achieved and will be sustained. Total cost: $25 million.
Ecuador	IBRD—$12 million. Technical assistance will be provided to prepare for the necessary reforms in the electricity and telecommunications sectors. Total cost: $16 million.
Georgia	IDA—$10.1 million. The institutional framework for financial sector reforms will be prepared, institutional economic management capacities strengthened, and activities to help accelerate privatization financed. Total cost: $10.9 million.
Guatemala	IBRD—$9.4 million. The financial management capacity of the government will be strengthened, thereby helping restore public confidence in public sector integrity and competence. Total cost: $10.5 million.
Indonesia	IBRD—$28 million. Indonesia will be helped in assessing strategic priorities for reducing infrastructure bottlenecks and developing an updated strategy for public-private partnerships and suitable frameworks for private participation in infrastructure provision. Total cost: $33.6 million.
Kenya	IDA—$25.4 million. The first phase of the government's civil service reform program will be supported. Total cost: $157 million.
Mauritania	IDA—$30 million. Structural measures needed to develop the private sector, strengthen the financial sector, and promote growth in fishing and mining will be supported.
§‡ Mexico	IBRD—$500 million. About 10 million people are to benefit from rural investments that will finance basic social and economic infrastructure, provide potable water to small localities, rehabilitate and maintain roads, and support income-generating projects. Total cost: $1,095 million.
Nicaragua	IDA—$23 million. Long- and short-term consultants, training, and information technology will be financed to support the government's institutional restructuring-reform program. Total cost: $33.5 million.
Nicaragua	IDA—$6.3 million. Funds from IDA reflows will be provided to supplement the second Economic Recovery Credit approved in fiscal 1994.

Russia	IBRD—$16.8 million. Support will be provided for the development and installation of an effective and efficient national system of tax administration. Total cost: $27.4 million.
Senegal	IDA—$12.5 million. The government will be assisted in implementing its strategy to strengthen the private sector's supply response to the recent improvement of the policy environment and to enable it to take advantage of new opportunities. Total cost: $20.3 million.
Turkmenistan	IBRD—$25 million. Constraints to the design and implementation of a reform program will be alleviated, and the institutional framework for mobilizing and coordinating technical assistance will be strengthened. Total cost: $26 million.
Uganda	IDA—$36.4 million. Greater local institutional and human capacity will be established to develop and implement public policy and support the growth of the private sector. Total cost: $42.2 million.

SOCIAL SECTOR

§‡ Cambodia	IDA—$20 million. Small-scale projects for the rehabilitation and reconstruction of social and economic infrastructure, as well as for other socially productive activities—all of which will benefit the poor—will be financed. Total cost: $22.2 million.
§ Kazakhstan	IBRD—$41.1 million. Continued availability of social services, including provision of an effective social safety net for the vulnerable and poor, will be ensured by promoting the orderly divestiture of social assets from enterprises to municipalities. Total cost: $54.7 million.
§‡ Kyrgyz Republic	IDA—$17 million. Mechanisms to identify the poor will be improved and social programs made more effective and efficient in targeting and delivering social assistance. Total cost: $20.8 million.
§ Macedonia, former Yugoslav Republic of	IDA—$14 million. Labor redeployment in communities affected by enterprise restructuring will be supported, and a program that better targets social assistance to the poor will be developed, thus helping to sustain the government's reform program. Total cost: $17.1 million.
§‡ Mexico	IBRD—$500 million. Essential social services (in education and health) will be protected and existing social safety net measures strengthened to cushion the poor from the effects of the economic crisis. Total cost: $2,000 million.
§‡ Romania	IBRD—$55.4 million. Reforms in social insurance and assistance programs will be implemented, the capacity of labor offices to administer claims for unemployment benefits strengthened, and an adult training system developed. Total cost: $95.2 million.

TELECOMMUNICATIONS

Indonesia	IBRD—$325 million. Implementation of an ongoing telecommunications sector-reform program, aimed at bringing sector performance up to international competitive levels, will be supported. Total cost: $1,412.6 million.

TRANSPORTATION

§ Albania — IDA—$15 million. Rural roads, now in very poor condition due to lack of maintenance, will be rehabilitated by contractors using labor-intensive methods that will generate 12,000 manyear jobs—benefiting especially the poor and the unemployed—over a three-year period. Total cost: $33.6 million.

‡ Algeria — IBRD—$130 million. The backlog of roads and bridges in need of rehabilitation and maintenance will be reduced. Total cost: $230 million.

Brazil — IBRD—$102 million. An integrated urban transport system for the Recife metropolitan area will be developed, while services will be decentralized from the federal to the state level. Total cost: $203.8 million.

Brazil — IBRD—$99 million. An integrated urban transport system for the Belo Horizonte metropolitan area will be developed, while services will be decentralized from the federal to the state level. Total cost: $197.3 million.

Cameroon — IDA—$10.2 million. The transport-sector reform program—which aims at improving mobilization and allocation of resources, maintenance of transport infrastructure, and overall sectoral efficiency—will be supported. Total cost: $23.9 million.

Chad — IDA—$12.7 million. Funds will be provided to supplement the Second Transport Sector Project approved in fiscal 1993.

Chile — IBRD—$120 million. Key, innovative subcomponents of the Ministry of Public Works' 1995–98 Road Investment and Maintenance Program will be financed. Total cost: $2,075.3 million.

‡ China — IBRD—$400 million. A seventh railways project will address key issues in railway reform and critical constraints in railway capacity. Total cost: $1,747.5 million.

China — IBRD—$210 million. Capacity of six inland waterways will be expanded to remove bottlenecks and promote economic development. Total cost: $556.8 million.

China — IBRD—$150 million. Development of road infrastructure in the Xinjiang Uygur Autonomous Region will be supported. Total cost: $317.5 million.

Croatia — IBRD—$80 million. The modernization and transformation of the transport sector will be supported and accelerated, with special emphasis on the main road network and the Croatian Roads Authority. Total cost: $567.8 million.

§ Gabon — IBRD—$5.2 million. Institutional management capacity in the transport and urban sectors will be strengthened, a transport-sector strategy and investment plan established, and labor-intensive methods for urban civil works tested. Total cost: $8.3 million.

‡ Haiti — IDA—$50 million. The government will be assisted in implementing a comprehensive five-year road-maintenance and rehabilitation program on the intercity road network and in Port-au-Prince. Total cost: $125 million.

Hungary — IBRD—$38 million. Urban transport reforms undertaken by the city of Budapest and the Budapest Transport Company will be supported. Total cost: $67.1 million.

Korea, Republic of	IBRD—$100 million. The major environmental concerns in Korean maritime transport will be addressed, and the level of noise, air pollution, and traffic congestion in Pusan reduced. Total cost: $1,107 million.
Korea, Republic of	IBRD—$100 million. The potential of Pusan's transport services will be met by introducing a congestion-management system, expanding capacity, and institutional development. Total cost: $365.4 million.
Macedonia, former Yugoslav Republic of	IBRD—$24 million. The country's transit crisis, caused by the closing of the Serbian and Greek borders to the transport of goods, will be addressed by the upgrading of east-west transit corridors. Total cost: $38.7 million.
Malawi	IDA—$16.2 million. The government's program for revitalizing the Nacala rail route, restructuring and eventually privatizing Malawi Railways, and commercializing and privatizing Malawi Lake Services will be financed. Total cost: $29 million.
Mauritius	IBRD—$30.5 million. Environmentally sound improvements to the efficiency and competitiveness of port services will be supported. Total cost: $100.2 million.
§ Morocco	IBRD—$57.6 million. By improving more than 3,000 kilometers of unpaved rural roads and paved branch roads, access by the rural poor to social services and markets will be improved. Total cost: $194.1 million.
Russia	IBRD—$329 million. Essential urban transport capacity in fourteen cities will be preserved by linking financing of urgently needed replacement vehicles and spare parts to the implementation of reforms. Total cost: $391 million.
§ Tunisia	IBRD—$51.5 million. About 300 kilometers of gravel roads will be rehabilitated, and some 715 kilometers of priority rural roads will be upgraded. Total cost: $88.7 million.

URBAN DEVELOPMENT

Algeria	IBRD—$51 million. Economic, social, and physical assets destroyed by the August 1994 earthquake in Mascara province will be restored. Total cost: $83.6 million.
Argentina	IBRD—$225 million. Financial support and incentives will be provided for the provinces to undertake their own public sector-reform programs consistent with the national program. Total cost: $321 million.
Argentina	IBRD—$210 million. Public sector management at the provincial and municipal levels will be made more effective through improved financing mechanisms for municipal investments. Total cost: $600 million.
§ Brazil	IBRD—$140 million. Some 50,000 poor families in Ceará state's small towns and medium-sized cities will be provided with basic municipal infrastructure, and water will be brought to unserved localities through the construction of earthen dams. Total cost: $240 million.
‡ Burkina Faso	IDA—$37 million. Primary urban infrastructure networks will be rehabilitated, urban services directly benefiting the poor developed, and urban institutional capacity strengthened. Total cost: $49.7 million.

	Burkina Faso	IDA—$10 million. Finance will be supplied to supplement the Second Urban Project approved in fiscal 1990.
§‡	Côte d'Ivoire	IDA—$40 million. Capital improvements, including priority works for small municipalities and low-income squatter settlements, together with municipal capacity-building measures, will be financed. Total cost: $48.7 million.
	Georgia	IDA—$18 million. Investments will be made so as to arrest further deterioration of, and stabilize critical municipal infrastructure in, a number of selected cities. Total cost: $19.7 million.
§‡	Guinea-Bissau	IDA—$22 million. Rehabilitation of transport infrastructure and urban infrastructure will create jobs for unskilled workers, improve health and sanitation conditions, and lower transport costs. Total cost: $33.5 million.
§‡	Indonesia	IBRD—$136 million. Inhabitants of five Kalimantan cities, especially those in poor kampungs, will directly benefit from improvements in the quality, reliability, and accessibility of urban infrastructure services. Total cost: $262 million.
§‡	Indonesia	IBRD—$72.5 million. A pilot test in some 1,200 of the poorest villages in Java will seek to improve living standards of about 3 million people while building public works. Total cost: $83.8 million.
‡	Mali	IDA—$10 million. Finance will be supplied to supplement the Public Works and Capacity Building Project approved in fiscal 1992.
‡	Niger	IDA—$10 million. Funds will be provided to supplement the Public Works and Employment Project approved in fiscal 1991.
	Russia	IBRD—$400 million. The government's efforts to develop housing markets with choice for consumers and competition among private suppliers will be supported. Total cost: $758.7 million.
‡	Sri Lanka	IDA—$39 million. Municipal solid waste management and services in the Colombo area will be improved, and wastewater pollution will be reduced in two industrial areas through the construction of sewer networks. Total cost: $49 million.
‡	Swaziland	IBRD—$29 million. The first phase of a program aimed at increasing urban management efficiency and improving living conditions of low-income urban households will be supported. Total cost: $51.5 million.

WATER SUPPLY AND SEWERAGE

§	Azerbaijan	IDA—$61 million. Emergency short-term improvements will be made to Baku's water-supply system, particularly in lower-income areas. Institutional capacity building is included. Total cost: $94.9 million.
‡	India	IBRD—$275.8 million. The supply of water to Madras will be increased, and significant improvements made in its distribution and conservation. Total cost: $421 million.
	Korea, Republic of	IBRD—$75 million. Efforts to address in Pusan city and Chunbuk province environmental, institutional, and technological concerns regarding wastewater and specified waste disposal will be supported. Total cost: $305.1 million.

‡	Malawi	IDA—$79.2 million. Implementation of the water resources-management policy and strategies recently adopted by the government, together with capacity development and sector investments, will be financed. Total cost: $94.1 million.
‡	Paraguay	IBRD—$46.5 million. The health conditions and quality of life of some 250,000 people living in the greater Asunción area will improve through the expansion of sewerage facilities and the reduction of sewage disposal in the Paraguay river. Total cost: $72.2 million.
‡	Peru	IBRD—$150 million. Water conservation will be promoted, the privatization of Lima's water and sewerage utility supported, Lima's water-supply and sewerage system rehabilitated, and water and sanitation services to the urban poor expanded. Total cost: $306.2 million.
§	Senegal	IDA—$100 million. An estimated 1.8 million people will benefit from a project that will increase the production of safe drinking water in Dakar and increase the number of connections to the city's sewer system. Total cost: $290.1 million.
§‡	Sierra Leone	IDA—$36 million. Water supply and sanitation services in Freetown will be improved, and the poor's accessibility to them will be increased. Total cost: $46.5 million.
	Trinidad and Tobago	IBRD—$25 million. Technical assistance will be provided to help strengthen the institutions involved in the management of the country's water resources. Total cost: $33.1 million.
	Tunisia	IBRD—$58 million. Safe and accessible water will be provided to about 200,000 people living in rural areas, and water services in Greater Tunis will be rehabilitated and expanded. Total cost: $110.9 million.
	Turkey	IBRD—$100 million. Antalya's water-supply network will be rehabilitated and extended, a new sewerage network and a preliminary wastewater-treatment plant provided, and the stormwater-drainage system upgraded. Total cost: $244.6 million.
‡	Zambia	IDA—$33 million. Water supply and sanitation systems in nine urban areas will be rehabilitated, while community-based demonstration projects in seven peri-urban areas will provide water and access to sanitation for about 250,000 low-income people. Total cost: $46.6 million.

Economic Development Institute

While much of the work of the World Bank Group is involved in the transfer of capital to developing countries, the Economic Development Institute (EDI) focuses on the transfer of knowledge. During fiscal 1995, the EDI held 167 conferences, seminars, and workshops in all regions of the world, with a particular focus on sub-Saharan Africa and the former Soviet Union (FSU). Reflecting the diverse challenges of development, EDI programs covered a sweep of subject areas, ranging from girls' education to macroeconomic management.

Operating under a strategy of "investing in ideas and people," EDI's expanded mission is to assist countries to synthesize and adapt the lessons of worldwide development experience. The EDI increasingly emphasizes policy issues in its programs, while maintaining its historic mission of providing basic skills training in client countries. Much of the skills education occurs through training-of-trainers programs, in which the EDI works with partner institutions to spur training efforts that can be sustained in client countries with minimal support from Washington, D.C.

New audiences, new formats. As part of its newly defined mission, the EDI worked with both new audiences and new formats in fiscal 1995.

For example, a two-day workshop in Tanzania offered parliamentarians a detailed discussion of Malaysia's experience with private sector development; and in Ukraine, the EDI held a seminar on economic reform for parliamentarians—part of a larger economic education campaign launched by the EDI, the World Bank resident mission, and the Ukrainian government.

The EDI's fiscal 1995 programs were supported by the publication of forty-seven titles. Making use of new information technologies, the EDI is working with videos, teleconferencing, Internet connections, and CD-ROMs. The new formats give EDI programs broader reach and provide useful follow-up to seminars and conferences.

Timely ideas. In an effort to address concerns policymakers find most urgent, the EDI mounted programs that respond to economic and political upheavals around the world. On the heels of the financial crisis in Mexico—with its attendant fallout for other emerging markets—the EDI held a global conference in Washington, D.C. on how to manage economic reforms amid volatile capital flows. EDI then designed programs for particular countries focusing on ways to apply lessons drawn from the Mexican crisis.

Following elections in South Africa, the EDI mounted a number of programs there, including an interactive workshop on sustainable fiscal poli-

cies. Participants included parliamentarians, journalists, and government officials.

Human resources. The EDI extended its work in grassroots development, gender concerns, and social issues. It worked with governments, particularly in the FSU, to help design programs to support the unemployed and to build a sturdier social safety net. In line with the World Bank's larger commitment to the education of girls, the institute held workshops in Africa, Asia, and Washington, D.C. aimed at convincing policymakers of the importance of promoting girls' education and at providing education planners with practical approaches for doing so.

The EDI's Grassroots Management Training program, first carried out as a pilot program in Tanzania and Malawi, was extended to Burkina Faso, India, Nigeria, and Senegal. Under this program, the EDI trains local trainers to pass on grassroots management practices to poor, often illiterate women who operate tiny enterprises.

Sustaining the environment. As awareness of environmental challenges increases globally, the EDI has integrated environmental perspectives into its training programs at both national and regional levels. It held programs on environmental policies in Africa, including some targeted to particular sectors. In South Asia and the Central Asian republics, the EDI carried out programs on land use, deforestation, and biodiversity. The institute has also run training activities on managing the resettlement of people displaced by development projects.

Because more effective water management is a priority, the EDI has designed a series of national, regional, and international seminars to help policymakers better deal with the twin perils of increased demands for water and deteriorating water quality.

Supporting the transition to markets. The EDI is actively supporting countries that are making the transition from centrally planned economies by working with policymakers on matters such as civil service reform, project management, and privatization.

The Joint Vienna Institute (JVI), cosponsored by the Bank and four other international agencies, conducted courses that give key officials the skills they need to implement reforms. In addition, the JVI manages four regional centers—in Kiev, Moscow, Prague, and Tashkent—that offer introductory courses in market economics and financial analysis.

Scholarship and fellowship programs. The World Bank Graduate Scholarship Program, which supports graduate studies for mid career officials of members countries, awarded 106 scholarships for fiscal 1995. A special program funded by the government of Japan saw a group of twenty-five graduate with a master's degree in Economic Policy Management from Columbia University. Classes of about thirty students began studies at McGill University and the University of Auvergne under a program jointly initiated by the EDI and the African Capacity Building Foundation. Also under the special scholarship program, twenty participants pursued advanced studies in Japan through the policy-management program at Tsukuba University and the infrastructure-management program at Yokohama National University.

Research at the World Bank

The World Bank is now more than fifty years old, it has adapted to a changing world over that time span, and Bank research continues to evolve to support the Bank's changing role.

In the 1950s and 1960s, the Bank's work focused on financing discrete projects and infrastructure. As developing countries became the Bank's sole clients in the 1970s, policies to alleviate poverty and promote equity and rural development became priorities for both Bank operations and research. With the instability of the international environment and the onset of the debt crisis in the 1980s, the need for broad macroeconomic adjustment and policy advice became paramount. The Bank's lending supported that adjustment, and the Bank's research program examined how it had been done in successful cases and suggested what packages of reforms would be most likely to yield desired outcomes.

In the 1990s, multilateral lending has declined as a share of total capital flows. Private net flows of funds to developing countries have grown from $42 billion in 1989 to an estimated $173 billion in 1994. While the majority of the Bank's poorer member countries have received little of that private money, in many countries the Bank's role is beginning to shift from primary purveyor of capital to a source of related services—investment guarantees, aid coordination, technical assistance, and sectoral and macroeconomic advice. The basis for this expanding advisory role comes from both the findings of Bank research and operational experience. The Bank's expanding membership and declining resources for research require that current studies focus selectively on the priority issues that now recur in dialogue with client countries:

• how to sustain growth while protecting the poor and the environment;

• how to enhance the inflow and impact of foreign capital flows, and, for some, how to deal with a legacy of debt;

• how to encourage the development of the private sector;

• how to reduce and decentralize government activities; and

• how to promote the welfare of the poor and protect the vulnerable in these processes.

The research program assists operational staff in advising on proposed policies, projects, and problems in a host of developing or transitional countries. In many African countries, for instance, Bank staff find that negative rates of savings and investment since the early 1980s have precluded economic growth. Researchers in the African and Asian regional offices are examining how traditional lenders support rural savings and investment, and how to integrate those numerous informal agents with formal channels to better reach the poor. Lower incomes contribute to high fertility rates, which further lower parents' investment in their children's education. Bank research has examined where this cycle of low education and income can most effectively be interrupted and has suggested policies to do so.

The research departments provide comprehensive statistical information that allows operations staff and policymakers to compare the status of a country or region with other countries and regions and to point out in which areas national policy may be hampering development and poverty reduction. The International Economics Department (IEC) also monitors the international economy and analyzes international economic linkages. In 1994, IEC staff analyzed economic imbalances and potential financial volatility and, in the aftermath of the Mexican devaluation, they contributed to a review and monitoring system that encompasses several developing countries to warn of potential destabilizing trends. The department also examined the implications of the Uruguay Round of international trade negotiations and predicted substantial growth in trade and income for developing countries by the end of the ten-year implementation period—if all nations fully put in place the agreed changes.

Bank research also leads the way in examining critical new policy issues, including those dealing with transition economies, comparability, and pension programs.

The transition to a market economy. The Bank's research staff have been involved in this area since China opened up its economy in the 1980s; since 1990, it has been heavily involved with assisting countries of the former Soviet Union in their transition to a market economy.

Drawing on years of experience in advising on economywide policy reform, Bank research has analyzed and advised on a range of issues in transitional economies, including fiscal decentralization, taxation, finance and bankruptcy, agricultural development, labor markets, corporate finance, and social safety nets.

Comparing neighbors and nations. The Bank's Living Standards Measurement Studies (LSMS) program provides some of the first comprehensive information about the lives of rich and poor families in many developing countries. The data illuminate many important issues: In a recent study, for instance, LSMS data show why targeting is necessary if subsidies are to reach the poor without bankrupting governments. At the national level, the International Comparisons Program is being extended in Bank research to account for differences in exchange rates and consumption practices when comparing incomes and production across countries.

Dealing with aging populations. Successful development entails people having fewer children, educating them better, and living longer. But this imposes a cost—that of smaller working-age populations supporting a large number of the elderly. As a result, government-backed pension programs are near collapse in many countries. Recently completed research recommends ways to predict realistically what can be contributed by the labor force, private capital markets, and the public treasury to balance the need for savings, insurance, and safety nets for the poor.

The Administrative Budget and World Bank Administration

The Bank's total budget for fiscal 1995, as approved by the executive directors in fiscal 1994, was $1,420.3 million. It was subsequently increased to $1,421.6 million, with board approval, to accommodate the Bank's contribution of $1.3 million to the Task Force on Multilateral Development Banks. Late in fiscal 1995, the directors approved a total budget for fiscal 1996 of $1,382.2 million *(see Appendix 6)*. The net administrative budget for fiscal 1996, which takes into account reimbursements and fee revenues that offset the costs of programs not financed from the regular budget, shows a 6.4 percent decline in real terms over the fiscal 1995 budget. The net administrative budgets for the two-year period, fiscal 1996–97, are to be reduced by approximately 12 percent.

The budget for fiscal 1996 and the programs it funds were designed to enhance the Bank's development effectiveness by exercising selectivity and greater focus on work programs, increased emphasis on results and partnerships with clients and other development agencies, and more efficient use of resources.

The budget provides sufficient resources to implement work programs that are consistent with and derived from the development-assistance strategies and policy directions approved by the executive directors. They are based on three key objectives:

• The provision of financial assistance and services to reduce poverty on a sustainable basis;

• the delivery of lending and other services in an increasingly cost effective, responsive, and flexible manner; and

• increased attention on results in the field, where the Bank's actions ultimately matter.

The reduction in the budgets in the next two fiscal years will be accompanied by corresponding reductions in staffing. Bank units began to plan for these changes during fiscal 1995, and the impacts, notably on redundancies and attrition rates, were already evident by the year's end. Regular and fixed-term staff on board at the end of fiscal year 1995—excluding staff on special leave and leave without pay—numbered 6,059, down from 6,185 at the end of fiscal 1994. Of that number 3,983 were higher-level staff (4,034 at June 30, 1994). Some 59 percent of the higher-level staff were from industrialized countries; 41 percent were from developing countries—the same breakdown as in fiscal 1994. At the end of fiscal 1995, long-term consultants numbered 1,112 (1,166 on June 30, 1994).

As a result of downsizing and changes in skills needs, some 590 staff are expected to be declared redundant by the end of fiscal 1996.

The redundancy payments are expected to be made by fiscal 1998. The estimated cost of this plan is $131 million. This is more than offset by anticipated savings of about $78 million in fiscal 1996 and $143 million in fiscal 1997. To assist redundant staff, a Job Search Center was set up that provides individualized consultations, workshops, and seminars on visa issues, financial planning, job searching, and how to start a business.

To further refine the skills mix needed to address the challenges posed by a rapidly changing global economy, the Bank recruited 186 higher-level staff, of whom 29 percent were from developing countries and 38 percent were women. Thirty-nine of the Bank's recruits were selected through the Young Professionals Program; eleven were from developing countries, and twenty were women.

During fiscal year 1995, the Bank began implementation of a program to help the institution better manage change and to engender excellence in its business practices. Efforts focused on improving the business-process efficiency in service units and in front line operations and at reducing costs. In addition, the quality of personnel services was improved, and a major overhaul of the Bank's training programs was begun.

Core business-redesign pilot projects are now being implemented throughout the East Asia and Pacific region and Development Economics. Sizable improvements in the quality and timeliness of projects are expected, as well as cost savings of as much as 20 percent. Redesign projects in three other regions were initiated. In the support services, business-redesign activities, begun in fiscal 1994, continued. Cost savings of about 7 percent have been realized. The redesign of personnel services focused on improved recruitment/internal staffing, more relevant training, faster personnel-transaction processing, and more effective support for front line managers. A redesigned personnel team structure will provide higher quality advice to managers and help staff with their careers.

Major improvements to the management-succession process were put in place, including identifying successors for senior positions, providing training for candidates exhibiting high potential, and putting into place a mentoring program for outside recruits. A Management Assessment Center was established jointly with the International Monetary Fund for division chiefs. Steps were taken to improve performance evaluation, primarily through follow-up and advice to managers on individual performance issues.

The new Headquarters Construction Project progressed satisfactorily, on schedule and within budget. The approved $314 million budget includes partial upgrading of two existing buildings.

A medium-term strategy for headquarters office space, designed to reduce leased space, was completed. Office space was placed on chargeback during the year to encourage more efficient use of space, new space-design options were tested, and a number of internal services were redesigned (printing and procurement, for example, with similar work in progress for others). Processes have been streamlined, customer focus improved, management overhead reduced, and costs reduced by $3 million yearly; office supplies and space lease-advisory functions were outsourced; contracted-out services were increased and management of contracts tightened; a new Corporate Card program is expected to save $1 million over three years; and negotiations with airlines, hotels, and the Bank's travel contractor have led to cost-avoidance of about $9 million annually.

The Health Services Department (HSD) launched a comprehensive Breast Care Program to increase early detection of breast cancers and reduce medical costs: More than 900 staff have participated. An on-site clinic was opened to help staff members with episodic, acute illnesses and provide referrals to a specialist. Utilization of the clinic is high and is expected to reduce medical insurance costs. Negotiation of preferred rates at local hospitals is expected to reduce insurance costs by $600,000.

The Bank is working to harness technology to improve efficiency and support its role as a leading source of development information. Installation of a Bankwide "Enterprise" electronic network is scheduled to be completed by December 1995. It is expected to facilitate work collaboration and information exchange both within the Bank and with field offices, member countries, and others. Bankwide technology standards have been established; communications with field offices are being upgraded; and new work tools, including a new electronic mail system, electronic filing and document-management systems, and software that facilitates communication among people in different locations, are being examined.

International Finance Corporation (IFC)

The IFC registered another record year in fiscal 1995, maintaining the pattern of expansion established over the past decade. Over the past four years, total financing for IFC's own account increased by an annual average of 16 percent. This steady rate of growth reflects the strong demand for its financing and services brought on by the expansion in private sector economic activities in many member countries. Sectors of particular growth and strength for the IFC during fiscal 1995 included infrastructure (power, telecommunications, and transport), capital markets development, and privatization work.

Financing approved for the IFC's own account was $2.9 billion for 212 projects, compared with almost $2.5 billion for 231 projects in fiscal 1994. It was also a record year for the IFC's resource-mobilization activities: $2.6 billion in financing was approved through loan syndications and the underwriting of securities issues and investment funds. Projects approved by the IFC had total investment costs of $18.9 billion, meaning other investors and lenders provided a total of $5.56 for every dollar approved by the IFC. Projects were approved in sixty-seven countries, compared with sixty-five countries in fiscal 1994. In addition, a number of projects were regional or international in scope.

In July 1994, the IFC's board of directors approved a new policy on disclosure of information for the corporation. Like the Bank's policy, that of the IFC seeks to ensure that its activities are undertaken with transparency and accountability. The fundamental principle of the policy is a presumption of disclosure where disclosure would not materially harm the business and competitive interests of clients.

The IFC's 1995 financial performance was more in line with historic levels after having achieved a record level in fiscal 1994. Fiscal 1995 net income was $188 million, reflecting lower equity sales and capital gains due to the weakness and uncertain conditions in most emerging markets in the second half of the fiscal year. The IFC earned a return of 5.5 percent on its net worth, which reached $3.6 billion at June 30, 1995. New commitments signed during the year totaled $2.4 billion, up from $1.8 billion in fiscal 1994. Disbursements were also up, to $1.8 billion, and the IFC's total disbursed portfolio reached $7.3 billion as of June 30, 1995. The corporation borrowed $2.4 billion in the international markets and $45 million from the IBRD. The IFC issued bonds in ten currencies.

In fiscal 1995, the corporation's membership increased to 165 countries with the additions of Armenia, Georgia, Moldova, and Tajikistan.

Details of the IFC's fiscal year can be found in its Annual Report, published separately.

Multilateral Investment Guarantee Agency (MIGA)

During fiscal 1995, MIGA's board of directors concurred with the president's decision on forty-six insurance projects conveyed to it. Since MIGA's inception, the board has considered 171 projects. MIGA's net income before provisioning increased 140 percent to $12.8 million in fiscal 1995.

Seven additional countries became members of the agency in fiscal 1995, increasing the number of MIGA member countries to 128. An additional twenty-four developing countries and economies in transition are in the process of fulfilling membership requirements; MIGA has 152 signatories to its Convention.

Guarantee program. In fiscal 1995, MIGA's guarantee-program results exceeded fiscal 1994 records for the number of guarantee contracts executed (fifty-four versus thirty-eight), total amount of coverage issued ($672 million versus $372.6 million), number of developing countries benefited (twenty-one versus fourteen), and amount of income earned from premiums

and commitment fees ($14.4 million versus $9.9 million). In addition, MIGA has seven commitment letters outstanding, with $210 million in potential coverage, which also surpassed the five commitment letters for potential maximum coverage of $167 million outstanding at the end of fiscal 1994.

The contracts issued in fiscal 1995 facilitated total direct investment of about $2.5 billion and created an estimated 8,800 jobs in developing member countries. MIGA issued, for the first time, significant amounts of coverage ($142 million) for infrastructure investments, including its first power and toll road projects.

Other milestones reached in fiscal 1995 were:
• MIGA signed its 155th contract of guarantee;
• these contracts facilitated an estimated $8.6 billion in total foreign private investment;
• the outstanding maximum contingent liability exceeded $1.6 billion;
• MIGA issued its first guarantees in Costa Rica, Ecuador, Honduras, Morocco, the Philippines, the Slovak Republic, South Africa, Venezuela, and Viet Nam; and
• MIGA received its 2,250th preliminary application for coverage.

Technical assistance activities. MIGA offers technical assistance to help developing countries promote private investment opportunities more effectively. It does this through direct support of investment-promotion activities; dissemination of information on investment opportunities; and capacity building of investment-promotion agencies (IPAs). The underlying focus of these services is the introduction of new management and marketing techniques to help developing member states maximize the effectiveness of their programs in attracting foreign direct investment.

MIGA's investment-promotion assistance involves organization of investment conferences, preparatory executive training programs, strategy workshops, and follow-up investment-promotion missions. Wherever possible, MIGA seeks to support activities on a sectoral and multicountry basis. Two major conferences of this nature were organized during fiscal 1995—

for the tourism sector in the Middle East and the mining sector in sub-Saharan Africa. The latter, held in Toronto, Canada, followed a similar, highly successful conference convened by MIGA in fiscal 1994.

During fiscal 1995, MIGA organized several activities to promote investment between developing countries, which included investment missions from Africa and South America to Southeast Asia.

MIGA is pioneering the use of new marketing and communications technologies as vehicles for information dissemination on investment opportunities in developing countries. This includes the development of CD-ROMs on investment opportunities in specific regions and sectors. MIGA also made considerable progress in developing a global electronic information exchange and communications network on investment opportunities (IPA *net*), to be carried over the Internet. This network will link IPAS, business associations, financial institutions, and other intermediaries involved in the promotion or facilitation of foreign investment and will become operational during fiscal 1996. MIGA is also spearheading the development of joint programs for IPAS through a global association.

Details about MIGA's activities in fiscal 1995 appear in its Annual Report, published separately.

International Centre for Settlement of Investment Disputes

The International Centre for Settlement of Investment Disputes (ICSID) is a separate international organization established under the Convention on the Settlement of Investment Disputes between States and Nationals of Other States (the Convention), which was opened for signature in 1965 and entered into force the following year.

ICSID seeks to encourage greater flows of international investment by providing facilities for the conciliation and arbitration of disputes between governments and foreign investors. In addition, ICSID undertakes advisory, research, and publications activities in the area of foreign investment law.

During fiscal 1995, ICSID's membership continued to grow with the ratification of the Convention by Argentina, Bolivia, Mozambique, Nicaragua, Spain, and Venezuela. As of June 30, 1995, 119 countries had become members of ICSID. An additional fifteen countries had signed but not yet ratified the Convention.

During the year, two new requests for arbitration were registered. As of June 30, 1995, five cases were pending before the centre.

ICSID's publications include a semiannual law journal, "ICSID Review—Foreign Investment Law Journal," and multivolume collections of *Investment Laws of the World* and *Investment Treaties*. Two issues of the law journal and three releases of the investment laws and treaties collections were published in fiscal 1995.

Details of ICSID's activities during fiscal year 1995 appear in its Annual Report, which is published separately.

IBRD Financial Highlights

In the fiscal year ending June 30, 1995, the IBRD achieved solid financial results, of which highlights included:

• disbursements to countries of $12.7 billion;

• medium- and long-term borrowing the equivalent of $9.0 billion in seven currencies, four after swaps; and

• net income of $1,354 million, well within the range that satisfies the IBRD's financial objectives.

In the first quarter of fiscal 1995, net income earned during fiscal 1994 was allocated as follows:

• $285 million to the general reserve, which was intended to maintain the IBRD's reserves-to-loan ratio at the end of fiscal 1995 at 13.85 percent, excluding amounts allocated for prefunding of interest waivers;

• $220 million to the general reserve for prefunding of interest waivers to be granted in fiscal 1995;

• $300 million to IDA; and

• $246 million to surplus.

In the second quarter of fiscal 1995, the board of governors approved a grant of $20 million out of surplus for emergency assistance to Rwanda.

Financial Policies

Conversion from 1982 loan terms to 1989 loan terms. In December 1994, the executive directors approved a proposal to encourage the IBRD's borrowers to convert the variable lending rate (VLR) 1982

loans to VLR 1989 loans. The VLR 1982 loan terms were based on all IBRD funding. The VLR 1989 loan terms allocate specific funding to the Bank's currency-pool products. The purpose is to facilitate interest risk management by the IBRD and to enhance its ability to offer borrowers new loan products. Two actions are being taken to promote loan conversions:

• A one-time, 10 basis point waiver of annual interest charges spread over two interest periods for loans that are converted is being credited to each borrower that converts all of its VLR 1982 loans to VLR 1989 loan terms (borrowers that had previously done so will also receive this waiver).

• When the executive directors consider future annual interest waivers for eligible borrowers, the IBRD will adjust any such waivers for VLR 1982 loans whenever the VLR 1982 loan rate is below the VLR 1989 loan rate in order to equalize the two.

At the end of fiscal 1995, conversions following this initiative amounted to $28,470 million, or approximately 73 percent of the unconverted volume outstanding at December 31, 1994.

Single currency loan pilot program reviewed. In May 1995, the executive directors of the Bank approved a proposal that, effective immediately, provides all IBRD borrowers the option of choosing the currency in which their loans are denominated. Prior to this, a choice of currencies had

been offered under a two-year, $3 billion pilot program.

Under the pilot program, only "eligible" borrowers were permitted to choose the currency—United States dollars, deutsche mark, yen, pounds sterling, or French francs—in which their loans were denominated. To be eligible, a borrower (or subborrower) had to be an autonomous entity with revenues in the same currency as the loan.

With the expanded program, this eligibility criterion was dropped; now, governments can also borrow in a single currency. In addition, the prospective currency options were expanded to include any currency or composite currency for which there is sufficient borrower demand and in which the IBRD can efficiently borrow from the market. A fixed rate single-currency loan option was also agreed to; under the pilot scheme, only a floating rate single currency loan was offered. The IBRD, therefore, now provides three standard lending instruments to countries:

• a floating rate single currency loan tied to the six-month LIBOR rate of the chosen currency;

• a fixed rate single currency loan tied to the fixed rate equivalent of six-month LIBOR in each loan currency; and

• the previous standard, a variable rate currency-pool loan, whose lending rate is calculated each semester on the

IBRD's cost of outstanding borrowings that are funding these loans.

The directors agreed to impose a cap on the amount of single currency loans a borrowing country could undertake: 50 percent of a country's annual lending program, or $100 million, whichever is higher. The management of the Bank will bring the issue of the lending cap back to the executive board for further discussion within a year's time, with the intention of phasing it out progressively or removing it entirely when circumstances warrant.

It was also agreed that eligibility for the new program required that member governments (and individual borrowers, if applicable), must have converted all their outstanding loans under VLR 1982 to VLR 1989.

Directors affirmed that the future design of single currency loan products should consider variations on the fixed rate option. They also emphasized the importance of adequate staff training to ensure that the Bank's lending products are offered to borrowers in such a way that borrowers can make informed choices to reduce their risks.

As of June 30, 1995, $3,775 million of single currency loans had been approved, including $1,507 million under the expanded program.

Accumulated provisions for loan losses. The level of loan-loss provision is based on an assessment of the collectibility of loans in nonaccrual status, together with an evaluation of collectibility risks in the remainder of the portfolio. For fiscal year 1995, loan-loss provisions were maintained at a level equal to 3 percent of total loans disbursed and outstanding plus the present value of callable guarantees for an amount equivalent to $3,740 million at the end of the fiscal year.

Loans

Disbursements. Gross disbursements by the IBRD to countries during fiscal 1995 were $12,672 million, up $2,225 million from fiscal 1994's total of $10,447 million. Net disbursements, excluding prepayments, to current borrowers were $2,238 million, an increase of $1,275 million over the previous year's total of $963 million.

Lending rate. Under VLR 1989, the interest rate was 7.10 percent for the first semester and 7.09 percent for the second semester of fiscal 1995. By comparison, the interest rates for VLR 1982 were 7.11 percent and 7.13 percent for the first and second semesters, respectively, of fiscal 1995.

The single currency lending rate in United States dollars (the only currency with outstanding loans) applicable in the second semester of 1995 was 6.98 percent. This rate was based on the IBRD's cost of LIBOR-based funding in that currency.

Interest waivers. During fiscal 1995, the IBRD continued to waive 25 basis points of the semester interest rate on loans to all borrowers that had made all loan-service payments within thirty days of their due date. (Approximately 86 percent of the IBRD's total volume of outstanding loans is currently eligible for the interest-spread waiver.) This waiver was in addition to the continuation during the year of a waiver of part of the IBRD's commitment fee on undisbursed balances that resulted in a reduction of that fee from 75 to 25 basis points.

Loans in nonaccrual status. At the end of fiscal 1995, five member countries (Iraq, Liberia, Sudan, Syria, and Zaire), as well as two successor republics of the former Socialist Federal Republic of Yugoslavia (the Federal Republic of Yugoslavia (Serbia and Montenegro) and Bosnia-Herzegovina) were in nonaccrual status. Loans in nonaccrual accounted for 2.1 percent of the total IBRD portfolio at the end of fiscal 1995.

Liquid Assets Management

At the end of fiscal 1995, the IBRD's liquidity totaled $18.4 billion (of which $1.2 billion was segregated as "held-to-maturity"), equivalent to about 46 percent of anticipated net cash requirements over the next three fiscal years. At the end of fiscal 1994, liquidity amounted to $19.2 billion. The IBRD's primary objective in holding such liquidity is to ensure flexibility in the timing of its borrowings should borrowing ability be adversely affected by temporary conditions in the capital markets.

The IBRD's liquid assets are invested exclusively in fixed-income markets and are actively traded with the exception of the British pound holdings, which have been matched to the duration of underlying liabilities. This portfolio is classified as held-to-maturity. Portfolio-management activities are fully supported by comprehensive risk-management and monitoring procedures covering both credit risk and interest-rate risk. Trading performance of actively managed portfolios is measured daily against detailed benchmark portfolios.

Continued enhancements in the management of the IBRD's liquid assets included integration of computer systems across trading, accounting, and control functions; and improvements in performance-measurement and risk-monitoring systems.

During fiscal 1995, the IBRD's financial return on its portfolio was 5.71 percent, including one synthetic instrument. The financial return on investments in fiscal 1994 was 3.56 percent. The portfolio continues to be managed in relation to a benchmark strategy of one-year duration except for the held-to-maturity portfolio, whose average duration was six years as of June 30, 1995.

Borrowings and Liability Management

The objectives of the IBRD's borrowing and liability-management strategy are to ensure the long-term availability of funds to the IBRD for lending and liquidity and to minimize the costs of funds for the IBRD and its borrowers. The IBRD seeks to ensure the availability of funds by developing borrowing capacity in markets in advance of need and by diversifying its borrowings by currency, country, source, and maturity to provide maximum flexibility in funding. It also seeks to strengthen the continuing appeal of its securities by offering features that are tailored to satisfy investors' asset preferences and by positioning its securities advantageously in each capital market (for example, from a regulatory-tax and investment-classification perspective).

Within the framework of the currency composition of borrowings required to fund its lending products, the IBRD seeks to minimize the cost of borrowed funds by using, among other things, currency swaps to obtain cost savings compared with the cost of direct borrowings in target currencies; structured financings converted to conventional liabilities using over-the-counter financial derivatives; the use of short-term and variable rate instruments; and prepayments or market repurchases of borrowings, which, by varying margins, exceed the costs of refinancing.

Medium-term and long-term (MLT) funding. During fiscal year 1995, the IBRD raised $9.0 billion through MLT borrowings in seven currencies *(see Table 6-1)*. After $1.0 billion of currency swaps and a notional par volume of $782 million of interest-rate swaps, all of the year's borrowings, except for $216 million raised in United States dollars to fund single currency loans and minor residuals in vehicle currencies, were fixed rate liabilities denominated in United States dollars, yen, deutsche mark, and Swiss francs. The average maturity of all this funding, including the MLT funding held at floating rates, was 7.4 years, and the after-swap cost was 6.32 percent *(see Table 6-2)*.

Noteworthy among the transactions in the IBRD's core currencies during the past year was the reopening of the IBRD's second deutsche mark global bond, which marked the first time the IBRD had reopened one of its global bonds since the product's inception in 1989. The initial size of the second deutsche mark global bond issue was DM2 billion, and the reopening, which was launched to enhance the liquidity of the issue, added DM500 million to the size of the borrowing. Also noteworthy was an innovative feature introduced with the IBRD's third deutsche mark global bond, a market-based arrangement to facilitate the use of these bonds for repurchase (repo) transactions. To achieve this objective, a core group of underwriters for this issue agreed to become market makers in the repo market for these bonds and to post repo rates on electronic screens accessible to other market participants. This was the first time such a commitment had been made for such securities in the deutsche mark repo market.

TABLE 6-1. IBRD BORROWINGS, FISCAL YEAR 1995

(amounts in millions)

Type	Issue	Currency of issue		US dollar equivalent [a]
Medium- and long-term public offerings				
Global	7.125% five-year bonds, due 1999	US$	1,500	1,492.1
	7.25% five-year bonds, due 1999	DM	2,500	1,617.6
	4.75% ten-year bonds, due 2004	¥	200,000	2,045.8
	7.125% ten-year bonds, due 2005	DM	3,000	2,169.9
Eurobond market	10.125% three-year notes, due 1998	$A	100	78.4
	10.625% three-year bonds, due 1997	Lit	300,000	197.7
	11% three-year bonds, due 1998	Lit	250,000	150.6
	Zero-coupon note, due 1996	Lit	200,000	106.5
	4.5% five-year notes, due 1999	US$	200	184.0
	10.625% three-year bonds, due 1998	Lit	500,000	307.0
Germany	Zero-coupon note, due 2024	DM	500	36.1
Luxembourg	8.125% ten-year bonds, due 2004	Lux F	2,000	66.8
Switzerland	5.5% five-year bonds, due 1999	Sw F	200	159.0
	5.375% six-year bonds, due 2000	Sw F	200	157.3
	5.375% five-year bonds, due 2000	Sw F	200	159.3
Total medium- and long-term public offerings				8,928.1
Medium- and long-term private placements				
Germany	Zero-coupon note, due 2025	DM	400	31.4
	Zero-coupon note, due 2025	DM	300	25.3
United States	2.51% five-year notes, due 1999	US$	50	41.5
Total medium- and long-term private placements				98.2
Total medium- and long-term borrowings, fiscal 1995				9,026.3
Short-term borrowings outstanding [b]				
Central bank facility [c]		US$	2,599.8	2,599.8
Discount notes		US$	1,211.8	1,211.8
Others [d]				
		US$	20	20.0
		Lit [e]	138,000	84.9
Short-term borrowings outstanding				3,916.5

a. Medium- and long-term borrowing amounts based on gross proceeds, expressed at exchange rates prevailing at the time of launch.

b. Maturing within one year; short-term borrowings are shown at face value.

c. These issues were placed with central banks, government agencies, and international organizations.

d. Executed under the IBRD's Global Multicurrency Note Program.

e. Swapped into deutsche mark.

TABLE 6-2. IBRD BORROWINGS, AFTER SWAPS, FISCAL YEAR 1995

(amounts in millions of US dollars equivalent)

Item	Before swaps			Currency swaps (amount)	After swaps			
	Amount	%	Maturity (years)		Amount	%	Maturity (years)	Cost (%)
Medium- and long-term borrowings								
U.S. dollars	1,717.6	19	5.0	216.4	1,934.0	21	4.8	7.30
Japanese yen	2,045.8	23	10.0	77.2	2,123.0	24	9.7	4.46
Deutsche mark	3,880.3	43	8.4	598.5	4,478.8	50	7.7	6.92
Swiss francs	475.6	5	5.3	0.0	475.6	5	5.3	5.27
Others[a]	907.0	10	3.3	(892.1)	14.9	0	3.4	10.42
Total	9,026.3	100	7.4		9,026.3	100	7.4	6.32[b]
Short-term borrowings outstanding								
Central bank facility (U.S. dollars)	2,599.8	66	0.5					5.81
Discount notes (U.S. dollars)	1,211.8	31	0.3					5.96
Other[c]								
U.S. dollars	20.0	1	0.6					7.01
Italian lire, swapped into deutsche mark	84.9	2	0.7					4.92
Total[d]	3,916.5	100	0.4					5.85

NOTE: *Details may not add to totals because of rounding.*

a. Represents borrowings in Australian dollars, Italian lire, and Luxembourg francs.

b. Excludes the cost of $216 million of single currency loan funding held at floating rates.

c. Executed under the IBRD's Global Multicurrency Note Program.

d. Short-term borrowings outstanding on June 30, 1994, totaled $3,311 million; short-term borrowings are shown at face value.

During the past fiscal year, the IBRD prepaid an aggregate volume of $721 million of borrowings, including borrowings in yen, Swiss francs, and French francs. In addition, it redeemed $60 million of United States dollar and yen borrowings through market repurchases.

At the end of the fiscal year, MLT funding outstanding amounted to $104.5 billion, or 96 percent ($107.8 billion, or 97 percent after swaps) of total debt outstanding. As of June 30, 1995, the average maturity of total MLT debt was 5.6 years, and its average cost, after swaps, was 6.3 percent.

Short-term funding. As of June 30, 1995, short-term borrowings outstanding were $3.9 billion before and after swaps. These comprised $2.6 billion from official sources through the IBRD's central bank facility, $1.2 billion from market funding in United States dollar notes, and $0.1 billion from global multicurrency notes. The cost of these borrowings was 5.85 percent compared with 4.94 percent at the end of fiscal 1994.

On June 30, 1995, short-term and variable rate funding aggregated $4.3 billion equivalent, representing about 3 percent of total outstanding debt.

Capital

On June 30, 1995, the total subscribed capital of the IBRD was $176.4 billion, or 96 percent of authorized capital of $184 billion. During fiscal year 1995, subscriptions to the $74.8 billion general capital increase (GCI), approved in April 1988, continued on schedule. Twenty countries subscribed an aggregate $6.4 billion. A total of 51,754 GCI shares ($6.2 billion, or 8 percent of total allocations, including additional GCI shares allocated to new members that joined the IBRD after April 1988) remain to be subscribed. At the end of fiscal 1995, the permissible increase of net disbursements ("headroom") was $75.3 billion, or 38 percent of the IBRD's lending limit.

Reserves. On June 30, 1995, reserves amounted to $17.2 billion, and the reserves-to-loan ratio stood at 14.3 percent.

IDA Finances

In October 1994, the executive directors discussed a report on the use of resources during the first year of IDA-10 (fiscal year 1994), took note of it, and encouraged a candid look in the future at implementation and design problems and at establishing firmer linkages between IDA programs and results on the ground *(see Box 6-1).*

IDA's commitment authority. IDA is mainly funded by donor contributions, and such funds

are "replenished" by an agreement among donors every three years. Fiscal year 1995 was the second year of the tenth replenishment of IDA (IDA-10), the agreed size of which was SDR13 billion. IDA's commitment authority is based on these donor contributions, which are made available in three annual tranches, and other resources available to IDA (mainly repayments from past credits and net income transfers from the IBRD).

As of June 30, 1995, the donor funds made available for the IDA-10 period (fiscal 1994–96) totaled SDR7,642 million. During fiscal 1995, the association received formal notifications to contribute to IDA-10 from Belgium, Portugal, and Spain, which increased commitment authority by SDR208 million. Part of the second tranche of IDA-10 contributions is not yet available, as the United States' payment to IDA-10 was about 8 percent less than the agreed schedule, and two other donors (Germany and Canada) exercised their right to withhold their contributions proportionately to the shortfall in the United States' payment.

Other resources made available during the year included the transfer of SDR207 million from the IBRD's fiscal 1994 net income and

BOX 6-1. REVIEW OF THE FISCAL 1994 IDA PROGRAM

The review covered IDA's efforts during fiscal 1994 in the three major areas defined by donors: IDA's experience and progress in poverty reduction, its efforts to stimulate sustainable growth through improvements in the quality and level of investment in IDA countries, and IDA's enhanced activities on environmental sustainability. The pervading influence of these priorities was demonstrated by the fact that 80 percent of the fiscal 1994 lending operations directly addressed at least one of these objectives, while most addressed more than one. The remainder addressed specific country priorities considered essential for growth.

The $6.6 billion in commitments during fiscal 1994 was the highest annual lending ever achieved by IDA. Commitments fell short of expectations, however, because civil strife or inadequate progress in the adoption of policy reforms curtailed lending in sev-

eral countries. A partially offsetting factor was the policy breakthrough achieved by the countries of the CFA zone, which, in January 1994 decided to change the parity of the CFA franc vis-à-vis the French franc. In the first six months of 1994, IDA provided approximately $1 billion in quick-disbursing credits and adjustment operations to these countries.

The $5.5 billion in disbursements during fiscal 1994 was also the highest ever for IDA—reflecting better portfolio management and an increase in adjustment lending. Adjustment operations remained within guidelines, and most had a poverty focus.

To build on progress in developing country-specific strategies, further emphasis is being given to incorporating results from poverty assessments, national environmental action programs, and other country-specific analytical work into IDA operations.

SDR931 million of commitment authority against current and future repayments from past credits. Of the latter amount, SDR800 million is for ordinary credits and another SDR131 million is for the Fifth Dimension program. Therefore, the total available resources for the IDA-10 period increased to SDR10,303 million in fiscal 1995.

Against these resources, the association made IDA-10 commitments of SDR3,829 million during fiscal 1995. Of this amount, 39 percent went to Africa, 25 percent to South Asia, 19 percent to East Asia and Pacific, 10 percent to Europe and Central Asia, 6 percent to Latin America and the Caribbean, and 1 percent to the Middle East and North Africa.

IDA's commitment fee. For each fiscal year, the level of commitment fee is set by the executive directors based on an annual review of IDA's financial position. The commitment fee for fiscal 1996 was set at 0 percent for all IDA credits. IDA's commitment fee had been 0 percent from fiscal year 1989 through fiscal 1995.

FINANCIAL STATEMENTS OF THE
INTERNATIONAL BANK FOR RECONSTRUCTION AND DEVELOPMENT

BALANCE SHEET

June 30, 1995 and June 30, 1994
Expressed in millions of U.S. dollars

	1995	1994
Assets		
Due from Banks		
Unrestricted currencies	$ 40	$ 216
Currencies subject to restrictions—Note A	549	544
	589	760
Investments—Notes C and D		
Trading	19,936	21,306
Held-to-maturity	1,203	—
	21,139	21,306
Securities Purchased Under Resale Agreements	246	577
Nonnegotiable, Noninterest-bearing Demand Obligations on Account of Subscribed Capital (subject to restrictions—Note A)	1,610	1,507
Amounts Receivable to Maintain Value of Currency Holdings—Note A	1,106	1,133
Other Receivables		
Amounts receivable from currency swaps—Notes C and D	16,735	18,222
Amounts receivable from investment securities sold	1,762	2,389
Amounts receivable from covered forwards—Notes C and D	1,307	1,503
Accrued income on loans	2,538	2,294
Accrued interest on investments	159	106
	22,501	24,514
Loans Outstanding		
(see Summary Statement of Loans, Notes B and C)		
Total loans	179,453	164,300
Less loans approved but not yet effective	11,982	11,349
Less undisbursed balance of effective loans	43,972	43,660
Loans outstanding	123,499	109,291
Less accumulated provision for loan losses	3,740	3,324
Loans outstanding net of accumulated provision	119,759	105,967
Other Assets		
Unamortized issuance costs of borrowings	485	494
Miscellaneous	1,259	1,245
	1,744	1,739
Total assets	$168,694	$157,503

	1995	1994
Liabilities		
Borrowings (see Summary Statement of Borrowings, Notes C and D)		
Short-term	$ 3,898	$ 3,304
Medium- and long-term	104,507	95,615
	108,405	98,919
Securities Sold Under Agreements to Repurchase and Payable For Cash Collateral Received	2,567	1,927
Amounts Payable to Maintain Value of Currency Holdings—Note A	24	6
Other Liabilities		
Amounts payable for currency swaps—Notes C and D	19,985	20,332
Amounts payable for investment securities purchased	2,231	3,381
Amounts payable for covered forwards—Notes C and D	1,306	1,484
Accrued charges on borrowings	2,857	2,725
Payable for Board-approved transfers—Note E	135	1,204
Accounts payable and miscellaneous liabilities	723	579
	27,237	29,705
Total liabilities	138,233	130,557

Equity

Capital Stock (see Statement of Subscriptions to Capital Stock and Voting Power, Note A)

	1995	1994
Authorized capital (1,525,248 shares—June 30, 1995 and June 30, 1994)		
Subscribed capital (1,462,574 shares—June 30, 1995; 1,409,235 shares—June 30, 1994)	176,438	170,003
Less uncalled portion of subscriptions	165,580	159,338
	10,858	10,665
Deferred Amounts to Maintain Value of Currency Holdings—Note A	770	332
Payments on Account of Pending Subscriptions—Note A	23	87
Retained Earnings (see Statement of Changes in Retained Earnings, Note E)	15,502	14,468
Cumulative Translation Adjustment (see Statement of Changes in Cumulative Translation Adjustment)	3,308	1,394
Total equity	30,461	26,946
Total liabilities and equity	$168,694	$157,503

The Notes to Financial Statements are an integral part of these Statements.

STATEMENT OF INCOME

For the fiscal years ended June 30, 1995 and June 30, 1994
Expressed in millions of U.S. dollars

	1995	1994
Income		
Income from loans—Note B		
Interest	$8,069	$7,707
Commitment charges	118	115
Income from investments—Note C		
Trading		
Interest	891	837
Net (losses)/gains		
Realized	(23)	(29)
Unrealized	168	(127)
Held-to-maturity		
Interest	78	—
Income from securities purchased under resale agreements	61	86
Other income	10	11
Total income	9,372	8,600
Expenses		
Borrowing expenses		
Interest—Note C	6,842	6,549
Prepayment costs	7	31
Amortization of issuance costs and other borrowing costs	105	76
Interest on securities sold under agreements to repurchase and payable for cash collateral received	83	46
Administrative expenses—Notes F, G, and H	842	731
Provision for loan losses—Note B	12	—
Other expenses	8	6
Total expenses	7,899	7,439
Operating Income	1,473	1,161
Less contributions to special programs—Note F	119	110
Net Income	$1,354	$1,051

STATEMENT OF CHANGES IN RETAINED EARNINGS

For the fiscal years ended June 30, 1995 and June 30, 1994
Expressed in millions of U.S. dollars

	1995	1994
Retained earnings at beginning of the fiscal year	$14,468	$14,032
Transfer to International Development Association—Note E	(300)	(465)
Transfer to Debt Reduction Facility for IDA-Only Countries—Note E	—	(100)
Transfer to Trust Fund for Gaza—Note E	—	(50)
Transfer for Emergency Assistance for Rwanda—Note E	(20)	—
Net income for the fiscal year	1,354	1,051
Retained earnings at end of the fiscal year	$15,502	$14,468

STATEMENT OF CHANGES IN CUMULATIVE TRANSLATION ADJUSTMENT

For the fiscal years ended June 30, 1995 and June 30, 1994
Expressed in millions of U.S. dollars

	1995	1994
Cumulative translation adjustment at beginning of the fiscal year	$1,394	$ 541
Translation adjustment for the fiscal year	1,914	853
Cumulative translation adjustment at end of the fiscal year	$3,308	$1,394

The Notes to Financial Statements are an integral part of these Statements.

STATEMENT OF CASH FLOWS

For the fiscal years ended June 30, 1995 and June 30, 1994
Expressed in millions of U.S. dollars

	1995	1994
Cash flows from lending, investing, and development activities		
Loans		
Disbursements	$(12,803)	$(10,502)
Principal repayments	11,301	10,350
Principal prepayments	625	970
Investments: Held-to-maturity		
Purchases	(8,160)	—
Maturities	6,952	—
Payments to the International Development Association	(1,427)	(452)
Payments to Debt Reduction Facility for IDA-Only Countries	(25)	(23)
Payments to Trust Fund for Gaza and for Emergency Assistance for Rwanda	(45)	—
Net cash (used in) provided by lending, investing, and development activities	(3,582)	343
Cash flows from financing activities		
Medium- and long-term borrowings		
New issues	9,986	8,178
Retirements	(11,578)	(9,121)
Net cash flows from short-term borrowings	563	(504)
Net cash flows from currency swaps	(413)	(176)
Net cash flows from capital transactions	107	199
Net cash used in financing activities	(1,335)	(1,424)
Cash flows from operating activities		
Net income	1,354	1,051
Adjustments to reconcile net income to net cash provided by operating activities		
Depreciation and amortization	279	197
Provision for loan losses	12	—
Changes in other assets and liabilities		
(Increase) decrease in accrued income on loans and investments	(58)	92
Increase in miscellaneous assets	(67)	(24)
Decrease in accrued charges on borrowings	(186)	(180)
Increase in accounts payable and miscellaneous liabilities	82	85
Net cash provided by operating activities	1,416	1,221
Effect of exchange rate changes on unrestricted cash and liquid investments	1,489	586
Net (decrease) increase in unrestricted cash and liquid investments	(2,012)	726
Unrestricted cash and liquid investments at beginning of the fiscal year	19,199	18,473
Unrestricted cash and liquid investments at end of the fiscal year	$ 17,187	$ 19,199
Composed of		
Investments held in trading portfolio	$ 19,936	$ 21,306
Unrestricted currencies	40	216
Net payable for investment securities purchased/sold	(469)	(992)
Net receivable from covered forwards	1	19
Net payable for securities purchased/sold under resale/repurchase agreements and payable for cash collateral received	(2,321)	(1,350)
	$ 17,187	$ 19,199
Supplemental disclosure		
Increase (decrease) in ending balances resulting from exchange rate fluctuations		
Loans outstanding	$ 13,331	$ 5,658
Borrowings	10,310	3,952
Currency swaps	1,553	1,084
Investments: Held-to-maturity	(5)	—

The Notes to Financial Statements are an integral part of these Statements.

Summary Statement of Loans

June 30, 1995
Expressed in millions of U.S. dollars

Borrower or guarantor	Total loans	Loans approved but not yet effective[1]	Undisbursed balance of effective loans[2]	Loans outstanding[3]	Percentage of total loans outstanding
Algeria	$ 3,177	$ —	$ 1,111	$ 2,066	1.67
Argentina	7,312	1,125	1,255	4,932	3.99
Armenia	13	—	9	4	*
Bahamas, The	20	—	3	17	0.01
Bangladesh	62	—	—	62	0.05
Barbados	46	—	25	21	0.02
Belarus	183	—	67	116	0.09
Belize	61	12	19	30	0.02
Bolivia	120	—	—	120	0.10
Bosnia-Herzegovina/ Federal Republic of Yugoslavia[4]	1,837	—	—	1,837	1.49
Botswana	118	—	2	116	0.09
Brazil	11,336	412	4,100	6,824	5.53
Bulgaria	784	148	163	473	0.38
Cameroon	785	—	56	729	0.59
Chile	2,603	155	388	2,060	1.67
China	13,876	1,660	4,972	7,244	5.87
Colombia	3,768	62	888	2,818	2.28
Congo	129	—	4	125	0.10
Costa Rica	449	—	100	349	0.28
Côte d'Ivoire	1,875	—	89	1,786	1.45
Croatia	348	120	129	99	0.08
Cyprus	144	—	62	82	0.07
Czech Republic	694	—	257	437	0.35
Dominica	1	1	—	—	—
Dominican Republic	391	28	59	304	0.25
Ecuador	1,613	12	534	1,067	0.86
Egypt	1,837	81	262	1,494	1.21
El Salvador	387	—	59	328	0.27
Estonia	114	30	43	41	0.03
Fiji	66	—	24	42	0.03
Gabon	147	—	26	121	0.10
Ghana	71	—	—	71	0.06
Guatemala	299	9	107	183	0.15
Guyana	42	—	—	42	0.03
Honduras	510	—	7	503	0.41
Hungary	3,154	38	686	2,430	1.97
Iceland	4	—	—	4	*
India	15,508	276	3,988	11,244	9.10
Indonesia	18,575	1,243	3,741	13,591	11.00
Iran, Islamic Republic of	887	—	624	263	0.21
Iraq	55	—	—	55	0.04
Jamaica	822	—	190	632	0.51
Jordan	972	60	167	745	0.60
Kazakhstan	585	299	68	218	0.18
Kenya[5]	517	—	—	517	0.42
Korea, Republic of	3,271	175	618	2,478	2.01
Latvia	128	14	58	56	0.05
Lebanon	366	91	170	105	0.09
Lesotho	116	—	65	51	0.04
Liberia	170	—	—	170	0.14
Lithuania	127	52	10	65	0.05
Macedonia, former Yugoslav Republic of	118	—	24	94	0.08
Madagascar	14	—	—	14	0.01
Malawi	66	—	—	66	0.05
Malaysia	1,453	—	284	1,169	0.95
Mauritania	13	—	—	13	0.01
Mauritius	260	47	56	157	0.13
Mexico	19,966	1,999	3,481	14,486	11.73

Borrower or guarantor	Total loans	Loans approved but not yet effective[1]	Undisbursed balance of effective loans[2]	Loans outstanding[3]	Percentage of total loans outstanding
Moldova	$ 193	$ 30	$ 30	$ 133	0.11
Morocco	5,598	58	1,427	4,113	3.33
Nicaragua	80	—	—	80	0.06
Nigeria	4,431	—	818	3,613	2.93
Oman	30	—	—	30	0.02
Pakistan	4,687	216	1,148	3,323	2.69
Panama	347	25	117	205	0.17
Papua New Guinea	418	—	106	312	0.25
Paraguay	416	97	152	167	0.14
Peru	2,575	296	559	1,720	1.39
Philippines	6,922	18	1,406	5,498	4.45
Poland	3,979	—	1,889	2,090	1.69
Portugal	137	—	14	123	0.10
Romania	1,522	230	435	857	0.69
Russia	4,721	2,042	1,845	834	0.68
St. Kitts and Nevis	3	2	*	1	*
St. Lucia	9	6	1	2	*
St. Vincent and the Grenadines	3	2	1	*	*
Senegal	43	—	—	43	0.03
Seychelles	9	—	3	6	*
Sierra Leone	3	—	—	3	*
Slovak Republic	326	—	47	279	0.23
Slovenia	228	—	59	169	0.14
Sri Lanka	57	—	—	57	0.05
Sudan	6	—	—	6	*
Swaziland	50	29	—	21	0.02
Syrian Arab Republic	453	—	—	453	0.37
Tanzania	108	—	—	108	0.09
Thailand	2,609	190	479	1,940	1.57
Trinidad and Tobago	133	6	56	71	0.06
Tunisia	2,638	65	687	1,886	1.53
Turkey	7,482	100	1,894	5,488	4.44
Turkmenistan	25	25	—	—	—
Ukraine	691	146	160	385	0.31
Uruguay	790	16	197	577	0.47
Uzbekistan	248	66	115	67	0.05
Venezuela	2,878	148	904	1,826	1.48
Zaire	97	—	—	97	0.08
Zambia	197	—	—	197	0.16
Zimbabwe	824	—	215	609	0.49
Subtotal	178,331	11,962	43,814	122,555	99.23
Caribbean Development Bank[6]	42	20	12	10	0.01
International Finance Corporation	1,080	—	146	934	0.76
Total—June 30, 1995	$179,453	$11,982	$43,972	$123,499	100.00
Total—June 30, 1994	$164,300	$11,349	$43,660	$109,291	

* Indicates amounts less than $0.5 million or 0.005 percent.

NOTES

1. Loans totaling $5,198 million ($5,196 million—June 30, 1994) have been approved by the IBRD, but the related agreements have not been signed. Loan agreements totaling $6,784 million ($6,153 million—June 30, 1994) have been signed, but the loans do not become effective and disbursements thereunder do not start until the borrowers and guarantors, if any, take certain actions and furnish certain documents to the IBRD.

2. Of the undisbursed balance, the IBRD has entered into irrevocable commitments to disburse $1,834 million ($1,861 million—June 30, 1994).

3. Total loans outstanding as at June 30, 1995 include $106,371 million ($89,588 million—June 30, 1994) at variable interest rates and $17,128 million ($19,703 million—June 30, 1994) at fixed interest rates.

4. See Notes to Financial Statements—Notes A and B.

5. Includes portions of loans made to corporations of the former East African Community.

6. These loans are for the benefit of The Bahamas, Barbados, Grenada, Guyana, Jamaica, Trinidad and Tobago, and territories of the United Kingdom (Associated States and Dependencies) in the Caribbean Region, who are severally liable as guarantors to the extent of subloans made in their territories.

Summary Statement of Loans (continued)

June 30, 1995 and June 30, 1994
Expressed in millions of U.S. dollars

Summary of Currencies Repayable on Loans Outstanding

Currency	1995	1994
Austrian schillings	$ 216	$ 189
Belgian francs	268	235
Canadian dollars	165	164
Danish kroner	87	75
Deutsche mark	30,053	26,142
European currency units	16	17
Finnish markkaa	59	48
French francs	861	783
Indian rupees	26	26
Irish pounds	29	28
Italian lire	176	183
Japanese yen	44,722	37,175
Kuwaiti dinars	52	154
Luxembourg francs	41	35
Malaysian ringgit	46	41
Netherlands guilders	3,016	2,701
Norwegian kroner	72	65
Portuguese escudos	25	22
Pounds sterling	263	258
Saudi Arabian riyals	90	91
South African rand	41	41
Spanish pesetas	126	116
Swedish kronor	75	72
Swiss francs	13,068	11,855
United States dollars	29,886	28,753
Other currencies	20	22
Loans outstanding	$123,499	$109,291

Maturity Structure of Loans Outstanding

Period	
July 1, 1995 through June 30, 1996	$ 14,380
July 1, 1996 through June 30, 1997	13,155
July 1, 1997 through June 30, 1998	13,406
July 1, 1998 through June 30, 1999	13,228
July 1, 1999 through June 30, 2000	12,227
July 1, 2000 through June 30, 2005	40,675
July 1, 2005 through June 30, 2010	15,133
July 1, 2010 through June 30, 2015	1,295
Total	$123,499

The Notes to Financial Statements are an integral part of these Statements.

June 30, 1995 and June 30, 1994
Expressed in millions of U.S. dollars

Medium- and Long-term Borrowings and Swaps

	Medium- and long-term borrowings			Swap agreements [a]			Net currency obligations	
	Principal outstanding [b]		Weighted average cost (%)	Currency swap payables (receivables)		Weighted average cost (return) (%)		
	1995	1994	1995	1995	1994	1995	1995	1994
Australian dollars	$ 322	$ 504	11.63	$ (319)	$ (505)	(11.58)	$ 3	$ (1)
Austrian schillings	205	295	7.81	—	(73)	—	205	222
Belgian francs	353	523	7.08	(339)	(471)	(9.22)	14	52
Canadian dollars	1,549 [d]	1,745 [d]	8.71	(1,348)	(1,548)	(7.87) [c]	201	197
Danish kroner	—	48	—	—	(47)	—	—	1
Deutsche mark	14,456 [d]	11,111 [d]	6.95	11,826	11,848	7.10 [c]	26,282	22,959
European currency units	1,701 [d]	2,111 [d]	6.91	(1,518)	(1,953)	(6.83)	183	158
Finnish markkaa	141	114	9.68	(139)	(112)	(9.70)	2	2
French francs	1,169	1,421	9.17	(821)	(857)	(8.75) [c]	348	564
Greek drachma	66	63	15.22	(66)	(62)	(15.22)	—	1
Hong Kong dollars	336	401	7.42	(333)	(400)	(7.40)	3	1
Irish pounds	65	61	7.75	(65)	(60)	(7.75)	—	1
Italian lire	3,642 [d]	3,506 [d]	10.55	(3,614)	(3,490)	(10.50) [c]	28	16
Japanese yen	42,039 [d]	35,617 [d]	5.25	690	549	12.10 [c]		
				(1,246)	(1,585)	(7.47) [c]	41,483	34,581
Kuwaiti dinars	—	102	—	—	—	—	—	102
Luxembourg francs	140	92	7.74	(105)	(60)	(7.65)	35	32
Netherlands guilders	3,259	3,087	7.27	500	559	6.92		
				(1,597)	(1,395)	(7.70)	2,162	2,251
New Zealand dollars	168	148	12.40	(167)	(148)	(12.40)	1	—
Norwegian kroner	40	36	9.55	—	—	—	40	36
Portuguese escudos	296	267	10.79	(293)	(264)	(10.80)	3	3
Pounds sterling	2,308 [d]	2,797 [d]	9.62	(1,130)	(1,415)	(8.07) [c]	1,178	1,382
Spanish pesetas	866	1,001	11.44	(856)	(987)	(11.44)	10	14
Swedish kronor	124	118	11.43	(123)	(118)	(11.42)	1	—
Swiss francs	6,077	5,758	6.05	4,729	4,442	5.45 [c]	10,806	10,200
United States dollars	25,168 [d, e]	24,713 [d, e]	7.99	2,146	2,934	9.00 [c]		
				(2,569)	(2,672)	(7.82) [c]	24,745 [g]	24,975
Principal at face value	104,490	95,639	6.80 [f]					
Plus net unamortized premiums (discounts)	17	(24)						
Total	$104,507	$95,615						

SUMMARY STATEMENT OF BORROWINGS (continued)

June 30, 1995 and June 30, 1994
Expressed in millions of U.S. dollars

Medium- and Long-term Borrowings and Swaps (continued)

a. See Notes to Financial Statements—Notes C and D.
b. Includes zero-coupon borrowings that have been recorded at their discounted values. The aggregate face amounts and discounted values of these borrowings at June 30, 1995 and June 30, 1994 are:

In millions of U.S. dollar equivalents

Currency	Aggregate face amount		Discounted value	
	1995	1994	1995	1994
Canadian dollars	$ 145	$ 145	$ 132	$120
Deutsche mark	2,303	1,260	486	319
Italian lire	184	64	167	51
Japanese yen	1,189	—	1,033	—
Swiss francs	1,130	973	310	253
United States dollars	2,834	2,874	591	572

c. Includes income and expense from interest rate swaps. At June 30, 1995 and June 30, 1994, the IBRD has entered into interest rate swap agreements with respect to notional principal amounts as follows:

In millions

Currency	Currency amount		U.S. dollar equivalent	
	1995	1994	1995	1994
Canadian dollars	149	149	$ 109	$ 108
Deutsche mark	14,293	14,991	10,289	9,442
French francs	984	984	202	182
Italian lire	200,000	200,000	123	127
Japanese yen	155,038	152,350	1,843	1,522
Pounds sterling	100	100	158	155
Swiss francs	1,124	1,124	977	841
United States dollars	2,435	3,681	2,435	3,681

As at June 30, 1995, 93 percent (95 percent—June 30, 1994) of the above notional principal amounts of these interest rate swap agreements are from floating rates into fixed rates.

d. Includes the following variable interest rate borrowings at June 30, 1995 and June 30, 1994, which through swaps have been transformed into the financial equivalent of fixed rate borrowings:

In millions

Currency	Currency amount		U.S. dollar equivalent	
	1995	1994	1995	1994
Canadian dollars	100	100	$ 73	$ 72
Deutsche mark	550	425	396	268
European currency units	640	640	857	774
Italian lire	550,000	550,000	337	351
Japanese yen	144,500	149,500	1,718	1,494
Pounds sterling	25	25	40	39
United States dollars	1,563	1,602	1,563	1,602

e. Includes $178 million ($175 million—June 30, 1994) borrowed from the Interest Subsidy Fund. The Interest Subsidy Fund, which obtained its resources from voluntary contributions from member governments, was established to subsidize the interest payments to the IBRD on selected loans.
f. The weighted average cost of medium- and long-term borrowings outstanding at June 30, 1995, after adjustment for swap activities, was 6.53 percent (6.72 percent—June 30, 1994).
g. Includes borrowings of $408 million equivalents for which effective interest rate has not yet been fixed. These amounts are allocated to single currency loans.

Maturity Structure of Medium- and Long-term Borrowings

Period	
July 1, 1995 through June 30, 1996	$ 10,450
July 1, 1996 through June 30, 1997	14,084
July 1, 1997 through June 30, 1998	15,168
July 1, 1998 through June 30, 1999	8,198
July 1, 1999 through June 30, 2000	15,646
July 1, 2000 through June 30, 2005	30,747
July 1, 2005 through June 30, 2010	2,723
July 1, 2010 through June 30, 2015	1,784
July 1, 2015 through June 30, 2020	3,830
July 1, 2020 through June 30, 2025	1,521
Thereafter	339
Total	$104,490

Short-term Borrowings

	Principal outstanding		Weighted average cost (%)
	1995	1994	1995
Short-term Notes (U.S. dollars)			
Principal outstanding at face value	$1,212	$ 691	
Net unamortized discounts and premiums	(20)	(8)	
Subtotal	1,192	683[a]	5.96
Short-term Notes (Japanese yen)	—	21[a]	
Global Multicurrency Notes			
U.S. dollars	20	—	7.01
Italian lire[b]	86	—	5.46
Subtotal	106	—	
Central Bank Facility (U.S. dollars)	2,600	2,600	5.81
Total	$3,898	$3,304	5.85

NOTES

a. Includes interest rate swap agreements with respect to notional principal amounts of $262 million U.S. dollars and $21 million equivalent of Japanese yen.

b. Has been swapped from Italian lire to Deutsche mark. The U.S. dollar equivalents of the swap payable and receivable are $94 million and $86 million, respectively.

The Notes to Financial Statements are an integral part of these Statements.

Statement of Subscriptions to Capital Stock and Voting Power

June 30, 1995
Expressed in millions of U.S. dollars

Member	Shares	Subscriptions Percentage of total	Subscriptions Total amounts	Subscriptions Amounts paid in (Note A)	Subscriptions Amounts subject to call (Note A)	Voting power Number of votes	Voting power Percentage of total
Afghanistan	300	0.02	$ 36	$ 3.6	$ 33	550	0.04
Albania	830	0.06	100	3.6	97	1,080	0.07
Algeria	9,252	0.63	1,116	67.1	1,049	9,502	0.63
Angola	2,676	0.18	323	17.5	305	2,926	0.19
Antigua and Barbuda	292	0.02	35	0.4	35	542	0.04
Argentina	17,911	1.22	2,161	132.2	2,028	18,161	1.21
Armenia	1,139	0.08	137	5.9	132	1,389	0.09
Australia	21,610	1.48	2,607	171.4	2,436	21,860	1.45
Austria	11,063	0.76	1,335	80.7	1,254	11,313	0.75
Azerbaijan	1,646	0.11	199	9.7	189	1,896	0.13
Bahamas, The	1,071	0.07	129	5.4	124	1,321	0.09
Bahrain	1,103	0.08	133	5.7	127	1,353	0.09
Bangladesh	4,854	0.33	586	33.9	552	5,104	0.34
Barbados	948	0.06	114	4.5	110	1,198	0.08
Belarus	3,323	0.23	401	22.3	379	3,573	0.24
Belgium	28,983	1.98	3,496	215.8	3,281	29,233	1.94
Belize	586	0.04	71	1.8	69	836	0.06
Benin	487	0.03	59	2.5	56	737	0.05
Bhutan	479	0.03	58	1.0	57	729	0.05
Bolivia	1,785	0.12	215	10.8	205	2,035	0.14
Botswana	615	0.04	74	2.0	72	865	0.06
Brazil	24,946	1.71	3,009	185.1	2,824	25,196	1.67
Bulgaria	5,215	0.36	629	36.5	593	5,465	0.36
Burkina Faso	487	0.03	59	2.5	56	737	0.05
Burundi	402	0.03	48	1.8	47	652	0.04
Cambodia	214	0.01	26	2.6	23	464	0.03
Cameroon	857	0.06	103	6.6	97	1,107	0.07
Canada	44,795	3.06	5,404	334.9	5,069	45,045	2.99
Cape Verde	508	0.03	61	1.2	60	758	0.05
Central African Republic	484	0.03	58	2.5	56	734	0.05
Chad	484	0.03	58	2.5	56	734	0.05
Chile	6,931	0.47	836	49.6	787	7,181	0.48
China	44,799	3.06	5,404	335.0	5,069	45,049	2.99
Colombia	6,352	0.43	766	45.2	721	6,602	0.44
Comoros	282	0.02	34	0.3	34	532	0.04
Congo	520	0.04	63	2.9	60	770	0.05
Costa Rica	233	0.02	28	1.9	26	483	0.03
Côte d'Ivoire	2,516	0.17	304	16.4	287	2,766	0.18
Croatia	2,293	0.16	277	17.3	259	2,543	0.17
Cyprus	1,461	0.10	176	8.4	168	1,711	0.11
Czech Republic	6,308	0.43	761	45.9	715	6,558	0.44
Denmark	10,251	0.70	1,237	74.6	1,162	10,501	0.70
Djibouti	314	0.02	38	0.7	37	564	0.04
Dominica	504	0.03	61	1.1	60	754	0.05
Dominican Republic	1,174	0.08	142	9.8	132	1,424	0.09
Ecuador	2,771	0.19	334	18.2	316	3,021	0.20
Egypt	7,108	0.49	858	50.9	807	7,358	0.49
El Salvador	141	0.01	17	1.7	15	391	0.03
Equatorial Guinea	401	0.03	48	1.6	47	651	0.04
Eritrea	333	0.02	40	0.9	39	583	0.04
Estonia	518	0.04	63	2.8	60	768	0.05
Ethiopia	978	0.07	118	4.7	113	1,228	0.08
Fiji	987	0.07	119	4.8	114	1,237	0.08
Finland	8,560	0.59	1,033	61.9	971	8,810	0.58
France	69,397	4.74	8,372	520.4	7,851	69,647	4.62

Member	Subscriptions					Voting power	
	Shares	Percentage of total	Total amounts	Amounts paid in (Note A)	Amounts subject to call (Note A)	Number of votes	Percentage of total
Gabon	554	0.04	$ 67	$ 3.6	$ 63	804	0.05
Gambia, The	305	0.02	37	0.7	36	555	0.04
Georgia	1,584	0.11	191	9.3	182	1,834	0.12
Germany	72,399	4.95	8,734	542.9	8,191	72,649	4.82
Ghana	856	0.06	103	10.3	93	1,106	0.07
Greece	945	0.06	114	11.4	103	1,195	0.08
Grenada	531	0.04	64	1.4	63	781	0.05
Guatemala	1,123	0.08	136	9.3	126	1,373	0.09
Guinea	725	0.05	88	5.0	82	975	0.06
Guinea-Bissau	303	0.02	37	0.6	36	553	0.04
Guyana	1,058	0.07	128	5.3	122	1,308	0.09
Haiti	599	0.04	72	3.7	69	849	0.06
Honduras	360	0.02	43	1.3	42	610	0.04
Hungary	8,050	0.55	971	58.0	913	8,300	0.55
Iceland	1,258	0.09	152	6.8	145	1,508	0.10
India	44,795	3.06	5,404	333.7	5,070	45,045	2.99
Indonesia	14,981	1.02	1,807	110.3	1,697	15,231	1.01
Iran, Islamic Republic of	23,686	1.62	2,857	175.8	2,682	23,936	1.59
Iraq	2,808	0.19	339	27.1	312	3,058	0.20
Ireland	5,271	0.36	636	37.1	599	5,521	0.37
Israel	4,750	0.32	573	33.2	540	5,000	0.33
Italy	44,795	3.06	5,404	334.8	5,069	45,045	2.99
Jamaica	2,578	0.18	311	16.8	294	2,828	0.19
Japan	93,770	6.41	11,312	703.5	10,608	94,020	6.24
Jordan	1,388	0.09	167	7.8	160	1,638	0.11
Kazakhstan	1,675	0.11	202	15.0	187	1,925	0.13
Kenya	2,461	0.17	297	15.9	281	2,711	0.18
Kiribati	261	0.02	31	0.1	31	511	0.03
Korea, Republic of	9,372	0.64	1,131	67.9	1,063	9,622	0.64
Kuwait	13,280	0.91	1,602	97.4	1,505	13,530	0.90
Kyrgyz Republic	621	0.04	75	3.9	71	871	0.06
Lao People's Democratic Republic	100	0.01	12	1.2	11	350	0.02
Latvia	777	0.05	94	5.6	88	1,027	0.07
Lebanon	340	0.02	41	1.1	40	590	0.04
Lesotho	372	0.03	45	1.3	44	622	0.04
Liberia	463	0.03	56	2.6	53	713	0.05
Libya	7,840	0.54	946	57.0	889	8,090	0.54
Lithuania	846	0.06	102	6.3	96	1,096	0.07
Luxembourg	1,652	0.11	199	9.8	190	1,902	0.13
Macedonia, former Yugoslav Republic of	427	0.03	52	3.2	48	677	0.04
Madagascar	1,422	0.10	172	8.1	164	1,672	0.11
Malawi	1,094	0.07	132	5.6	126	1,344	0.09
Malaysia	8,244	0.56	995	59.5	935	8,494	0.56
Maldives	469	0.03	57	0.9	56	719	0.05
Mali	652	0.04	79	4.3	74	902	0.06
Malta	1,074	0.07	130	5.4	124	1,324	0.09
Marshall Islands	263	0.02	32	0.1	32	513	0.03
Mauritania	505	0.03	61	2.7	58	755	0.05
Mauritius	1,242	0.08	150	6.7	143	1,492	0.10
Mexico	18,804	1.29	2,268	139.0	2,129	19,054	1.26
Micronesia, Federated States of	479	0.03	58	1.0	57	729	0.05
Moldova	1,368	0.09	165	7.6	157	1,618	0.11
Mongolia	466	0.03	56	2.3	54	716	0.05

Member	Shares	Subscriptions Percentage of total	Total amounts	Amounts paid in (Note A)	Amounts subject to call (Note A)	Voting power Number of votes	Percentage of total
Morocco	4,973	0.34	$ 600	$ 34.8	$ 565	5,223	0.35
Mozambique	930	0.06	112	4.8	107	1,180	0.08
Myanmar	2,484	0.17	300	16.1	284	2,734	0.18
Namibia	855	0.06	103	6.4	97	1,105	0.07
Nepal	968	0.07	117	4.6	112	1,218	0.08
Netherlands	35,503	2.43	4,283	264.8	4,018	35,753	2.37
New Zealand	7,236	0.49	873	51.9	821	7,486	0.50
Nicaragua	608	0.04	73	2.1	71	858	0.06
Niger	478	0.03	58	2.4	55	728	0.05
Nigeria	12,655	0.87	1,527	92.7	1,434	12,905	0.86
Norway	9,982	0.68	1,204	72.6	1,132	10,232	0.68
Oman	1,561	0.11	188	9.1	179	1,811	0.12
Pakistan	9,339	0.64	1,127	67.8	1,059	9,589	0.64
Panama	385	0.03	46	3.2	43	635	0.04
Papua New Guinea	726	0.05	88	5.0	83	976	0.06
Paraguay	1,229	0.08	148	6.6	142	1,479	0.10
Peru	5,331	0.36	643	37.5	606	5,581	0.37
Philippines	6,844	0.47	826	48.9	777	7,094	0.47
Poland	10,908	0.75	1,316	79.6	1,236	11,158	0.74
Portugal	5,460	0.37	659	38.5	620	5,710	0.38
Qatar	1,096	0.07	132	9.0	123	1,346	0.09
Romania	4,011	0.27	484	30.5	453	4,261	0.28
Russia	44,795	3.06	5,404	333.9	5,070	45,045	2.99
Rwanda	587	0.04	71	3.6	67	837	0.06
St. Kitts and Nevis	275	0.02	33	0.3	33	525	0.03
St. Lucia	552	0.04	67	1.5	65	802	0.05
St. Vincent and the Grenadines	278	0.02	34	0.3	33	528	0.04
São Tomé and Principe	278	0.02	34	0.3	33	528	0.04
Saudi Arabia	44,795	3.06	5,404	335.0	5,069	45,045	2.99
Senegal	1,163	0.08	140	9.7	131	1,413	0.09
Seychelles	263	0.02	32	0.2	32	513	0.03
Sierra Leone	403	0.03	49	1.8	47	653	0.04
Singapore	320	0.02	39	3.9	35	570	0.04
Slovak Republic	3,216	0.22	388	23.0	365	3,466	0.23
Slovenia	1,261	0.09	152	9.5	143	1,511	0.10
Solomon Islands	513	0.04	62	1.2	61	763	0.05
Somalia	552	0.04	67	3.3	63	802	0.05
South Africa	13,462	0.92	1,624	98.8	1,525	13,712	0.91
Spain	23,686	1.62	2,857	175.6	2,682	23,936	1.59
Sri Lanka	3,817	0.26	461	26.1	434	4,067	0.27
Sudan	850	0.06	103	7.2	95	1,100	0.07
Suriname	412	0.03	50	2.0	48	662	0.04
Swaziland	440	0.03	53	2.0	51	690	0.05
Sweden	14,974	1.02	1,806	110.2	1,696	15,224	1.01
Switzerland	26,606	1.82	3,210	197.2	3,012	26,856	1.78
Syrian Arab Republic	1,236	0.08	149	10.5	139	1,486	0.10
Tajikistan	1,060	0.07	128	5.3	123	1,310	0.09
Tanzania	727	0.05	88	7.9	80	977	0.06
Thailand	6,349	0.43	766	45.2	721	6,599	0.44
Togo	620	0.04	75	3.9	71	870	0.06
Tonga	277	0.02	33	0.3	33	527	0.03
Trinidad and Tobago	1,495	0.10	180	13.4	167	1,745	0.12
Tunisia	719	0.05	87	5.7	81	969	0.06
Turkey	7,379	0.50	890	52.9	837	7,629	0.51
Turkmenistan	526	0.04	64	2.9	61	776	0.05

Member	Shares	Percentage of total	Total amounts	Amounts paid in (Note A)	Amounts subject to call (Note A)	Number of votes	Percentage of total
			Subscriptions			**Voting power**	
Uganda	617	0.04	$ 74	$ 4.4	$ 70	867	0.06
Ukraine	10,908	0.75	1,316	79.3	1,237	11,158	0.74
United Arab Emirates	2,385	0.16	288	22.6	265	2,635	0.17
United Kingdom	69,397	4.74	8,372	539.5	7,832	69,647	4.62
United States	255,590	17.48	30,833	1,964.4	28,869	255,840	16.98
Uruguay	1,578	0.11	190	14.1	176	1,828	0.12
Uzbekistan	2,493	0.17	301	16.1	285	2,743	0.18
Vanuatu	586	0.04	71	1.8	69	836	0.06
Venezuela	11,427	0.78	1,379	118.5	1,260	11,677	0.77
Viet Nam	543	0.04	66	6.6	59	793	0.05
Western Samoa	298	0.02	36	0.5	35	548	0.04
Yemen, Republic of	1,241	0.08	150	10.5	139	1,491	0.10
Zaire	2,643	0.18	319	25.4	294	2,893	0.19
Zambia	1,577	0.11	190	15.6	175	1,827	0.12
Zimbabwe	3,325	0.23	401	22.4	379	3,575	0.24
Total—June 30, 1995*	1,462,574	100.00	$176,438	$10,857.5	$165,580	1,507,074	100.00
Total—June 30, 1994	1,409,235		$170,003	$10,664.8	$159,338	1,453,485	

Note: * May differ from the sum of individual figures due to rounding.

The Notes to Financial Statements are an integral part of these Statements.

NOTES TO FINANCIAL STATEMENTS

ORIGIN AND AFFILIATED ORGANIZATIONS

The International Bank for Reconstruction and Development (IBRD) is an international organization which commenced business in 1946. The principal purpose of the IBRD is to promote economic development in its member countries, primarily by providing loans and related technical assistance for specific projects and for programs of economic reform in developing member countries. The activities of the IBRD are supplemented by those of three affiliated organizations, the International Development Association (IDA), the International Finance Corporation (IFC), and the Multilateral Investment Guarantee Agency (MIGA). The IDA's purpose is to promote economic development in the less developed areas of the world included in the IDA's membership by providing financing on terms which are more flexible and bear less heavily on the balance of payments than those of conventional loans. The IFC's purpose is to encourage the growth of productive private enterprises in its member countries through loans and equity investments in such enterprises without a member's guarantee. The MIGA was established to encourage the flow of investments for productive purposes among member countries and, in particular, to developing member countries by providing guarantees against noncommercial risks for foreign investment in its developing member countries.

SUMMARY OF SIGNIFICANT ACCOUNTING AND RELATED POLICIES

The IBRD's financial statements are prepared in conformity with the accounting principles generally accepted in the United States and with International Accounting Standards.

During the first quarter of fiscal year 1995, the IBRD adopted a new accounting interpretation that requires receivables and payables from certain financial transactions be presented on a gross basis in the financial statements when the right and intent to offset are not present. The effect is that both Total Assets and Total Liabilities are increased by $17,523 million ($19,193 million—June 30, 1994).

Reclassifications: Certain reclassifications of the prior year's information have been made to conform to the current year's presentation. In prior years, deferred amounts receivable and payable to maintain value of currency holdings had been classified as an asset and a liability, respectively. These amounts have been reclassified in the balance sheet as a component of Equity. The effect has been to reduce Total Assets by $542 million, decrease Total Liabilities by $874 million, and increase Total Equity by $332 million at June 30, 1994 from those amounts previously reported. This reclassification has no impact on the legal obligation of the members to maintain the value of their capital. In addition, in prior years the Accumulated Provision for Loan Losses was recorded as a liability. This amount has been reclassified as a reduction of assets. The effect

of this reclassification has been to reduce Total Assets and Total Liabilities by $3,324 million at June 30, 1994 from the amounts previously reported. This reclassification does not reflect a change in the provisioning policy, but has been made to conform with industry practice.

Translation of Currencies: The IBRD's financial statements are expressed in terms of U.S. dollars solely for the purpose of summarizing the IBRD's financial position and the results of its operations for the convenience of its members and other interested parties.

The IBRD is an international organization which conducts its business in the currencies of all of its members. The IBRD's resources are derived from its capital, borrowings, and accumulated earnings in those various currencies. The IBRD has a number of general policies aimed at minimizing exchange-rate risk in a multicurrency environment. The IBRD matches its borrowing obligations in any one currency (after swap activities) with assets in the same currency, as prescribed by its Articles of Agreement, primarily by holding or lending the proceeds of its borrowings in the same currencies in which they are borrowed. In addition, the IBRD periodically undertakes currency conversions to more closely match the currencies underlying its Retained Earnings with those of the outstanding loans. With respect to its other resources, the IBRD does not convert one currency into another except for small amounts required to meet certain obligations and operational needs.

Assets and liabilities are translated at market exchange rates at the end of the period. Income and expenses are translated at the market exchange rate at the dates on which they are recognized or at average market exchange rates in effect during each month. Translation adjustments, with the exception of those relating to capital subscriptions described in Note A, are charged or credited to Equity.

Valuation of Capital Stock: In the Articles of Agreement, the capital stock of the IBRD is expressed in terms of "U.S. dollars of the weight and fineness in effect on July 1, 1944" (1944 dollars). Following the abolition of gold as a common denominator of the monetary system and the repeal of the provision of the U.S. law defining the par value of the U.S. dollar in terms of gold, the pre-existing basis for translating 1944 dollars into current dollars or into any other currency disappeared. The Executive Directors of the IBRD have decided, until such time as the relevant provisions of the Articles of Agreement are amended, that the words "U.S. dollars of the weight and fineness in effect on July 1, 1944" in Article II, Section 2(a) of the Articles of Agreement of the IBRD are interpreted to mean the Special Drawing Right (SDR) introduced by the International Monetary Fund, as the SDR was valued in terms of U.S. dollars immediately before the introduction of the basket method of valuing the SDR on July 1, 1974, such value being $1.20635 for one SDR.

Retained Earnings: Retained Earnings consists of allocated amounts (Special Reserve, General Reserve, and Surplus) and unallocated Net Income.

The Special Reserve consists of loan commissions set aside pursuant to Article IV, Section 6 of the Articles of Agreement which are to be held in liquid assets. These assets may be used only for the purpose of meeting liabilities of the IBRD on its borrowings and guarantees in the event of defaults on loans made, participated in, or guaranteed by the IBRD. The Special Reserve assets are included under Investments in the Trading portfolio, comprising obligations of the United States Government, its agencies, and other official entities. The allocation of such commissions to the Special Reserve was discontinued in 1964 with respect to subsequent loans and no further additions are being made to it.

The General Reserve consists of earnings from prior fiscal years which, in the judgment of the Executive Directors, should be retained in the IBRD's business.

Surplus consists of earnings from prior fiscal years which are retained by the IBRD until a further decision is made on their disposition or the conditions of transfer for specified uses have been met.

Unallocated Net Income consists of earnings in the current fiscal year. Commencing in 1950, a portion or all of the unallocated Net Income has been allocated to the General Reserve. Additionally, upon approval of the Board of Governors, transfers have been made out of unallocated Net Income to the IDA (or facilities administered by the IDA), the Global Environment Trust Fund, Technical Assistance Trust Fund for the Union of Soviet Socialist Republics, and Surplus.

Loans: All of the IBRD's loans are made to or guaranteed by members, except loans to the IFC. The majority of the IBRD's loans have repayment obligations in various currencies determined on the basis of a currency pooling system, which is designed to equalize exchange-rate risks among borrowers. The IBRD also offers single currency loans. Except for certain loans which were converted to the currency pooling system, loans negotiated prior to July 1980 and all single currency loans are repayable in the currencies disbursed. Interest on all loans is accrued in the currencies outstanding.

Incremental direct costs associated with originating loans are expensed as incurred as such amounts are considered immaterial.

The IBRD does not reschedule interest or principal payments on its loans or participate in debt rescheduling agreements with respect to its loans. In exceptional cases, however, such as when implementation of a financed project has been delayed, the loan amortization schedule may be modified to avoid substantial repayments prior to project completion. It is the policy of the IBRD to place in nonaccrual status all loans made to or guaranteed by a member of the IBRD if principal, interest, or other charges with respect to any such loan are overdue by more than six months, unless the IBRD management determines that the overdue amount will be collected in the immediate future. In addition, if development credits by the IDA to a member government are placed in nonaccrual status, all loans to that member government will also be placed in nonaccrual status by the IBRD. On the date a member's loans are placed in nonaccrual status, unpaid interest and other charges accrued on loans outstanding to the member are deducted from the income of the current period. Interest and other charges on nonaccruing loans are included in income only to the extent that payments have actually been received by the IBRD. On the date a member pays in full all overdue amounts, its loans emerge from nonaccrual status, its eligibility for new loans is restored, and all its overdue interest and other charges including those from prior years are recognized as income in the current period.

The IBRD determines the Accumulated Provision for Loan Losses based on an assessment of collectibility risk in the total loan portfolio, including loans in nonaccrual status. The accumulated provision is periodically adjusted based on a review of the prevailing circumstances and would be used to meet actual losses on loans. Adjustments to the accumulated provision are recorded as a charge or credit to income.

Investments: During the first quarter of fiscal year 1995, the IBRD adopted a new accounting standard that requires investments to be classified into trading, available-for-sale, or held-to-maturity portfolios. In the second quarter of the fiscal year, the IBRD commenced investing in certain securities with the intention of holding such securities to maturity to align the investment portfolio with the debt funding these investments in specific currencies. Remaining investment securities are held in a trading portfolio and classified as an element of liquidity in the Statement of Cash Flows due to their nature and the IBRD's policies governing the level and use of such investments.

The IBRD carries its investment securities and related financial instruments in the trading portfolio at market value and investment securities in the held-to-maturity portfolio at amortized cost. For investments in the trading portfolio, both realized and unrealized gains and losses are included in Income from Investments. From time to time, the IBRD enters into forward contracts for the sale or purchase of investment securities; these transactions are recorded at the time of commitment.

Fair Value Disclosures: Financial instruments for which market quotations are available have been valued at the prevailing market value. Financial instruments for which market quotations are not readily available have been valued using methodologies and assumptions that necessarily require the use of subjective judgments. Accordingly, the actual value at which such financial instruments could be exchanged in a current transaction or whether they are actually exchangeable is not determinable.

NOTE A—CAPITAL STOCK, RESTRICTED CURRENCIES, MAINTENANCE OF VALUE, AND MEMBERSHIP

Capital Stock: At June 30, 1995, the IBRD's capital comprised 1,525,248 (1,525,248—June 30, 1994) authorized shares, of which 1,462,574 (1,409,235—June 30, 1994) shares had been subscribed. Each share has a par value of 0.1 million 1974 SDRs, valued at the rate of $1.20635 per 1974 SDR. Of the subscribed capital, $10,858 million ($10,665 million—June 30, 1994) has been paid in, and the remaining $165,580 million ($159,338 million—June 30, 1994) is subject to call only when required to meet the obligations of the IBRD created by borrowing or guaranteeing loans. As to $141,150 million ($136,002 million—June 30, 1994), the restriction on calls is imposed by the Articles of Agreement and as to $24,430 million ($23,336 million—June 30, 1994), by resolutions of the Board of Governors.

Restricted Currencies: The portion of capital subscriptions paid in to the IBRD is divided into two parts: (1) $1,086 million ($1,067 million—June 30, 1994) initially paid in gold or U.S. dollars and (2) $9,772 million ($9,598 million—June 30, 1994) paid in cash or noninterest-bearing demand obligations denominated either in the currencies of the respective members or in U.S. dollars. The amounts mentioned in (1) above, and (i) $774 million ($779 million—June 30, 1994) which were repurchased by members with U.S. dollars, and (ii) $364 million ($284 million—June 30, 1994) which were the proceeds from encashments of U.S. dollar-denominated notes which are included in the amounts mentioned in (2) above, are freely usable by the IBRD in any of its operations. The portion of the amounts paid in U.S. dollar-denominated notes are encashed by the IBRD in accordance with the schedules agreed between the members and the IBRD. The remaining amounts paid in the currencies of the members, referred to as restricted currencies, are usable by the IBRD in its lending operations only with the consent of the respective members, and for administrative expenses. The equivalent of $5,967 million ($5,444 million—June 30, 1994) has been used for lending purposes, with such consent.

Maintenance of Value: Article II, Section 9 of the Articles of Agreement provides for maintenance of the value, as at the time of subscription, of such restricted currencies, requiring (1) the member to make additional payments to the IBRD in the event that the par value of its currency is reduced or the foreign exchange value of its currency has, in the opinion of the IBRD, depreciated to a significant extent in its territories and (2) the IBRD to reimburse the member in the event that the par value of its currency is increased.

Since currencies no longer have par values, maintenance of value amounts are determined by measuring the foreign exchange value of a member's currency against the standard of value of the IBRD capital based on the 1974 SDR. Members are required to make payments to the IBRD if their currencies depreciate significantly relative to the standard of value. Furthermore, the Executive Directors have adopted a policy of reimbursing members whose currencies appreciate significantly in terms of the standard of value.

The net maintenance of value amounts relating to restricted currencies out on loan are included in Deferred Amounts to Maintain Value of Currency Holdings and shown as a component of Equity since maintenance of value becomes effective only as such currencies are repaid to the IBRD.

Membership: On February 25, 1993, the IBRD's Executive Directors decided that the Socialist Federal Republic of Yugoslavia (SFRY) had ceased to be a member of the IBRD and that the Republic of Bosnia and Herzegovina, the Republic of Croatia, the former Yugoslav Republic of Macedonia, the Republic of Slovenia, and the Federal Republic of Yugoslavia (Serbia and Montenegro) (FRY) are authorized to succeed to the SFRY's membership when certain requirements are met including entering into a final agreement with the IBRD on the IBRD's loans made to or guaranteed by the SFRY which the particular successor Republic would assume. Three of the five successor Republics—the Republics of Croatia and Slovenia and the former Yugoslav Republic of Macedonia—have since become members of the IBRD. The paid-in portion of the SFRY's subscribed capital allocated to the other successor Republics (the Republic of Bosnia and Herzegovina and the Federal Republic of Yugoslavia (Serbia and Montenegro)) is included under Payments on Account of Pending Subscriptions until the requirements of succession have been met.

NOTE B—LOANS, COFINANCING AND GUARANTEES

Loans: On August 2, 1994, the IBRD's Executive Directors approved a one-year interest waiver of 25 basis points on disbursed and outstanding loans for all payment periods commencing in the fiscal year ending June 30, 1995 for all eligible borrowers. Also, on August 2, 1994, the Executive Directors approved a one-year commitment fee waiver of 50 basis points on undisbursed loans to all borrowers for all payment periods commencing in the fiscal year ending June 30, 1995. Similar waivers were in effect for the fiscal year ended June 30, 1994. On December 20, 1994, the IBRD's Executive Directors approved a proposal to encourage the IBRD's borrowers to convert their respective loans from 1982 terms to 1989 terms. Loans on 1982 terms are based on the weighted average cost of all IBRD debt drawn down after June 30, 1982 while loans on 1989 terms are based on the weighted average cost of borrowings funding these loans. The purpose of the conversion is to facilitate interest risk management by the IBRD and to enhance its ability to offer borrowers new loan products. To each borrower that converts all its loans from 1982 loan terms to 1989 loan terms, a one-time 10 basis point waiver of annual interest charges for two consecutive six-month interest periods will be given. Borrowers that had opted for such conversion before December 20, 1994 were also given this waiver. For the fiscal year ended June 30, 1995 the combined effect of these waivers was to reduce Net Income by $251 million ($238 million—June 30, 1994).

In connection with the cessation of the membership of the SFRY discussed in Note A, in February 1993 the IBRD reached an agreement with FRY for the apportionment and service of debt due to the IBRD on loans made to or guaranteed by the SFRY and assumed by the FRY, which confirmed a February 1992 interim agreement between the SFRY (then consisting of the Republics of Bosnia and Herzegovina, Macedonia, Montenegro and Serbia) and the IBRD pertaining, among other things, to such loans. As of the date hereof, no debt-service payments have been received by the IBRD from the FRY. With respect to the Republic of Bosnia and Herzegovina, a preliminary understanding was reached in June 1993 on the loans made to or guaranteed by the SFRY to be assumed by that Republic. Until an agreement is reached, loans benefitting that Republic are included with the loans assumed by the FRY in accordance with the IBRD's above-mentioned agreement with the FRY.

At June 30, 1995, no loans payable to the IBRD other than those referred to in the following paragraphs were overdue by more than three months.

At June 30, 1995, the loans made to or guaranteed by certain member countries and two other countries— the FRY and the Republic of Bosnia and Herzegovina— with an aggregate principal balance outstanding of $2,618 million ($2,363 million—June 30, 1994), of which $1,411 million ($1,009 million—June 30, 1994) was overdue, were in nonaccrual status. As at such date, overdue interest and other charges in respect of these loans totaled $864 million ($628 million—June 30, 1994). If these loans had not been in nonaccrual status, income from loans for the fiscal year ended June 30, 1995 would have been higher by $156 million ($149 million—June 30, 1994). A summary of

member countries and other countries with loans or guarantees in nonaccrual status follows:

In millions

	June 30, 1995		
Country	Principal out-standing	Principal and charges overdue	Nonaccrual since
Bosnia-Herzegovina/ Federal Republic of Yugoslavia	$1,837	$1,405	September 1992
Iraq	55	61	December 1990
Liberia	170	253	June 1987
Sudan	6	2	January 1994
Syrian Arab Republic	453	511	February 1987
Zaire	97	43	November 1993
Total	$2,618	$2,275	

During the fiscal year ended June 30, 1995, no loans came out of nonaccrual status. For the fiscal year ended June 30, 1994, the increase in loan income from loans to countries coming out of nonaccrual status during the fiscal year was $52 million.

An analysis of the changes to the Accumulated Provision for Loan Losses for the fiscal years ending June 30, 1995 and June 30, 1994 appears below:

In millions

	1995	1994
Balance, beginning of the fiscal year	$3,324	$3,150
Provision for loan losses	12	—
Translation adjustments	404	174
Balance, end of the fiscal year	$3,740	$3,324

Under an IDA program established in September 1988, a portion of principal repayments to the IDA are allocated on an annual basis to provide supplementary IDA credits to IDA-eligible countries that are no longer able to borrow on IBRD terms but have outstanding IBRD loans approved prior to September 1988. Such supplementary IDA credits are allocated to countries that meet specified conditions, in proportion to each country's interest payments due that year on its pre-September 1988 IBRD loans. To be eligible for such IDA supplemental credits, a member country must meet the IDA's eligibility criteria for lending, must be ineligible for IBRD lending, and must not have had an IBRD loan approved within the past twelve months. To receive a supplemental credit from the program, a member country cannot be more than 60 days overdue on its debt-service payments to the IBRD and the IDA and must have an IDA-supported structural adjustment program in place. As at June 30, 1995, the IDA had approved credits of $1,179 million ($974 million—June 30, 1994) under this program from inception, of which $1,128 million ($846 million—June 30, 1994) had been disbursed to the eligible countries.

Cofinancing and Guarantees: The IBRD has entered into agreements syndicated by other financial institutions either by a direct participation in, or a partial guarantee of, loans for the benefit of member countries or a partial guarantee of securities issued by an entity eligible for IBRD loans. The IBRD's direct participations in syndicated loans are included in reported loan balances.

Guarantees of $1,610 million at June 30, 1995 ($1,181 million—June 30, 1994) were not included in reported loan balances. $173 million of these guarantees were subject to call at June 30, 1995 ($173 million—June 30, 1994).

The IBRD has partially guaranteed the timely payment of interest amounts on certain loans that have been sold. At June 30, 1995, these guarantees, approximating $4 million ($4 million—June 30, 1994), were subject to call.

Statutory Lending Limit: Under the Articles of Agreement, the total amount outstanding of guarantees, participations in loans, and direct loans made by the IBRD may not be increased to an amount exceeding 100 percent of the sum of subscribed capital, reserves, and surplus. On the IBRD's Balance Sheet, Reserves and Surplus correspond to items labelled Retained Earnings, Cumulative Translation Adjustment, and Accumulated Provision for Loan Losses. The IBRD's Executive Directors have issued guidelines pursuant to which all guarantees issued by the IBRD will be counted towards this limit at the time they first become callable, irrespective of the likelihood of an actual call. At June 30, 1995, such total amount was $123,676 million or 62 percent (58 percent—June 30, 1994) of the Statutory Lending Limit.

NOTE C—FINANCIAL INSTRUMENTS

Investments

As part of its overall portfolio management strategy, the IBRD invests in government and agency obligations, time deposits, and related financial instruments with off-balance sheet risk including futures, forward contracts, covered forward contracts, options, and short sales.

Government and Agency Obligations: These obligations include marketable bonds, notes, and other obligations. Obligations issued or unconditionally guaranteed by governments of countries require a minimum credit rating of AA, if denominated in a currency other than the home currency; otherwise no rating is required. Obligations issued by an agency or instrumentality of a government of a country, a multilateral organization, or any other official entity require a credit rating of AAA.

Time Deposits: Time deposits include certificates of deposit, bankers' acceptances, and other obligations issued or unconditionally guaranteed by banks and other financial institutions.

Futures and Forwards: Futures and forward contracts are contracts for delayed delivery of securities or money market instruments in which the seller agrees to make delivery at a specified future date of a specified instrument, at a specified price or yield.

Covered Forwards: Covered forwards are agreements in which cash in one currency is converted into a different currency and, simultaneously, a forward exchange agreement is executed providing for a future exchange of the two currencies in order to recover the currency converted.

Options: Options are contracts that allow the holder of the option to purchase or sell a financial instrument at a specified price within a specified period of time from or to the seller of the option. The purchaser of an option pays a premium at the outset to the seller of the option, who then bears the risk of an unfavorable change in the price of the financial instrument underlying the option. The IBRD only invests in exchange-traded options.

Short Sales: Short sales are sales of securities not held in the IBRD's portfolio at the time of the sale. The IBRD must purchase the security at a later date and bears the risk that the market value of the security will move adversely between the time of the sale and the time the security must be delivered.

Trading Portfolio: Investment securities in the trading portfolio are carried at market value. A summary of the trading portfolio by instrument at June 30, 1995 is as follows:

In millions

	1995		
	As at June 30	Average daily balance during the fiscal year	Net gains (losses) for the fiscal year
Government and agency obligations	$11,419	$10,117	$174
Time deposits	8,507	8,699	*
Futures and forwards	10	10	(26)
Options	*	*	(3)
Total trading investments	$19,936	$18,826	$145
Net covered forwards	$ 1	$ 1	$ —
Repurchase agreements	(2,567)	(1,612)	—
Short sales	(77)	(444)	—
Resale agreements	246	1,215	—

* Indicates amounts less than $0.5 million.

A summary of the currency composition of Investments held in the trading portfolio, net Receivable/Payable for Covered Forwards, and the net of Securities Purchased Under Resale Agreements and Securities Sold Under Agreements to Repurchase and Payable for Cash Collateral Received at June 30, 1995 and June 30, 1994 is as follows:

In millions of U.S. dollar equivalents

	1995				1994			
	Investments	Net covered forwards	Net repurchases and resales	Total	Investments	Net covered forwards	Net repurchases and resales	Total
Deutsche mark	$ 1,638	$ 587	$ (45)	$ 2,180	$ 1,484	$ 624	$ 260	$ 2,368
Japanese yen	6,872	(106)	—	6,766	5,332	—	—	5,332
United States dollars	10,449	(763)	(2,313)	7,373	11,679	(1,485)	(1,591)	8,603
Other currencies	977	283	37	1,297	2,811	880	(19)	3,672
Total	$19,936	$ 1	$(2,321)	$17,616	$21,306	$ 19	$(1,350)	$19,975

The annualized rate of return on average investments in the Trading portfolio, net of agreements to repurchase and cash collateral received, held during the fiscal year ended June 30, 1995, including both realized and unrealized gains and losses, was 5.58 percent (3.56 percent—June 30, 1994).

Held-to-maturity portfolio: Investment securities in the Held-to-maturity portfolio are carried at amortized cost. The book and fair values of investment securities in the Held-to-maturity portfolio at June 30, 1995 were:

In millions

	June 30, 1995			
	Securities—Held-to-maturity			
	Carrying value	Gross unrealized gains	Gross unrealized losses	Fair value
Government and agency obligations	$1,085	$19	$—	$1,104
Time deposits	118	—	—	118
Total	$1,203	$19	$—	$1,222

As at June 30, 1995, the Held-to-maturity portfolio comprised investments in Pounds sterling only.

The expected maturities of investment securities in the Held-to-maturity portfolio at June 30, 1995 are summarized below:

In millions

	June 30, 1995		
	Carrying value	Fair value	Net unrealized gains
July 1, 1995 through June 30, 1996	$ 118	$ 118	$—
July 1, 1996 through June 30, 2000	170	174	4
July 1, 2000 through June 30, 2005	242	248	6
Thereafter	673	682	9
Total	$1,203	$1,222	$19

The annualized rate of return on average investments in the Held-to-maturity portfolio, held during the fiscal year ended June 30, 1995, was 8.11 percent.

Loans

The table below reflects the carrying and estimated fair values of the loan portfolio, excluding the Accumulated Provision for Loan Losses, as at June 30, 1995 and June 30, 1994.

In millions

	1995		1994	
	Carrying value	Estimated fair value	Carrying value	Estimated fair value
Fixed rate loans	$ 17,128	$ 19,065	$ 19,703	$ 21,538
Variable rate loans	106,137	114,141	89,551	94,234
Single currency loans	234	235	37	37
Total	$123,499	$133,441	$109,291	$115,809

All of the IBRD's loans are made to or guaranteed by countries that are members of the IBRD, except for those loans made to the IFC. The IBRD does not currently sell its loans, nor is there a market of loans comparable to those made by the IBRD. The IBRD has never suffered a loss on any of its loans, although from time to time certain borrowers have found it difficult to make timely payments for protracted periods, resulting in their loans being placed in nonaccrual status. Several borrowers have emerged from nonaccrual status after a period of time by bringing up-to-date all principal payments and all interest payments, including interest and other charges on overdue principal payments. In an attempt to recognize the risk inherent in these overdue payments, the IBRD maintains a provision for loan losses. The balance of the Accumulated Provision for Loan Losses at June 30, 1995 was $3,740 million ($3,324 million—June 30, 1994).

Fixed rate loans: On loans negotiated prior to July 1982, the IBRD charges interest at fixed rates. The estimated fair value of these loans is based on discounted future cash flows using the rate at which the IBRD could undertake borrowings of comparable maturities at June 30, 1995 plus a 50 basis point spread.

Variable rate loans: In 1982 the IBRD mitigated its interest rate risk by moving from fixed rate to variable rate lending. The rate charged on variable rate loans is based on the IBRD's own cost of qualified borrowings plus a 50 basis point spread, resulting in a pass-through of its average borrowing costs to those members that benefit from IBRD loans. Since the interest rate for variable rate loans is based on the interest rate of the qualified borrowings, the fair value of variable rate loans has been estimated based on the relationship of the fair value to the carrying value of the underlying borrowings.

Single currency loans: In 1993 the IBRD introduced single currency loans. The rates charged on single currency loans are equal to the six-month reference interbank offered rate for the applicable currency prevailing on the semiannual reset date, plus a cost margin equal to the IBRD's weighted average margin relative to the six-month London Interbank Offered Rate on its borrowings funding single currency loans, calculated for the previous semester and averaged across currencies, plus an interest spread of 50 basis points. Since the interest rates for single currency loans are based on the interest rate of qualified borrowings, the fair value of single currency loans has been estimated based on the relationship of the fair value to the carrying value of underlying borrowings.

Borrowings

Currency swaps: Currency swaps are agreements in which proceeds of a borrowing are converted into a different currency and, simultaneously, a forward exchange agreement is executed providing for a schedule of future exchanges of the two currencies in order to recover the currency converted. The combination of a borrowing and a currency swap produces the financial equivalent of substituting a borrowing in the currency obtained in the initial conversion for the original borrowing.

Interest rate swaps: Interest rate swaps are agreements that transform a fixed rate payment obligation in a particular currency into a floating rate obligation in that currency and vice-versa.

Forward interest rate swaps: A forward interest rate swap is an agreement under which the cash flow exchanges of the underlying interest rate swaps would begin to take effect from a specified date.

Deferred rate setting agreements: The IBRD enters into deferred rate setting agreements in conjunction with some of its bond issues. These agreements provide for payments to be made to or by the IBRD reflecting gain or loss on one or more government securities or related financial instruments. These agreements allow the IBRD to fix the effective interest cost to the IBRD of all or a portion of the issues over a specified period of time after the issue date of the respective bond. The potential credit loss to the IBRD from nonperformance is limited to any amounts due, but unsettled, from the financial intermediary. However, periodic mark-to-market settlements on these agreements limit this risk. At June 30, 1995 and June 30, 1994, the effective interest cost of all principal amounts had been fixed.

Providing liquidity and minimizing the cost of funds are key objectives to the IBRD's overall borrowing strategy. The IBRD uses swaps in its borrowing strategy to lower the overall cost of its borrowings for those members who benefit from IBRD loans. The IBRD undertakes swap transactions with a list of authorized counterparties. Credit and maturity limits have been established for each counterparty.

Swaps are used to modify the interest rate and/or currency characteristics of the borrowing portfolio and are linked to the related borrowings at inception and remain so throughout the terms of their contracts. The interest component of a swap is recognized as an adjustment to the borrowing cost over the life of the contract. Upon termination, the change in a swap's market value is recorded as an adjustment to the carrying value of the underlying borrowing and recognized as an adjustment of the borrowing cost over the expected remaining life of the borrowing. In instances where the underlying borrowing is prepaid, the change in the associated swap's market value is recognized immediately as an adjustment to the cost of the underlying borrowing instrument.

The following table reflects the carrying and estimated fair values of the borrowings portfolio as at June 30, 1995 and June 30, 1994.

	1995		1994	
	Carrying value	Estimated fair value	Carrying value	Estimated fair value
Short-term	$ 3,898	$ 3,898	$ 3,304	$ 3,304
Medium- and long-term	104,507	113,119	95,615	101,280
Swaps				
Currency				
Payable	19,985	20,495	20,332	20,429
Receivable	(16,735)	(17,717)	(18,222)	(19,095)
Interest rate	—	1,059	—	874
Forward interest rate	—	23	—	19
Total	$111,655	$120,877	$101,029	$106,811

The estimated fair values are based on quoted market prices where such prices are available. Where no quoted market price is available, the fair value is estimated based on the cost at which the IBRD could currently undertake borrowings with similar terms and remaining maturities, using the secondary market yield curve. The fair value of swaps represent the estimated cost of replacing these contracts on that date.

The average cost of borrowings outstanding during the fiscal year ended June 30, 1995 was 6.62 percent (6.74 percent—June 30, 1994), reflecting a reduction in interest expense of $157 million ($234 million—June 30, 1994) as a result of swaps.

NOTE D—RISK EXPOSURE OF CERTAIN FINANCIAL INSTRUMENTS

For the purpose of risk management, the IBRD is party to a variety of financial instruments, certain of which involve elements of credit risk in excess of the amount recorded on the balance sheet. Credit risk represents the maximum potential accounting loss due to possible nonperformance by obligors and counterparties under the terms of the contracts. Additionally, the nature of the instruments involve contract value and notional principal amounts that are not reflected in the basic financial statements. For both on- and off-balance sheet securities, the IBRD limits trading to a list of authorized dealers and counterparties. Credit limits have been established for each counterparty by type of instrument and maturity category.

The credit risk exposure and contract value/notional amounts, as applicable, of these financial instruments as at June 30, 1995 and June 30, 1994 are given below.

In millions

	1995	1994
INVESTMENTS—TRADING PORTFOLIO		
Futures and forwards		
Long position	$ 4,039	$ 2,670
Short position	8,051	4,759
Credit exposure due to potential nonperformance by counterparties	6	10
Options		
Long position	19	613
Short position	—	825
Covered forwards		
Credit exposure due to potential nonperformance by counterparties	7	19
BORROWINGS		
Currency swaps		
Credit exposure due to potential nonperformance by counterparties	713	728
Interest rate swaps		
Notional principal	16,136	16,341
Credit exposure due to potential nonperformance by counterparties	57	111
Forward interest rate swaps		
Notional principal	300	497
Credit exposure due to potential nonperformance by counterparties	—	1

NOTE E—RETAINED EARNINGS AND ALLOCATION OF NET INCOME

Retained Earnings: Retained Earnings comprises the following elements as at June 30, 1995 and June 30, 1994:

In millions

	1995	1994
Special Reserve	$ 293	$ 293
General Reserve	13,629	13,124
Surplus	226	—
Unallocated Net Income for the fiscal year	1,354	1,051
Total	$15,502	$14,468

On August 2, 1994, the Executive Directors allocated $505 million of the net income earned in the fiscal year ended June 30, 1994 to the General Reserve. On October 6, 1994, the Board of Governors approved a transfer to the IDA, by way of grant, of $300 million in an equivalent amount in SDRs, out of the net income earned in the fiscal year ended June 30, 1994. On the same day the Board of Governors also approved a transfer of $246 million to Surplus. On November 28, 1994, the Board of Governors approved a transfer of $20 million for Emergency Assistance for Rwanda out of Surplus.

Transfers to International Development Association: The Board of Governors has approved aggregate transfers to the IDA totaling $4,273 million from unallocated Net Income for the fiscal years through June 30, 1993. On October 6, 1994, the Board of Governors approved a transfer to the IDA, by way of grant, of $300 million in an equivalent amount in SDRs. As at June 30, 1995, all transfers to the IDA had been paid. At June 30, 1994, $1,023 million remained payable to the IDA.

Transfers to Debt Reduction Facility for IDA-Only Countries: The Board of Governors approved aggregate transfers to the Debt Reduction Facility for IDA-Only Countries totaling $200 million through June 30, 1994. At June 30, 1995, $105 million remained payable ($131 million—June 30, 1994).

Transfer to Trust Fund for Gaza: The Board of Governors approved a transfer to the Trust Fund for Gaza, by way of grant, totaling $50 million through June 30, 1994. At June 30, 1995, $25 million remained payable ($50 million—June 30, 1994).

Transfer for Emergency Assistance for Rwanda: On November 28, 1994, the Board of Governors approved a transfer of $20 million for Emergency Assistance for Rwanda out of Surplus. At June 30, 1995, $5 million remained payable.

NOTE F—EXPENSES

On February 21, 1995, the Executive Directors approved the expenditure of $153 million for costs associated with planned staff reductions. At June 30, 1995, the revised estimate for the total cost of this plan was $131 million. The reductions, to meet changing client demands, are designed to improve the IBRD's and the IDA's efficiency while maintaining current operating levels. The planned staff reductions are expected to lower future years' administrative expenses by an amount greater than the associated cost. Under this plan, approximately 590 staff (originally budgeted at 568 staff) in various departments are to be declared redundant during fiscal year 1995 through fiscal year 1996. It is estimated that payments to meet termination costs from the planned reductions will be completed by the end of fiscal year 1998. As at June 30, 1995, 285 staff have been notified of pending separation under this plan at a cost of $51 million. $1 million has been charged against the accrual of $131 million. Included in the total charge of $131 million are costs associated with job search assistance, training, outplacement consulting, pension plan contributions, medical insurance contributions and related tax allowances.

Of the total charge of $131 million, $78 million has been included in Administrative Expenses for the fiscal year ended June 30, 1995 and $53 million has been charged to the IDA, consistent with normal cost apportionment procedures, through the management fee for the fiscal year 1995.

Administrative Expenses are net of the management fee of $571 million ($545 million—June 30, 1994) charged to the IDA and $111 million ($107 million—June 30, 1994) charged to reimbursable programs. Included in the amounts charged to reimbursable programs are allocated charges of $21 million ($21 million—June 30, 1994) charged to the IFC and $1 million ($1 million—June 30, 1994) charged to the MIGA.

Contributions to special programs represent grants for agricultural research, the control of onchocerciasis, and other developmental activities.

NOTE G—TRUST FUNDS

The IBRD, alone or jointly with the IDA, administers on behalf of donors, including members, their agencies and other entities, funds restricted for specific uses which include the cofinancing of IBRD lending projects, debt reduction operations for IBRD members, technical assistance for borrowers including feasibility studies and project preparation, global and regional programs and research and training programs. These funds are placed in trust and are not included in the assets of the

IBRD. The distribution of trust fund assets by executing agent is as follows:

	1995		1994	
	Total fiduciary assets (in millions)	Number of trust fund accounts	Total fiduciary assets (in millions)	Number of trust fund accounts
IBRD executed	$ 645	1,294	$ 433	1,228
Recipient executed	1,270	684	793	639
Total	$1,915	1,978	$1,226	1,867

The responsibilities of the IBRD under these arrangements vary and range from services normally provided under its own lending projects to full project implementation including procurement of goods and services. During the fiscal year 1995, the IBRD received $19 million ($17 million—June 30, 1994) as fees for administering trust funds. These fees have been recorded as a reduction of administrative expenses.

NOTE H—STAFF RETIREMENT PLAN

The IBRD has a defined benefit retirement plan (the Plan) covering substantially all of its staff. The Plan also covers substantially all the staff of the IFC and the MIGA. Under the Plan, benefits are based on the years of contributory service and the highest three-year average of pensionable remuneration as defined in the Plan, with the staff contributing a fixed percentage of pensionable remuneration, and the IBRD contributing the remainder of the actuarially determined cost of future Plan benefits. The IBRD uses the aggregate method for determining its contribution to the Plan. The amount of that contribution approximates the net periodic pension cost as detailed below. All contributions to the Plan and all other assets and income held for the purposes of the Plan are held by the IBRD separately from the other assets and income of the IBRD, IDA, IFC, and MIGA and can be used only for the benefit of the participants in the Plan and their beneficiaries, until all liabilities to them have been paid or provided for. Plan assets consist primarily of equity and fixed income securities, with smaller holdings of cash, real estate, and other investments.

Net periodic pension cost for the IBRD participants for the fiscal years ended June 30, 1995 and June 30, 1994 consisted of the following components:

In millions

	1995	1994
Service cost—benefits earned during the fiscal year	$ 186	$ 185
Interest cost on projected benefit obligation	348	310
Actual return on plan assets	(428)	(342)
Net amortization and deferral	(3)	(50)
Net periodic pension cost	$ 103	$ 103

The portion of this cost that relates to the IBRD and is included in Administrative Expenses for the fiscal year ended June 30, 1995 is $65 million ($63 million–June 30, 1994). The balance has been included in the management fee charged to the IDA.

The following table sets forth the Plan's funded status as at June 30, 1995 and June 30, 1994:

In millions

	1995	1994
Actuarial present value of benefit obligations		
Accumulated benefit obligation		
Vested	$(3,551)	$(3,092)
Nonvested	(22)	(43)
Subtotal	(3,573)	(3,135)
Effect of projected compensation levels	(1,866)	(1,743)
Projected benefit obligation	(5,439)	(4,878)
Plan assets at fair value	5,925	5,387
Plan assets in excess of projected benefit obligation	486	509
Remaining unrecognized net transition asset	(104)	(117)
Unrecognized prior service cost	82	91
Unrecognized net gain from past experience different from that assumed and from changes in assumptions	(464)	(483)
Prepaid pension cost	$ 0	$ 0

The weighted-average discount rate used in determining the actuarial present value of the projected benefit obligation was 8.25 percent (8.25 percent—June 30, 1994). The effect of projected compensation levels was calculated based on a scale that provides for a decreasing rate of salary increase depending on age, beginning with 12.7 percent at age 20 and decreasing to 6.2 percent at age 64. The expected long-term rate of return on assets was 9 percent (9 percent—June 30, 1994).

NOTES TO FINANCIAL STATEMENTS *(continued)*

NOTE I—RETIRED STAFF BENEFITS PLAN

The IBRD has a Retired Staff Benefits Plan (RSBP) that provides certain health care and life insurance benefits to retirees. All staff who are enrolled in the insurance programs while in active service and who meet certain requirements are eligible for benefits when they reach early or normal retirement age while working for the IBRD. The RSBP also covers the staff of the IFC and the MIGA.

Retirees contribute a level amount toward life insurance based on the amount of coverage. Retiree contributions toward health care are based on length of service and age at retirement. The IBRD annually contributes the remainder of the actuarially determined cost for future benefits. All contributions to the RSBP and all other assets and income held for purposes of the RSBP are held by the IBRD separately from the other assets and income of the IBRD, IDA, IFC, and MIGA and can be used only for the benefit of the participants in the RSBP and their beneficiaries until all liabilities to them have been paid or provided for. RSBP assets consist primarily of fixed income and equity securities.

Net periodic postretirement benefits cost for the IBRD participants for the fiscal years ended June 30, 1995 and June 30, 1994 consisted of the following components:

In millions

	1995	1994
Service cost—benefits earned during the fiscal year	$ 28	$ 25
Interest cost on accumulated postretirement benefit obligation	48	39
Actual return on plan assets	(40)	(49)
Net amortization and deferral	1	19
	$ 37	$ 34

The portion of this cost that relates to the IBRD and is included in Administrative Expenses for the fiscal year ended June 30, 1995 is $23 million ($21 million—June 30, 1994). The balance has been included in the management fee charged to the IDA.

The following table sets forth the RSBP's funded status as at June 30, 1995 and June 30, 1994:

In millions

	1995	1994
Accumulated postretirement benefit obligation		
Retirees	$(257)	$(228)
Fully eligible active plan participants	(125)	(119)
Other active plan participants	(292)	(297)
	(674)	(644)
Plan assets at fair value	770	702
Plan assets in excess of accumulated postretirement benefit obligation	96	58
Unrecognized prior service costs	(14)	(16)
Unrecognized net loss from past experience different from that assumed and from changes in assumptions	250	296
Prepaid postretirement benefit cost	$ 332	$ 338

Of the $332 million prepaid as at June 30, 1995 ($338 million—June 30, 1994), $301 million is attributable to the IBRD ($311 million—June 30, 1994) and is included in Miscellaneous Assets on the Balance Sheet. The remainder has been attributed to the IFC and the MIGA.

For June 30, 1995, the accumulated plan benefit obligation (APBO) was determined using health care cost trend rates of 11.2 to 15.1 percent, decreasing gradually to 5.1 percent in 2010 and thereafter. The health care cost trend rate used for June 30, 1994 was 12.2 to 16.4 percent decreasing gradually to 5.8 percent in 2010 and thereafter.

The health care cost trend rate assumption has a significant effect on the amounts reported. To illustrate, increasing the assumed health care cost trend rates by one percentage point would increase the APBO as at June 30, 1995 by $138 million and the net periodic postretirement benefit cost for the fiscal year by $19 million.

The weighted average discount rate used in determining the APBO was 7.5 percent (8.25 percent—June 30, 1994). The expected long-term rate of return on plan assets was 8.25 percent (8.25 percent—June 30, 1994).

Price Waterhouse (International Firm)	The Hague Beijing Hong Kong London	New York Tokyo Washington

Price Waterhouse

July 26, 1995

President and Board of Governors
 International Bank for Reconstruction
 and Development

In our opinion, the financial statements appearing on pages 140 through 164 of this Report present fairly, in all material respects, in terms of United States dollars, the financial position of the International Bank for Reconstruction and Development at June 30, 1995 and 1994, and the results of its operations and its cash flows for the years then ended in conformity with generally accepted accounting principles in the United States and with International Accounting Standards. These financial statements are the responsibility of management of the International Bank for Reconstruction and Development; our responsibility is to express an opinion on these financial statements based on our audits. We conducted our audits of these statements in accordance with generally accepted auditing standards, including International Standards on Auditing, which require that we plan and perform the audit to obtain reasonable assurance about whether the financial statements are free of material misstatement. An audit includes examining, on a test basis, evidence supporting the amounts and disclosures in the financial statements, assessing the accounting principles used and significant estimates made by management, and evaluating the overall financial statement presentation. We believe that our audits provide a reasonable basis for the opinion expressed above.

As described in the Summary of Significant Accounting and Related Policies in the Notes to Financial Statements, the International Bank for Reconstruction and Development changed its method of accounting for the offsetting of amounts related to certain contracts during the year ended June 30, 1995.

Price Waterhouse

(International Firm)

SPECIAL PURPOSE FINANCIAL STATEMENTS OF THE INTERNATIONAL DEVELOPMENT ASSOCIATION AND SPECIAL FUND

STATEMENTS OF SOURCES AND APPLICATIONS OF DEVELOPMENT RESOURCES

June 30, 1995 and June 30, 1994
Expressed in millions of U.S. dollars

	IDA		Special Fund	
	1995	**1994**	**1995**	**1994**
Applications of Development Resources				
Net Resources Available For Development Activities				
Cash and investments immediately available for disbursement				
Due from banks	$ 43	$ 65	$ 1	$ 2
Obligations of governments and other official entities—Notes B and F	1,851	1,368	—	5
Obligations of banks and other financial institutions—Notes B and F	2,257	876	333	267
Net (payable) receivable on investment securities transactions—Notes B and F	(128)	116		
	4,023	2,425	334	274
Cash and investments not immediately available for disbursement				
Due from banks	3	2		
Obligations of governments and other official entities—Notes B and F	938	136		
Obligations of banks and other financial institutions—Notes B and F	402	501		
	1,343	639	—	—
Restricted cash and notes	73	71		
Nonnegotiable, noninterest-bearing demand obligations	23,677	21,548	—	33
Receivable from the International Bank for Reconstruction and Development—Note D	—	1,023		
Other resources, net	153	95	—	—
Total net resources available for development activities	29,269	25,801	334	307
Resources Used For Development Credits				
(see Summary Statement of Development Credits, Notes E and F)				
Total development credits	98,285	87,880	—	21
Less undisbursed balance	26,253	25,070	—	21
Total resources used for development credits	72,032	62,810	—	—
Total applications of development resources	**$101,301**	**$88,611**	**$334**	**$307**

	IDA		Special Fund	
	1995	1994	1995	1994

Sources of Development Resources

Member subscriptions and contributions (see Statement of Voting Power, and Subscriptions and Contributions, Note C)

	IDA 1995	IDA 1994	Special Fund 1995	Special Fund 1994
Unrestricted	$ 92,485	$89,258	$203	$206
Restricted	287	286		
Subscriptions and contributions committed	92,772	89,544	203	206
Less subscriptions and contributions receivable—Note C	6,739	11,186		
Subscriptions and contributions paid in	86,033	78,358	203	206
Deferred amounts receivable to maintain value of currency holdings	(218)	(217)		
Payments on account of pending membership—Note C	9	9		
Transfer from the International Bank for Reconstruction and Development—Note D	4,581	4,176		
Cumulative translation adjustment on development credits	8,823	4,807		
Accumulated surplus (see Statements of Changes in Accumulated Surplus)	1,864	1,264	131	101
Securities sold under agreements to repurchase and payable for cash collateral received	209	214		
Total sources of development resources	**$101,301**	**$88,611**	**$334**	**$307**

The Notes to Special Purpose Financial Statements are an integral part of these Statements.

STATEMENTS OF CHANGES IN ACCUMULATED SURPLUS

For the fiscal years ended June 30, 1995 and June 30, 1994
Expressed in millions of U.S. dollars

	IDA		Special Fund	
	1995	1994	1995	1994
Income from development credits—Notes E and G	$ 489	$ 417		
Income from investments—Note B	289	168	$ 22	$ 18
Management fee charged by the International Bank for Reconstruction and Development—Note G	(571)	(545)		
Amortization of discount on subscription advances	(11)	(9)	(1)	—
Changes from operations	196	31	21	18
Effect of exchange rate changes on accumulated surplus	404	123	9	(1)
Net changes	600	154	30	17
Balance at beginning of the fiscal year	1,264	1,110	101	84
Balance at end of the fiscal year	$1,864	$1,264	$131	$101

The Notes to Special Purpose Financial Statements are an integral part of these Statements.

STATEMENTS OF CASH FLOWS

For the fiscal years ended June 30, 1995 and June 30, 1994
Expressed in millions of U.S. dollars

	IDA		Special Fund	
	1995	1994	1995	1994
Cash flows from development activities				
Development credit disbursements	$(5,700)	$(5,520)	$ (3)	$(11)
Development credit principal repayments	493	420		
Net cash used in development activities	(5,207)	(5,100)	(3)	(11)
Cash flows from member subscriptions and contributions	5,174	3,960	33	16
Cash flows from IBRD contributions	1,427	452		
Cash flows from operating activities				
Changes from operations	196	31	21	18
Adjustments to reconcile changes from operations to net cash provided by operating activities				
Amortization of discount on subscription advances	11	9	1	—
Net changes in other development resources	(281)	163		
Net cash (used in) provided by operating activities	(74)	203	22	18
Effect of exchange rate changes on cash and investments immediately available for disbursement	278	122	8	(1)
Net increase (decrease) in cash and investments immediately available for disbursement	1,598	(363)	60	22
Cash and investments immediately available for disbursement at beginning of the fiscal year	2,425	2,788	274	252
Cash and investments immediately available for disbursement at end of the fiscal year	$ 4,023	$ 2,425	$334	$274
Supplemental disclosure				
Increase in ending balances resulting from exchange rate fluctuations				
Development credits outstanding	$ 4,017	$ 1,542	—	—
Receivable from the IBRD	90	60	—	—

The Notes to Special Purpose Financial Statements are an integral part of these Statements.

Summary Statement of Development Credits

June 30, 1995

Expressed in millions of U.S. dollars

Borrower or guarantor	IDA Total development credits	IDA Undisbursed development credits[1]	IDA Development credits outstanding	Special Fund Total development credits	Special Fund Undisbursed development credits	Special Fund Development credits outstanding	Total Development credits outstanding	Total Percentage of development credits outstanding
Afghanistan	$ 75	$ —	$ 75	$ —	$ —	$ —	$ 75	0.10
Albania	223	126	97	—	—	—	97	0.13
Angola	281	214	67	—	—	—	67	0.09
Armenia	157	75	82	—	—	—	82	0.11
Azerbaijan	83	83	—	—	—	—	—	—
Bangladesh	7,380	1,589	5,791	7	—	7	5,798	8.05
Benin	699	207	492	13	—	13	505	0.70
Bhutan	31	8	23	—	—	—	23	0.03
Bolivia	1,180	442	738	—	—	—	738	1.02
Botswana	12	—	12	—	—	—	12	0.02
Burkina Faso	872	276	596	—	—	—	596	0.83
Burundi	839	229	610	—	—	—	610	0.85
Cambodia	110	53	57	—	—	—	57	0.08
Cameroon	515	57	458	—	—	—	458	0.64
Cape Verde	63	32	31	—	—	—	31	0.04
Central African Republic	507	85	422	—	—	—	422	0.59
Chad	551	170	381	—	—	—	381	0.53
Chile	11	—	11	—	—	—	11	0.02
China	10,061	3,200	6,861	88	—	88	6,949	9.65
Colombia	11	—	11	—	—	—	11	0.02
Comoros	86	23	63	—	—	—	63	0.09
Congo	182	—	182	—	—	—	182	0.25
Costa Rica	3	—	3	—	—	—	3	*
Côte d'Ivoire	918	205	713	—	—	—	713	0.99
Djibouti	55	7	48	—	—	—	48	0.07
Dominica	14	1	13	—	—	—	13	0.02
Dominican Republic	18	—	18	—	—	—	18	0.02
Ecuador	27	—	27	—	—	—	27	0.04
Egypt	1,418	420	998	—	—	—	998	1.39
El Salvador	21	—	21	—	—	—	21	0.03
Equatorial Guinea	61	6	55	—	—	—	55	0.08
Eritrea	28	5	23	—	—	—	23	0.03
Ethiopia	2,129	610	1,519	—	—	—	1,519	2.11
Gambia, The	198	35	163	—	—	—	163	0.23
Georgia	111	79	32	—	—	—	32	0.04
Ghana	3,444	1,158	2,286	52	—	52	2,338	3.25
Grenada	8	—	8	—	—	—	8	0.01
Guinea	1,102	237	865	—	—	—	865	1.20
Guinea-Bissau	264	51	213	6	—	6	219	0.30
Guyana	296	96	200	—	—	—	200	0.28
Haiti	546	164	382	15	—	15	397	0.55
Honduras	548	164	384	—	—	—	384	0.53
India	22,847	5,167	17,680	78	—	78	17,758	24.65
Indonesia	766	—	766	—	—	—	766	1.06
Jordan	70	—	70	—	—	—	70	0.10
Kenya	2,426	459	1,967	55	—	55	2,022	2.81
Korea, Republic of	84	—	84	—	—	—	84	0.12
Kyrgyz Republic	234	139	95	—	—	—	95	0.13
Lao People's Democratic Republic	465	175	290	—	—	—	290	0.40

	IDA			Special Fund			Total	
Borrower or guarantor	Total develop- ment credits	Undisbursed develop- ment credits[1]	Develop- ment credits out- standing	Total develop- ment credits	Undisbursed develop- ment credits	Develop- ment credits out- standing	Develop- ment credits out- standing	Percent- age of develop- ment credits out- standing
Lesotho	$ 236	$ 83	$ 153	$ —	$ —	$ —	$ 153	0.21
Liberia	115	3	112	—	—	—	112	0.16
Macedonia, former Yugoslav Republic of	145	100	45	—	—	—	45	0.06
Madagascar	1,429	349	1,080	43	—	43	1,123	1.56
Malawi	1,653	386	1,267	20	—	20	1,287	1.79
Maldives	55	19	36	—	—	—	36	0.05
Mali	1,128	267	861	16	—	16	877	1.22
Mauritania	478	148	330	—	—	—	330	0.46
Mauritius	17	—	17	—	—	—	17	0.02
Mongolia	97	40	57	—	—	—	57	0.08
Morocco	34	—	34	—	—	—	34	0.05
Mozambique	1,658	810	848	—	—	—	848	1.18
Myanmar	849	29	820	—	—	—	820	1.14
Nepal	1,477	454	1,023	—	—	—	1,023	1.42
Nicaragua	442	162	280	—	—	—	280	0.39
Niger	749	138	611	—	—	—	611	0.85
Nigeria	931	705	226	—	—	—	226	0.31
Pakistan	4,967	1,627	3,340	—	—	—	3,340	4.64
Papua New Guinea	111	—	111	—	—	—	111	0.15
Paraguay	36	—	36	—	—	—	36	0.05
Philippines	294	110	184	—	—	—	184	0.26
Rwanda	733	232	501	—	—	—	501	0.70
St. Kitts and Nevis	2	—	2	—	—	—	2	*
St. Lucia	12	6	6	—	—	—	6	0.01
St. Vincent and the Grenadines	4	2	2	6	—	6	8	0.01
São Tomé and Principe	75	22	53	—	—	—	53	0.07
Senegal	1,500	400	1,100	27	—	27	1,127	1.57
Sierra Leone	390	171	219	—	—	—	219	0.30
Solomon Islands	40	14	26	—	—	—	26	0.04
Somalia	448	*	448	—	—	—	448	0.62
Sri Lanka	1,955	480	1,475	—	—	—	1,475	2.05
Sudan	1,303	—	1,303	15	—	15	1,318	1.83
Swaziland	6	—	6	—	—	—	6	0.01
Syrian Arab Republic	44	—	44	—	—	—	44	0.06
Tanzania	3,086	906	2,180	—	—	—	2,180	3.03
Thailand	102	—	102	—	—	—	102	0.14
Togo	650	125	525	28	—	28	553	0.77
Tonga	6	1	5	—	—	—	5	0.01
Tunisia	51	—	51	—	—	—	51	0.07
Turkey	133	—	133	—	—	—	133	0.18
Uganda	2,592	808	1,784	—	—	—	1,784	2.48
Vanuatu	19	5	14	—	—	—	14	0.02
Viet Nam	858	625	233	—	—	—	233	0.32
Western Samoa	51	4	47	—	—	—	47	0.07
Yemen, Republic of	1,144	323	821	15	—	15	836	1.16

June 30, 1995
Expressed in millions of U.S. dollars

Borrower or guarantor	IDA			Special Fund			Total	
	Total development credits	Undisbursed development credits[1]	Development credits outstanding	Total development credits	Undisbursed development credits	Development credits outstanding	Development credits outstanding	Percentage of development credits outstanding
Zaire	$ 1,379	$ —	$ 1,379	$ —	$—	$ —	$ 1,379	1.91
Zambia	1,646	428	1,218	8	—	8	1,226	1.70
Zimbabwe	509	164	345	—	—	—	345	0.48
Subtotal members	97,669	26,193	71,476	492	—	492	71,968	99.91
West African Development Bank [2]	68	36	32	—	—	—	32	0.05
Caribbean Development Bank [3]	48	24	24	—	—	—	24	0.03
Subtotal regional development banks	116	60	56	—	—	—	56	0.08
Other [4]	8	—	8	—	—	—	8	0.01
Total—June 30, 1995 [5]	$97,793	$26,253	$71,540	$492	—	$492	$72,032	100.00
Total—June 30, 1994 [5]	$87,423	$25,070	$62,353	$478	$21	$457	$62,810	

* indicates amounts less than $0.5 million or 0.005 percent.

NOTES

1. Of the undisbursed balance at June 30, 1995, the IDA has entered into irrevocable commitments to disburse $270 million ($229 million—June 30, 1994).

2. These development credits are for the benefit of Benin, Burkina Faso, Côte d'Ivoire, Mali, Niger, Senegal, and Togo.

3. These development credits are for the benefit of Grenada and territories of the United Kingdom (Associated States and Dependencies) in the Caribbean region.

4. Represents development credits made at a time when the authorities on Taiwan represented China in the IDA (prior to May 15, 1980).

5. In the Statements of Sources and Applications of Development Resources at June 30, 1995, total development credits of $98,285 million ($87,880 million—June 30, 1994) and total development credits disbursed and outstanding of $72,032 million ($62,810 million—June 30, 1994) include development credits outstanding of $492 million ($457 million—June 30, 1994) which were originated under the Special Fund, since such amounts are repayable to the IDA (see Notes to Special Purpose Financial Statements—Note E).

Maturity Structure of Development Credits Outstanding

Period	IDA	Special Fund	Total
July 1, 1995 through June 30, 1996	$ 670	$ 5	$ 675
July 1, 1996 through June 30, 1997	670	5	675
July 1, 1997 through June 30, 1998	761	5	766
July 1, 1998 through June 30, 1999	931	5	936
July 1, 1999 through June 30, 2000	1,094	5	1,099
July 1, 2000 through June 30, 2005	8,892	39	8,931
July 1, 2005 through June 30, 2010	11,995	75	12,070
July 1, 2010 through June 30, 2015	13,534	75	13,609
July 1, 2015 through June 30, 2020	12,340	75	12,415
July 1, 2020 through June 30, 2025	10,206	75	10,281
July 1, 2025 through June 30, 2030	7,147	75	7,222
July 1, 2030 through June 30, 2035	3,037	53	3,090
July 1, 2035 through June 30, 2038	263	—	263
Total [1]	$71,540	$492	$72,032

NOTE

1. In the Statements of Sources and Applications of Development Resources at June 30, 1995, total development credits disbursed and outstanding of $72,032 million ($62,810 million—June 30, 1994) include development credits outstanding of $492 million ($457 million—June 30, 1994) which were originated under the Special Fund, since such amounts are repayable to the IDA (see Notes to Special Purpose Financial Statements—Note E).

The Notes to Special Purpose Financial Statements are an integral part of these Statements.

Statement of Voting Power, and Subscriptions and Contributions

June 30, 1995
Expressed in millions of U.S. dollars

Member[1]	IDA			Special Fund contributions
	Number of votes	Percentage of total	Subscriptions and contributions committed	
Part I Members				
Australia	136,489	1.34	$ 1,522.3	$ —
Austria	68,149	0.67	778.3	—
Belgium	120,087	1.18	1,557.0	49.5
Canada	310,558	3.05	3,821.4	158.3
Denmark	98,592	0.97	1,198.9	34.7
Finland	70,199	0.69	630.1	—
France	420,934	4.13	6,431.5	149.4
Germany	702,871	6.90	10,692.1	—
Iceland	24,438	0.24	17.1	—
Ireland	29,922	0.29	105.3	—
Italy	259,449	2.55	2,913.6	90.3
Japan	1,071,214	10.51	22,488.1	—
Kuwait	69,834	0.69	649.1	—
Luxembourg	25,738	0.25	50.6	—
Netherlands	220,346	2.16	3,461.4	—
New Zealand	30,062	0.29	104.7	—
Norway	99,285	0.97	1,129.4	40.0
Portugal	24,140	0.24	24.0	—
Russia	28,202	0.28	152.7	—
South Africa	30,089	0.30	85.2	—
Spain	54,398	0.53	431.1	—
Sweden	203,559	2.00	2,249.3	74.1
Switzerland[2]	87,723	0.86	1,035.4	
United Arab Emirates	1,367	0.01	5.6	—
United Kingdom	518,046	5.08	6,560.1	—
United States	1,563,036	15.34	21,831.5	—
Subtotal Part I Members[3]	6,268,727	61.51	89,925.9	596.4
Part II Members				
Afghanistan	13,557	0.13	1.3	—
Albania	19,711	0.19	0.3	—
Algeria	26,107	0.26	5.1	—
Angola	45,662	0.45	7.9	—
Argentina	96,503	0.95	58.0	—
Armenia	584	0.01	0.5	—
Azerbaijan	644	0.01	0.9	—
Bangladesh	59,796	0.59	7.3	—
Belize	1,788	0.02	0.2	—
Benin	5,297	0.05	0.6	—
Bhutan	12,233	0.12	0.1	—
Bolivia	29,974	0.29	1.4	—
Botswana	23,751	0.23	0.2	—
Brazil	167,452	1.64	94.3	—
Burkina Faso	19,065	0.19	0.7	—

	IDA			
Member[1]	Number of votes	Percentage of total	Subscriptions and contributions committed	Special Fund contributions
Burundi	22,702	0.22	$ 1.0	$ —
Cambodia	7,826	0.08	1.3	—
Cameroon	18,655	0.18	1.3	—
Cape Verde	4,948	0.05	0.1	—
Central African Republic	10,920	0.11	0.6	—
Chad	10,990	0.11	0.6	—
Chile	31,782	0.31	4.5	—
China	205,683	2.02	39.7	—
Colombia	34,350	0.34	22.5	—
Comoros	13,141	0.13	0.1	—
Congo	6,685	0.07	0.6	—
Costa Rica	12,323	0.12	0.3	—
Côte d'Ivoire	18,267	0.18	1.3	—
Croatia	28,806	0.28	5.5	—
Cyprus	27,932	0.27	1.1	—
Czech Republic	40,518	0.40	23.9	—
Djibouti	532	0.01	0.2	—
Dominica	15,017	0.15	0.1	—
Dominican Republic	25,496	0.25	0.6	—
Ecuador	23,540	0.23	0.8	—
Egypt	47,446	0.47	6.7	—
El Salvador	6,244	0.06	0.4	—
Equatorial Guinea	6,167	0.06	0.4	—
Eritrea	23,326	0.23	0.1	—
Ethiopia	21,353	0.21	0.7	—
Fiji	6,981	0.07	0.7	—
Gabon	2,093	0.02	0.6	—
Gambia, The	15,152	0.15	0.3	—
Georgia	22,523	0.22	0.9	—
Ghana	22,131	0.22	3.0	—
Greece	36,429	0.36	18.6	—
Grenada	18,930	0.19	0.1	—
Guatemala	25,473	0.25	0.5	—
Guinea	27,283	0.27	1.3	—
Guinea-Bissau	5,036	0.05	0.2	—
Guyana	18,160	0.18	1.0	—
Haiti	17,143	0.17	1.0	—
Honduras	21,451	0.21	0.4	—
Hungary	77,408	0.76	36.6	—
India	319,834	3.14	55.1	—
Indonesia	99,250	0.97	14.8	—
Iran, Islamic Republic of	15,455	0.15	5.7	—
Iraq	9,407	0.09	1.0	—
Israel	21,260	0.21	2.5	—
Jordan	24,627	0.24	0.4	—
Kazakhstan	806	0.01	1.8	—
Kenya	25,760	0.25	2.2	—
Kiribati	4,777	0.05	0.1	—
Korea, Republic of	41,411	0.41	117.3	—
Kyrgyz Republic	580	0.01	0.5	—

June 30, 1995
Expressed in millions of U.S. dollars

Member[1]	IDA			Special Fund contributions
	Number of votes	Percentage of total	Subscriptions and contributions committed	
Lao People's Democratic Republic	11,723	0.12	$ 0.6	$ —
Latvia	614	0.01	0.7	—
Lebanon	8,562	0.08	0.6	—
Lesotho	23,809	0.23	0.2	—
Liberia	22,771	0.22	1.1	—
Libya	7,771	0.08	1.3	—
Macedonia, former Yugoslav Republic of	15,759	0.15	1.0	—
Madagascar	11,198	0.11	1.2	—
Malawi	27,352	0.27	1.0	—
Malaysia	40,053	0.39	3.6	—
Maldives	22,904	0.22	*	—
Mali	22,407	0.22	1.2	—
Marshall Islands	4,906	0.05	*	—
Mauritania	10,885	0.11	0.6	—
Mauritius	28,664	0.28	1.2	—
Mexico	73,491	0.72	130.0	—
Micronesia, Federated States of	18,424	0.18	*	—
Moldova	612	0.01	0.7	—
Mongolia	5,039	0.05	0.3	—
Morocco	47,066	0.46	4.9	—
Mozambique	6,268	0.06	1.7	—
Myanmar	36,659	0.36	2.9	—
Nepal	25,966	0.25	0.7	—
Nicaragua	24,627	0.24	0.4	—
Niger	16,541	0.16	0.7	—
Nigeria	8,257	0.08	4.2	—
Oman	24,751	0.24	0.4	—
Pakistan	93,288	0.92	13.7	—
Panama	5,657	0.06	*	—
Papua New Guinea	13,050	0.13	1.1	—
Paraguay	11,419	0.11	0.4	—
Peru	12,813	0.13	2.2	—
Philippines	16,583	0.16	6.5	—
Poland	236,855	2.32	52.8	—
Rwanda	17,371	0.17	1.0	—
St. Kitts and Nevis	5,030	0.05	0.2	—
St. Lucia	22,475	0.22	0.2	—
St. Vincent and the Grenadines	514	0.01	0.1	—
São Tomé and Principe	4,714	0.05	0.1	—
Saudi Arabia	353,707	3.47	2,033.2	—
Senegal	27,775	0.27	2.2	—
Sierra Leone	12,667	0.12	1.0	—
Slovak Republic	20,893	0.20	7.0	—
Slovenia	18,956	0.19	3.0	—
Solomon Islands	518	0.01	0.1	—
Somalia	10,506	0.10	1.0	—
Sri Lanka	43,571	0.43	4.0	—
Sudan	22,886	0.22	1.3	—
Swaziland	11,073	0.11	0.4	—
Syrian Arab Republic	7,651	0.08	1.2	—

Member[1]	IDA Number of votes	IDA Percentage of total	IDA Subscriptions and contributions committed	Special Fund contributions
Tajikistan	20,568	0.20	$ 0.5	$ —
Tanzania	33,599	0.33	2.1	—
Thailand	43,571	0.43	4.3	—
Togo	21,847	0.21	1.0	—
Tonga	11,380	0.11	0.1	—
Trinidad and Tobago	770	0.01	1.6	—
Tunisia	2,793	0.03	1.9	—
Turkey	67,441	0.66	80.1	—
Uganda	21,093	0.21	2.2	—
Uzbekistan	746	0.01	1.5	—
Vanuatu	13,745	0.13	0.2	—
Viet Nam	8,889	0.09	1.9	—
Western Samoa	13,061	0.13	0.1	—
Yemen, Republic of	32,648	0.32	2.1	—
Zaire	12,164	0.12	3.8	—
Zambia	26,868	0.26	3.4	—
Zimbabwe	9,013	0.09	5.0	—
Subtotal Part II Members [3]	3,923,380	38.49	2,965.2	—
Total—June 30, 1995 [2, 3]	10,192,107	100.00	$92,891.1	$596.4
Total—June 30, 1994 [2]	9,668,041		$89,667.4	$596.4

* Indicates amounts less than $0.05 million.

NOTES
1. See Notes to Special Purpose Financial Statements—Note C for an explanation of the two categories of membership.
2. In the Statements of Sources and Applications of Development Resources at June 30, 1995, Member Subscriptions and Contributions Committed of $92,772 million ($89,544 million—June 30, 1994) does not include $512 million ($512 million—June 30, 1994) of Switzerland's subscription and contributions and includes Special Fund contributions of $386 million ($389 million—June 30, 1994) and repayments from credits financed by the Special Fund of $7 million (nil—June 30, 1994).
$512 million ($512 million—June 30, 1994) of Switzerland's subscription and contribution have not been included in the Statements of Sources and Applications of Development Resources since this represents the difference between the total cofinancing grants of $580 million provided by Switzerland directly to the IDA borrowers as cofinancing grants between the fourth and the ninth replenishments of the IDA resources, and the July 1992 contribution by Switzerland of $68 million.
Special Fund contributions of $386 million ($389 million—June 30, 1994) have been included, since the development credits that were funded using these resources are repayable to the IDA (see Notes to Special Purpose Financial Statements—Note C).
Repayments from credits financed by the Special Fund of $7 million (nil—June 30, 1994) have been included.
3. May differ from the sum of individual figures shown because of rounding.

The Notes to Special Purpose Financial Statements are an integral part of these Statements.

NOTE A—ORGANIZATION, OPERATIONS AND SIGNIFICANT ACCOUNTING AND RELATED POLICIES

ORIGIN AND AFFILIATED ORGANIZATIONS

IDA: The International Development Association (IDA) is an international organization established on September 24, 1960 to promote economic development in the less developed areas of the world included in the IDA's membership by providing financing on terms which are more flexible and bear less heavily on the balance of payments than those of conventional loans. The IDA has three affiliated organizations, the International Bank for Reconstruction and Development (IBRD), the International Finance Corporation (IFC), and the Multilateral Investment Guarantee Agency (MIGA). The principal purpose of the IBRD is to promote the economic development of its member countries, primarily by providing loans and related technical assistance for specific projects and for programs of economic reform in developing member countries. The IFC's purpose is to encourage the growth of productive private enterprises in its member countries through loans and equity investments in such enterprises without a member's guarantee. The MIGA was established to encourage the flow of investments for productive purposes among member countries and, in particular, to developing member countries by providing guarantees against noncommercial risks for foreign investment in its developing member countries.

Special Fund: On October 26, 1982, the IDA established the Special Fund constituted by funds contributed by members of the IDA and administered by the IDA to supplement the regular resources available for lending by the IDA. The arrangements governing the Special Fund may be amended or terminated by the IDA's Executive Directors subject to the agreement of a qualified majority of the contributors to the Special Fund. The resources of the Special Fund are kept separate from the resources of the IDA.

SUMMARY OF SIGNIFICANT ACCOUNTING AND RELATED POLICIES

Due to the nature and organization of the IDA and the Special Fund, these financial statements have been prepared for the specific purpose of reflecting the sources and applications of member subscriptions and are not intended to be a presentation in accordance with generally accepted accounting principles in the United States or with International Accounting Standards. These special purpose financial statements have been prepared to comply with Article VI, Section 11 (a) of the Articles of Agreement of the IDA.

The IDA's special purpose financial statements are prepared in accordance with the accounting policies outlined below.

Basis of Accounting

The IDA's special purpose financial statements are prepared on the accrual basis of accounting for development credit income, investment income, and administrative expenses. That is, the effects of transactions and other events are recognized when they occur (and not as cash or its equivalent is received or paid), and they are recorded in the accounting records and reported in the financial statements of the periods to which they relate.

Translation of Currencies

The IDA's special purpose financial statements are expressed in terms of U.S. dollars solely for the purpose of summarizing the IDA's financial position and the results of its operations for the convenience of its members and other interested parties.

IDA: The IDA is an international organization that conducts its business in the currencies of all of its members. Development resources and sources of development resources are translated at market rates of exchange at the end of the accounting period, except Member Subscriptions and Contributions, which are translated in the manner described below. Income and expenses are translated at the market rates of exchange at the dates on which they are recognized or at an average of the market rates of exchange in effect during each month. Translation adjustments relating to the revaluation of development credits denominated in Special Drawing Rights (SDRs) are charged or credited to Cumulative Translation Adjustment on Development Credits. Other translation adjustments are charged or credited to the Accumulated Surplus.

Special Fund: Development resources of the Special Fund are translated at market rates of exchange at the end of the period. Contributions are translated in the manner described below. Income is translated at market rates of exchange on dates of recognition of income. Translation adjustments are charged or credited to the Accumulated Surplus.

Member Subscriptions and Contributions

Recognition

IDA: Member Subscriptions and Contributions for each IDA replenishment are recorded in full as Subscriptions and Contributions Committed upon effectiveness of the relevant replenishment. Replenishments become effective when the IDA has received commitments from members for subscriptions and contributions of a specified portion of the full replenishment. Amounts not yet paid in, as at the date of effectiveness, are recorded as Subscriptions and Contributions Receivable and shown as a reduction of Subscriptions and Contributions Committed. These receivables come due throughout the replenishment period (generally three years) in accordance with an agreed maturity schedule. The actual payment of receivables when they become due from certain members is conditional upon the respective member's budgetary appropriation processes.

The Subscriptions and Contributions Receivable are settled through payment of cash or nonnegotiable, noninterest-bearing demand notes. If the receivable is settled in cash, the cash is recorded in Cash and Investments Not Immediately Available for Disbursement until such time as it becomes available in accordance with the replenishment agreement. The notes are encashed by the IDA as provided in the relevant replenishment resolution over the disbursement period of the credits committed under the replenishment, and the cash received is recorded in Cash and Investments Immediately Available for Disbursement.

In certain replenishments, members have had the option of paying all of their subscription and contribution amount in cash before it becomes due and receiving a discount. In these cases, the IDA and the member agree that the IDA will invest the cash and retain the income. The related subscription and contribution payment is recorded at the full undiscounted amount. The cash and investments are recorded in Cash and Investments Not Immediately Available for Disbursement until the date when the subscription and contribution amount would have become due, at which time it becomes available. The discount is recorded in Other Resources and amortized over the projected disbursement period for the replenishment's credits.

Under the Articles of Agreement and the arrangements governing replenishments, the IDA must take appropriate steps to ensure that over a reasonable period of time the resources provided by donors for lending by the IDA are used on an approximately pro rata basis. As discussed in the previous paragraph, donors sometimes contribute resources substantially ahead of their pro rata share. Unless otherwise agreed, the IDA does not disburse these funds ahead of donors' pro rata shares. Cash and Investments Not Immediately Available for Disbursement represents the difference between the amount contributed and the amount available for disbursements on a pro rata basis.

Transfers to the IDA from the IBRD are recorded as Sources of Development Resources and are receivable upon approval by the IBRD's Board of Governors.

For the purposes of its financial resources, the membership of the IDA is divided into two categories: (1) Part I members, which make payments of subscriptions and contributions provided to the IDA in convertible currencies that may be freely used or exchanged by the IDA in its operations, and (2) Part II members, most of which make payments of 10 percent of their initial subscriptions in freely convertible currencies, and the remaining 90 percent of their initial subscriptions, and all additional subscriptions and contributions, in their own currencies or in freely convertible currencies. Certain Part II members provide a portion of their subscriptions and contributions in the same

manner as mentioned in (1) above. The IDA's Articles of Agreement and subsequent replenishment agreements provide that the currency of any Part II member paid in by it may not be used by the IDA for projects financed by the IDA and located outside the territory of the member except by agreement between the member and the IDA. These subscriptions of Part II members are recorded as Restricted Cash and Notes.

Special Fund: Member Subscriptions and Contributions to the Special Fund are paid in cash and nonnegotiable, noninterest-bearing demand notes. The demand notes are encashed by the Special Fund as needed for disbursement on Special Fund credits. As Special Fund credits are disbursed, the portion of subscriptions and contributions related to those disbursements is reflected as part of the IDA's Member Subscriptions and Contributions, since repayments on all development credits become part of the general resources of the IDA.

Valuation

IDA: The subscriptions and contributions provided through the third replenishment are expressed in terms of "U.S. dollars of the weight and fineness in effect on January 1, 1960" (1960 dollars). Following the abolition of gold as a common denominator of the monetary system and the repeal of the provision of the U.S. law defining the par value of the U.S. dollar in terms of gold, the pre-existing basis for translating 1960 dollars into current dollars or any other currency disappeared. The Executive Directors of the IDA have decided, with effect on that date and until such time as the relevant provisions of the Articles of Agreement are amended, that the words "U.S. dollars of the weight and fineness in effect on January 1, 1960" in Article II, Section 2(b) of the Articles of Agreement of the IDA are interpreted to mean the SDR introduced by the International Monetary Fund as the SDR was valued in terms of U.S. dollars immediately before the introduction of the basket method of valuing the SDR on July 1, 1974, such value being equal to $1.20635 for one SDR (the 1974 SDR), and have also decided to apply the same standard of value to amounts expressed in 1960 dollars in the relevant resolutions of the Board of Governors.

The subscriptions and contributions provided through the third replenishment are expressed on the basis of the 1974 SDR. Prior to the decision of the Executive Directors, the IDA had valued these subscriptions and contributions on the basis of the SDR at the current market value of the SDR.

The subscriptions and contributions provided under the fourth replenishment and thereafter are expressed in members' currencies or SDRs and are payable in members' currencies. Beginning July 1, 1986, subscriptions and contributions made available for disbursement in cash to the IDA are translated at market rates of exchange on the dates they were made available. Prior to that date, subscriptions and contributions that had been disbursed or converted into other currencies were translated at market rates of exchange on dates of disbursement or conversion. Subscriptions and contributions not yet available for disbursements are translated at market rates of exchange at the end of the accounting period.

Article IV, Section 2(a) and (b) of the IDA's Articles of Agreement provides for maintenance of value payments on account of the local currency portion of the initial subscription whenever the par value of the member's currency or its foreign exchange value has, in the opinion of the IDA, depreciated or appreciated to a significant extent within the member's territories, so long as and to the extent that such currency shall not have been initially disbursed or exchanged for the currency of another member. The provisions of Article IV, Section 2(a) and (b) have by agreement been extended to cover additional subscriptions and contributions of the IDA through the third replenishment, but are not applicable to those of the fourth and subsequent replenishments.

The Executive Directors decided on June 30, 1987 that settlements of maintenance of value, which would result from the resolution of the valuation issue on the basis of the 1974 SDR, would be deferred until the Executive Directors decide to resume such settlements. These amounts are shown as Deferred Amounts Receivable to Maintain Value of Currency Holdings.

Special Fund: Beginning April 1, 1989, subscriptions and contributions received but not yet disbursed, as well as subscriptions and contributions disbursed or converted into other currencies, are translated at market rates of exchange on the dates they were made available for disbursement in cash to the Special Fund. Prior to that date, subscriptions and contributions that had been disbursed or converted into other currencies were translated at market rates of exchange at dates of disbursement or conversion. Subscriptions and contributions receivable are translated at market rates of exchange at the end of the accounting period.

Development Credits

All development credits are made to member governments or to the government of a territory of a member (except for development credits that have been made to regional development banks for the benefit of members or territories of members of the IDA). In order to qualify for lending on IDA terms, a country's per capita income must be below a certain level, and the country may have only limited or no creditworthiness for IBRD lending. Development credits carry a service charge of 0.75 percent, generally have 35- or 40-year final maturities and a 10-year grace period for principal payments. Development credits are carried in the financial statements at the full face amount of the borrowers' outstanding obligations.

It is the policy of the IDA to place in nonaccrual status all development credits made to a member government or to the government of a territory of a member if principal or charges with respect to any such development credit are overdue by more than six months, unless the IDA management determines that the overdue amount will be collected in the immediate future. In addition, if loans by the IBRD to a member government are placed in nonaccrual status, all development credits to that member government will also be placed in nonaccrual status by the IDA. On the date a member's development credits are placed in nonaccrual status, charges that had been accrued on development credits outstanding to the member that remained unpaid are deducted from the income from development credits of the current period. Charges on nonaccruing development credits are included in income only to the extent that payments have actually been received by the IDA. On the date a member pays in full all overdue amounts, the member's credits emerge from nonaccrual status, its eligibility for new credits is restored, and all overdue charges (including those from prior years) are recognized as income from development credits in the current period.

In fulfilling its mission, the IDA makes concessional loans to the poorest countries; therefore there is significant credit risk in the portfolio of development credits. Management continually monitors this credit risk. However, no provision for credit losses has been established because it is not practicable to determine such an amount in view of the nature and maturity structure of the credit portfolio. Should actual losses occur, they would be charged against the IDA's Accumulated Surplus. To date, the IDA has not suffered any losses on receivables from development credits.

IDA: The repayment obligations of the IDA's development credits funded from resources through the fifth replenishment are expressed in the development credit agreements in terms of 1960 dollars. In June 1987, the Executive Directors decided to value those development credits at the rate of $1.20635 per 1960 dollar on a permanent basis. Development credits funded from resources provided under the sixth replenishment and thereafter are denominated in SDRs; the principal amounts disbursed under such development credits are to be repaid in currency amounts currently equivalent to the SDRs disbursed.

Special Fund: Special Fund development credits are denominated in SDRs. The principal amounts disbursed under such development credits are to be repaid in currency amounts currently equivalent to the SDRs disbursed.

Special Fund development credits are made on the same terms as regular IDA development credits except that the proceeds of Special Fund development credits may be used only to finance expenditures for goods or services from (a) Part II members of the IDA; (b) Part I members contributing to the Special Fund; and (c)

Part I members contributing to the regular resources of the IDA through the IDA's FY84 Account who have notified the IDA that such contributions are to be treated in the same manner as contributions to the Special Fund for purposes of any future adjustment of the voting rights of the members of the IDA.

Investments

The IDA carries its investment securities and related financial instruments at market value. Both realized and unrealized gains and losses are included in Income from Investments.

NOTE B—INVESTMENTS

As part of its overall portfolio management strategy, the IDA invests in government and agency obligations, time deposits, and related financial instruments with off-balance sheet risk including futures, forward contracts, covered forward contracts, options, and short sales.

Government and Agency Obligations: These obligations include marketable bonds, notes, and other obligations. Obligations issued or unconditionally guaranteed by governments of countries require a minimum credit rating of AA if denominated in a currency other than the home currency; otherwise no rating is required. Obligations issued by an agency or instrumentality of a government of a country, a multilateral organization, or any other official entity require a credit rating of AAA.

Time Deposits: Time deposits include certificates of deposit, bankers' acceptances, and other obligations issued or unconditionally guaranteed by banks and other financial institutions.

Futures and Forwards: Futures and forward contracts are contracts for delayed delivery of securities or money market instruments in which the seller agrees to make delivery at a specified future date of a specified instrument at a specified price or yield.

Covered Forwards: Covered forwards are agreements in which cash in one currency is converted into a different currency and, simultaneously, a forward exchange agreement is executed providing for a future exchange of the two currencies in order to recover the currency converted.

Options: Options are contracts that allow the holder of the option to purchase or sell a financial instrument at a specified price within a specified period of time from or to the seller of the option. The purchaser of an option pays a premium at the outset to the seller of the option, who then bears the risk of an unfavorable change in the price of the financial instrument underlying the option. The IDA only invests in exchange-traded options.

Short Sales: Short sales are sales of securities not held in the IDA's portfolio at the time of the sale. The IDA must purchase the security at a later date and bears the risk that the market value of the security will move adversely between the time of the sale and the time the security must be delivered.

A summary of the IDA investment portfolio by instrument for Investments Immediately Available for Disbursement and Not Immediately Available for Disbursement at June 30, 1995 is as follows:

In millions

	Immediately available for disbursement			Not immediately available for disbursement		
	As at June 30, 1995	Average daily balance during the fiscal year	Net gains (losses) for the fiscal year	As at June 30, 1995	Average daily balance during the fiscal year	Net gains (losses) for the fiscal year
Government and agency obligations	$1,642	$1,334	$19	$ 937	$562	$48
Time deposits	2,252	1,610	—	402	393	—
Futures and forwards	1	1	(1)	1	*	*
Covered forwards	5	1	—	—	*	—
Options	*	*	*	*	*	*
Resale agreements	208	415	—	—	22	—
	$4,108	$3,361	$18	$1,340	$977	$48
Short Sales	$ (27)	$(46)	$—	$ —	$ *	$—
Repurchase Agreements	(64)	(102)	—	(145)	(63)	—

* Less than $0.5 million

As at June 30, 1995, the Special Fund had only time deposits in its investment portfolio.

A summary of the currency composition of Investments Immediately Available for Disbursement and Not Immediately Available for Disbursement at June 30, 1995 and June 30, 1994, is as follows:

In millions of U.S. dollar equivalents

	1995				1994			
	IDA			Special Fund	IDA			Special Fund
	Immediately available for disbursement	Not immediately available for disbursement	Total	Total	Immediately available for disbursement	Not immediately available for disbursement	Total	Total
Canadian dollars	$ 37	$ —	$ 37	$ 90	$ —	$ —	$ —	$ 73
Deutsche mark	1,587	236	1,823	—	1,242	95	1,337	—
French francs	330	123	453	51	172	53	225	37
Italian lire	—	—	—	95	33	—	33	90
Japanese yen	623	289	912	—	237	106	343	—
Pound sterling	288	95	383	—	103	42	145	—
Swedish kronor	—	—	—	59	16	—	16	44
United States dollars	1,243	597	1,840	—	336	341	677	—
Other currencies	—	—	—	38	105	—	105	28
	$4,108	$1,340	$5,448	$333	$2,244	$637	$2,881	$272

For the purpose of risk management, the IDA is party to a variety of financial instruments, certain of which involve elements of credit risk in excess of the amount reflected in the Statements of Sources and Applications of Development Resources. Credit risk represents the maximum potential accounting loss due to possible nonperformance by obligors and counterparties under the terms of the contracts. Additionally, the nature of the instruments involves contract value and notional principal amounts that are not reflected in the basic financial statements. For both on- and off-balance sheet securities, the IDA limits trading to a list of authorized dealers and counterparties. Credit limits have been established for each counterparty by type of instrument and maturity category.

The credit risk exposure and contract value/notional amounts, as applicable, of these financial instruments as at June 30, 1995 and June 30, 1994 are given below:

In millions

	1995	1994
Futures and Forwards		
Long position	$359	$299
Short position	561	862
Credit exposure due to potential nonperformance by counterparties	2	1
Covered forward contracts		
Credit exposure due to potential nonperformance by counterparties	5	6
Options		
Long position	35	310
Short position	—	216

NOTE C—MEMBER SUBSCRIPTIONS AND CONTRIBUTIONS

Subscriptions and Contributions Receivable:

The payment of subscriptions and contributions is conditional on the members' budgetary processes. At June 30, 1995 receivables from subscriptions and contributions was $6,739 million ($11,186 million—June 30, 1994) of which $475 million ($343 million—June 30, 1994) was due and $6,264 million ($10,843 million—June 30, 1994) was not yet due.

Subscriptions and contributions due as at June 30, 1995 were as follows:

In millions

Amounts initially due on	June 30, 1995
July 1, 1994 through June 30, 1995	$396.1
July 1, 1993 through June 30, 1994	0.9
July 1, 1992 through June 30, 1993	77.9
June 30, 1992 and earlier	0.3
Total	$475.2

Subscriptions and contributions not yet due as at June 30, 1995 will become due as follows:

In millions

July 1, 1995 through June 30, 1996	$6,034
July 1, 1996 through June 30, 1997	136
Thereafter	94
Total	$6,264

Membership: On February 25, 1993 the IBRD's Executive Directors decided that the Socialist Federal Republic of Yugoslavia (SFRY) had ceased to be a member of the IBRD and that the Republic of Bosnia and Herzegovina, the Republic of Croatia, the former Yugoslav Republic of Macedonia, the Republic of Slovenia, and the Federal Republic of Yugoslavia (Serbia and Montenegro) are authorized to succeed to the membership of the SFRY in the IBRD when certain requirements are met. In accordance with the Articles of Agreement of the IDA, on February 25, 1993 the SFRY ceased to be a member of the IDA due to the cessation of its membership in the IBRD. Three of the five successor Republics—the Republics of Croatia and Slovenia and the former Yugoslav Republic of Macedonia—have since become members of the IDA. As at June 30, 1995 the subscription and contributions allocated to the other successor Republics (the Republic of Bosnia and Herzegovina, and the Federal Republic of Yugoslavia (Serbia and Montenegro)) are included under Payments on Account of Pending Membership.

On May 29, 1992 Switzerland became a member of the IDA. Before that date Switzerland had contributed to the IDA an equivalent of $51 million. As agreed between the Swiss Confederation and the IDA, these grant contributions were converted to an IDA subscription. Further, during the commitment periods between the fourth and the ninth replenishments of the IDA resources, Switzerland had cofinanced projects by making available to the IDA borrowers untied grants in the aggregate amount of Swiss francs 1,055 million (historical U.S. dollar amount of $580 million). On July 7, 1992, as agreed between the Swiss Confederation and the IDA, these grant contributions were converted to an IDA subscription and contribution when Switzerland contributed a further $68 million, representing the present value of future reflows of the cofinancing grants if they had been made through the IDA on the IDA's repayment terms. At June 30, 1995, $512 million ($512 million—June 30, 1994), representing the difference between the total cofinancing grants of $580 million and the present value of future reflows of $68 million, have not been included in the Member Subscriptions and Contributions in the Statements of Sources and Applications of Development Resources.

Contributions to Special Fund: Member contributions to the Special Fund totaling $596 million at June 30, 1995 ($596 million—June 30, 1994) are reflected as Member Subscriptions and Contributions in the Statements of Sources and Applications of Development Resources. At June 30, 1995 the Special Fund total is reflected net of $386 million ($389 million—June 30, 1994), which represents development credit disbursements that are repayable to and included in Member Subscriptions and Contributions to the IDA. Further, $7 million (nil—June 30, 1994), representing repayments from development credits financed by the Special Fund, have been deducted from the Special Fund total and included in the Member Subscriptions and Contributions to the IDA.

NOTE D—TRANSFERS FROM THE IBRD

IDA: The IBRD's Board of Governors has approved aggregate transfers to the IDA totaling $4,273 million through June 30, 1994. Of the total amount, $80 million has been disbursed for grants for agricultural research, the control of onchocerciasis, and other developmental activities. On October 6, 1994 the IBRD's Board of Governors approved a further transfer of $300 million in an equivalent amount in SDRs to the IDA by way of a grant.

NOTE E—DEVELOPMENT CREDITS

IDA: At June 30, 1995 no development credits payable to the IDA other than those referred to in the following paragraphs were overdue by more than three months.

At June 30, 1995 the development credits made to or guaranteed by certain member countries with an aggregate principal balance outstanding of $3,376 million ($3,533 million—June 30, 1994), of which $65 million ($42 million—June 30, 1994) was overdue, were in nonaccrual status. As of such date, overdue charges in respect of these development credits totaled $66 million ($46 million—June 30, 1994). If these development credits had not been in nonaccrual status, income from development credits for the fiscal year ended June 30, 1995 would have been higher by $24 million ($31 million—June 30, 1994), which is net of charges received from such members during the year. A summary of member countries with credits or guarantees in nonaccrual status follows:

In millions

| Borrower | June 30, 1995 | | |
	Principal outstanding	Principal and charges overdue	Nonaccrual since
Afghanistan	$ 75	$ 5	June 1992
Liberia	112	13	April 1988
Somalia	448	27	July 1991
Sudan	1,318	39	January 1994
Syrian Arab Republic	44	9	April 1988
Zaire	1,379	38	November 1993
Total	$3,376	$131	

During the fiscal year ended June 30, 1995 Haiti and Rwanda paid off all their arrears, and therefore credits to them came out of nonaccrual status. As a result, income from development credits for the fiscal year ended June 30, 1995 increased by $7 million corresponding to income that would have been accrued in previous fiscal years. For the fiscal year ended June 30, 1994, the increase in income from development credits due to developing credits to countries coming out of nonaccrual status was $2 million.

Under a program established in September 1988, a portion of principal repayments to the IDA is allocated on an annual basis to provide supplementary IDA credits to IDA-eligible countries that are no longer able to borrow on IBRD terms but have outstanding IBRD loans approved prior to September 1988. Such supplementary IDA credits are allocated to countries that meet specified conditions, in proportion to each country's interest payments due that year on its pre-September 1988 IBRD loans. To be eligible for such supplemental credits from the IDA, a member country must meet the IDA's eligibility criteria for lending, must be ineligible for IBRD lending, and must not have had an IBRD loan approved within the last twelve months. To receive a supplemental credit from the program, a member country must be no more than sixty days overdue on its debt-service payments to the IBRD and the IDA and must have an IDA-supported structural adjustment program in place.

A summary of cumulative IDA credits committed and disbursed under this program from inception as at June 30, 1995 and June 30, 1994 is given below:

In millions

	1995	1994
Commitments	$1,179	$974
Less: Undisbursed	51	128
Disbursed and outstanding	$1,128	$846

Special Fund: Special Fund development credits disbursed and outstanding of $492 million at June 30, 1995 ($457 million—June 30, 1994) are included in the Statements of Sources and Applications of Development Resources of the IDA, since principal repayments on these development credits will become part of the general resources of the IDA.

NOTE F—DISCLOSURES ABOUT FAIR VALUE OF FINANCIAL INSTRUMENTS

Investments: Since the IDA carries its investments at market value, the carrying amount represents the fair value of the portfolio. These fair values are based on quoted market prices where available. If quoted market prices are not available, fair values are based on quoted market prices of comparable instruments. The fair value of short-term financial instruments approximates their carrying value.

Development Credits: The IDA development credits have a significant grant element because of the concessional nature of the IDA's terms. Discounting the IDA's credits using the standard 10 percent discount rate of the Development Assistance Committee (DAC) of the Organization for Economic Cooperation and Development provides an estimate for the grant element of the IDA credits. Using the 10 percent DAC discount rate indicates that the typical IDA credit contains a grant element of 75 percent to 80 percent of the nominal credit amount at the time the credit is committed.

This grant element calculation considers interest rates, maturity structures, and grace periods for the credits. It does not consider credit risk, portfolio seasoning, multilateral and sovereign credit preferences, and other risks or indicators that would be relevant in calculating face value. Estimating the impact of these factors is not practicable. However, the face value of Total Development Credits is substantially lower than the $98,285 million reflected on the Statements of Sources and Applications of Development Resources.

NOTE G—INCOME AND EXPENSES

IDA: The IDA pays a management fee to the IBRD representing its share of the administrative expenses incurred by the IBRD. In February 1995 the Executive Directors approved the expenditure of $153 million for costs associated with planned staff reductions. At June 30, 1995 the revised estimate for the total cost of this plan was $131 million. The reductions, to meet changing client demands, are designed to improve the IBRD's and the IDA's efficiency while maintaining current operating levels. The planned staff reductions are expected to lower future years' administrative expenses by an amount greater than the associated cost. The IDA's share of the $131 million in costs associated with the planned staff reductions is $53 million and has been included in the Management Fee charged by the IBRD for the fiscal year ended June 30, 1995.

Special Fund: The service and commitment charges payable by borrowers under Special Fund development credits are paid directly to the IDA to compensate it for services as administrator of the Special Fund. Income from investments of the Special Fund becomes part of the resources of the Special Fund.

NOTE H—TRUST FUNDS

The IDA, alone or jointly with the IBRD, administers on behalf of donors, including members, their agencies, and other entities, funds restricted for specific uses, which include the cofinancing of IDA lending projects, debt reduction operations for IDA members, technical assistance for borrowers including feasibility studies and project preparation, global and regional programs, and research and training programs. These funds are placed in trust and are not included in the development resources of the IDA. The distribution of trust fund assets by executing agent is as follows:

	1995		1994	
	Total fiduciary assets (in millions)	Number of trust fund accounts	Total fiduciary assets (in millions)	Number of trust fund accounts
IDA Executed	$263	445	$186	448
Recipient Executed	404	280	293	262
Total	$667	725	$479	710

The responsibilities of the IDA under these arrangements vary and range from services normally provided under its own lending projects to full project implementation including procurement of goods and services. The IDA receives fees for administering trust funds as a reduction of the Management Fee charged by the IBRD. During the fiscal year 1995, the IDA received $12 million ($11 million—June 30, 1994) as fees for administering trust funds.

REPORT OF INDEPENDENT ACCOUNTANTS ON SPECIAL PURPOSE FINANCIAL STATEMENTS

Price Waterhouse (International Firm)	The Hague	New York
	Beijing	Tokyo
	Hong Kong	Washington
	London	

Price Waterhouse

July 26, 1995

President and Board of Governors
 International Development Association and the
 Special Fund Administered by the International Development Association

We have audited the special purpose Statements of Sources and Applications of Development Resources as of June 30, 1995 and 1994, the Summary Statement of Development Credits and the Statement of Voting Power, and Subscriptions and Contributions as of June 30, 1995, and the related special purpose Statements of Changes in Accumulated Surplus and of Cash Flows for the years ended June 30, 1995 and 1994, expressed in terms of United States dollars, of the International Development Association (IDA) and of the Special Fund Administered by the International Development Association, which appear on pages 168 through 187 of this Report. These financial statements are the responsibility of management. Our responsibility is to express an opinion on these financial statements based on our audits.

We conducted our audits in accordance with generally accepted auditing standards, including International Standards on Auditing. Those standards require that we plan and perform the audit to obtain reasonable assurance about whether the financial statements are free of material misstatement. An audit includes examining, on a test basis, evidence supporting the amounts and disclosures in the financial statements. An audit also includes assessing the accounting principles used and significant estimates made by management, as well as evaluating the overall financial statement presentation. We believe that our audits provide a reasonable basis for our opinion.

The special purpose financial statements were prepared to reflect the sources and applications of development resources and the development credits, voting power, and subscriptions and contributions of IDA and the Special Fund Administered by IDA to comply with Article VI, Section 11(a) of the Articles of Agreement of IDA as described in Note A, and are not intended to be a presentation in conformity with generally accepted accounting principles in the United States or with International Accounting Standards.

In our opinion, the special purpose financial statements referred to above present fairly, in all material respects, in terms of United States dollars, the sources and applications of development resources as of June 30, 1995 and 1994, the development credits, voting power, and subscriptions and contributions of IDA and the Special Fund Administered by IDA at June 30, 1995 and the changes in their accumulated surplus and their cash flows for the years ended June 30, 1995 and 1994, on the basis of accounting described in Note A.

This report is intended solely for the information of the Board of Governors, management and members of IDA. However, under IDA's Articles of Agreement, this report is a matter of public record and its distribution is not limited.

Price Waterhouse
(International Firm)

Member	Governor	Alternate
Afghanistan	Abdul Karim Khalili	Mohammad Ehsan
Albania	Dylber Vrioni	Gjergj Konda
Algeria	Ahmed Benbitour	(vacant)
Angola	José Pedro de Morais	Antonio Gomes Furtado
Antigua and Barbuda †	Molwyn Joseph	Ludolph Brown
Argentina	Domingo Felipe Cavallo	Roque Benjamin Fernandez
Armenia	Hrant A. Bagratian	Armen Yeghiazarian
Australia	Ralph Willis	Gordon Bilney
Austria	Andreas Staribacher	Hans Dietmar Schweisgut
Azerbaijan	Elman Rustamov	Vagif K. Akhmedov
Bahamas, The †	Hubert A. Ingraham	Ruth Millar
Bahrain †	Ibrahim Abdul Karim	Rasheed M. Al-Maraj
Bangladesh	M. Saifur Rahman	Muhammad Lutfullahil Majid
Barbados †	Owen S. Arthur	George Reid
Belarus †	Nikolai Filippovich Rumas	Nikolai K. Lisai
Belgium	Philippe Maystadt	Alfons Verplaetse
Belize	Manuel Esquivel	Yvonne S. Hyde
Benin	Robert Tagnon	Rigobert Ladikpo
Bhutan	Dorji Tshering	Yeshey Zimba
Bolivia	Fernando Alvaro Cossio	Gabriela Candia de Mercado
Botswana	Festus G. Mogae	O.K. Matambo
Brazil	Pedro Sampaio Malan	Gustavo J. Laboissiere Loyola
Bulgaria †	Dimitar Kostov	Mileti Mladenov
Burkina Faso	Zephirin Diabre	T. Celestin Tiendrebeogo
Burundi	Toyi Salvator	Nestor Ntungwanayo
Cambodia	Keat Chhon	Sun Chan Thol
Cameroon	Justin Ndioro	Esther Dang Belibi
Canada	Paul Martin	Huguette Labelle
Cape Verde	Antonio Gualberto do Rosario	Alexandre Vieira Fontes
Central African Republic	Dogo Nendje Bhe	Emmanuel Dokouna
Chad	Mariam Mahamat Nour	Hassan Adoum Bakhit
Chile	Eduardo Aninat	José Pablo Arellano
China	Liu Zhongli	Jin Renqing
Colombia	Guillermo Perry	José Antonio Ocampo
Comoros	Said Youssouf Mondoha	Chabane Abdallah Halifa
Congo	Clement Mouamba	Antoine Banvidi
Costa Rica	Fernando Herrero Acosta	Rodrigo Bolanos Zamora
Côte d'Ivoire	N'Goran Niamien	Konan Victor Kouame
Croatia	Bozo Prka	Josip Kulisic
Cyprus	Christodoulos Christodoulou	Antonis Malaos

Member	Governor	Alternate
Czech Republic	Ivan Kocarnik	Jan Vit
Denmark	Poul Nielson	Ole Loensmann Poulsen
Djibouti	Mohamed Ali Mohamed	Hawa Ahmed
Dominica	Mary Eugenia Charles	Gilbert Williams
Dominican Republic	Hector Valdez Albizu	Luis Manuel Piantini
Ecuador	Mauricio Pinto Mancheno	Marcela Proano de Cartagena
Egypt	Kamal Ahmed El Ganzoury	Yousef Boutros Ghali
El Salvador	Ramon Gonzalez Giner	José Roberto Orellana Milla
Equatorial Guinea	Manuel-Enrique King Somo	Felipe Hinestrosa Ikaka
Eritrea	Haile Woldense	Gebreselassie Yosief
Estonia †	Mart Opmann	Enn Pant
Ethiopia	Alemayehu Daba	Abdulmejid Hussein
Fiji	Berenado Vunibobo	Rigamoto Taito
Finland	Iiro Viinanen	Mauri Eggert
France	Jean-Claude Trichet	Christian Noyer
Gabon	Pierre-Claver Maganga Moussavou	Richard Onouviet
Gambia, The	Bala Garba Jahumpa	Alieu M. N'gum
Georgia	David Iakobidze	Tengiz Geleishvili
Germany	Carl-Dieter Spranger	Juergen Stark
Ghana	Kwesi Botchwey	Kwesi Amissah-Arthur
Greece	Yannos Papantoniou	George Romeos
Grenada	George I. Brizan	Nolan K. Murray
Guatemala	Ana Ordonez de Molina	Willy W. Zapata Sagastume
Guinea	Michel Kamano	Kerfalla Yansane
Guinea-Bissau	Rui Dia de Sousa	Francisco Correia, Jr.
Guyana	Bharrat Jagdeo	Michael Sheer Chan
Haiti	Marie Michele Rey	Jean-Marie Cherestal
Honduras	Guillermo Bueso	Juan Ferrera
Hungary	Lajos Bokros	Almos Kovacs
Iceland	Finnur Ingolfsson	Fridrik Sophusson
India	Manmohan Singh	Montek Singh Ahluwalia
Indonesia	Mar'ie Muhammad	Boediono
Iran, Islamic Rep. of	Morteza Mohammad-Khan	Mehdi Navab Motlagh
Iraq	Issam Rashid Hwaish	Hashim Ali Obaid
Ireland	Ruairi Quinn	Paddy Mullarkey
Israel	Jacob A. Frenkel	David Brodet
Italy	Antonio Fazio	Mario Draghi
Jamaica †	Omar Davies	Wesley Hughes
Japan	Masayoshi Takemura	Yasuo Matsushita
Jordan	Rima Khalaf Hunaidi	Mohamed Smadi

Member	Governor	Alternate
Kazakhstan	Alexander S. Pavlov	Altai A. Tleuberdin
Kenya	W. Musalia Mudavadi	Benjamin Kipkoech Kipkulei
Kiribati	Beniamina Tinga	Bureti Williams
Korea, Republic of	Jae-Hyong Hong	Myung-Ho Kim
Kuwait	Nasser Abdullah Al-Roudhan	Bader Meshari Al-Humaidhi
Kyrgyz Republic	Kemelbek Nanaev	Askar I. Sarygulov
Lao People's Democratic Republic	Khamxay Souphanouvong	Pany Yathotou
Latvia	Indra Samite	Janis Zvanitajs
Lebanon	Fuad A.B. Siniora	El-Fadl Chalak
Lesotho	M. P. Senaoana	E. M. Matekane
Liberia	Amelia A. Ward	Wilson K. Tarpeh
Libya	Mohamed A. Bait El Mal	Bashir Ali Khallat
Lithuania †	Reijoldijus Sarkinas	Aleksandras Vasilauskas
Luxembourg	Marc Fischbach	Yves Mersch
Macedonia, former Yugoslav Republic of	Jane Miljovski	Hari Kostov
Madagascar	Tovonanahary Rabetsitonta	Bruno Betiana
Malawi	Aleke K. Banda	Charles D. Nthenda
Malaysia	Anwar Ibrahim	Clifford Francis Herbert
Maldives	Fathulla Jameel	Adam Maniku
Mali	Soumaila Cisse	Issaga Dembele
Malta †	John Dalli	Albert A. Attard
Marshall Islands	Ruben R. Zackhras	Michael Konelios
Mauritania	M. L. Ch'Bih Ould Cheikh Melainine	Mohamed Lemine Ould Deidah
Mauritius	Paramhamsa Nababsing	Dharam Dev Manraj
Mexico	Guillermo Ortiz	Jose Julian Sidaoui
Micronesia, Federated States of	Aloysius J. Tuuth	Asterio R. Takesy
Moldova	Valeriu Sergiu Kitsan	Dumitru Ursu
Mongolia	Demchigjavyn Molomzhamts	Erdeniin Byambajav
Morocco	Mohamed Kabbaj	Abdelfettah Benmansour
Mozambique	Adriano Afonso Maleiane	Samuel Canor Navele
Myanmar	Win Tin	Thein Aung Lwin
Namibia †	Saara Kuugongelwa	Godfrey Gaoseb
Nepal	Bharat Mohan Adhikari	R.B. Bhattarai
Netherlands	Gerrit Zalm	J. P. Pronk
New Zealand	Murray Horn	John Whitehead
Nicaragua	Emilio Pereira Alegria	José Evenor Taboada Arana
Niger	Almoustapha Soumaila	Boubacar Moumouni Saidou
Nigeria	Anthony A. Ani	Gidado Idris
Norway	Sigbjoern Johnsen	Kari Nordheim-Larsen
Oman	Qais Abdul-Munim Al-Zawawi	Mohammed Bin Musa Al Yousef

Member	Governor	Alternate
Pakistan	V. A. Jafarey	Aftab Ahmad Khan
Panama	Guillermo O. Chapman, Jr.	Olmedo Miranda, Jr.
Papua New Guinea	Christopher Haiveta	Gerea Aopi
Paraguay	Orlando Bareiro Aguilera	Hermes Gomez Ginard
Peru	Jorge Camet Dickmann	Alfredo Jalilie Awapara
Philippines	Roberto F. de Ocampo	Gabriel C. Singson
Poland	Hanna Gronkiewicz-Waltz	Witold Kozinski
Portugal	Eduardo de Almeida Catroga	Walter Marques
Qatar †	Mohammed bin Khalifa Al-Thani	Abdullah Khalid Al-Attiyah
Romania †	Florin Georgescu	Vladimir Soare
Russian Federation	Anatoli Chubais	Yevgeni Yasin
Rwanda	Marc Rugenera	Pierre Claver Gashumba
St. Kitts and Nevis	Kennedy A. Simmonds	William V. Herbert
St. Lucia	John G. M. Compton	Zenith James
St. Vincent and the Grenadines	James F. Mitchell	Dwight Venner
São Tomé and Principe	Carlos Quaresma Baptista de Sousa	Adelino Castelo David
Saudi Arabia	Mohammad Abalkhail	Hamad Al-Sayari
Senegal	Papa Ousmane Sakho	Awa Thiongane
Seychelles †	Danielle de St. Jorre	Emmanuel Faure
Sierra Leone	John A. Karimu	Samura Kamara
Singapore †	Richard Hu Tsu Tau	Ngiam Tong Dow
Slovak Republic	Sergej Kozlik	Vladimir Masar
Slovenia	Mitja Gaspari	Bozo Jasovic
Solomon Islands	Christopher Columbus Abe	Manasseh Sogavare
Somalia	(vacant)	(vacant)
South Africa	Christo Ferro Liebenberg	Christian Lodewyk Stals
Spain	Pedro Solbes Mira	Alfredo Pastor Bodner
Sri Lanka	Chandrika Bandaranaika Kamaratunga	A. S. Jayawardena
Sudan	Abd Alla Hassan Ahmed	Mohamed Khair El Zubair
Suriname †	Humphrey S. Hildenberg	Stanley B. Ramsaran
Swaziland	Themba N. Masuku	Musa D. Fakudze
Sweden	Goran Persson	Pierre Schori
Switzerland	Jean-Pascal Delamuraz	Flavio Cotti
Syrian Arab Republic	Mohammed Khaled Al-Mahayni	Adnan Al-Satti
Tajikistan	Murotali M. Alimardanov	Sharif M. Rakhimov
Tanzania	Horace Kolimba	Peter J. Ngumbullu
Thailand	Tarrin Nimmanahaeminda	Aran Thammano
Togo	Yandja Yentchabre	Kwassi Klutse
Tonga	Kinikinilau Tutoatasi Fakafanua	'Aisake V. Eke
Trinidad and Tobago	Wendell Mottley	T. Ainsworth Harewood

Member	Governor	Alternate
Tunisia	Mohamed Ghannouchi	Taoufik Baccar
Turkey	Ayfer Yilmaz	Bulent Ozgun
Turkmenistan †	Hudaiberdy A. Orazov	Annadurdy Khadjiev
Uganda	Jehoash Mayanja-Nkangi	Emmanuel T. Mutebile
Ukraine †	Ihor Mitiukov	Olexander Vesselovsky
United Arab Emirates	Hamdan bin Rashid Al-Maktoum	Ahmed Humaid Al-Tayer
United Kingdom	Kenneth Clarke	Baroness Chalker of Wallasey
United States	Robert E. Rubin	Joan E. Spero
Uruguay †	Luis Mosca	Ariel Davrieux
Uzbekistan	Bakhtiyar S. Hamidov	Vyacheslav A. Golyshev
Vanuatu	Willie Jimmy	Antoine Pikoune
Venezuela †	Luis Raul Matos Azocar	Edgar Humberto Paredes Pisani
Viet Nam	Cao Sy Kiem	Le Van Chau
Western Samoa	Tuilaepa S. Malielegaoi	Epa Tuioti
Yemen, Republic of	Abdul Kader Bajamal	Anwar Rizq Al-Harazi
Zaire	Pay-Pay W. S. Pierre	Kakese Mulume-Nda-Mumi
Zambia	Ronald Damson Siame Penza	James M. Mtonga
Zimbabwe	A. M. Chambati	Leonard Ladislas Tsumba

† Not a member of IDA

EXECUTIVE DIRECTORS AND ALTERNATES OF THE WORLD BANK AND THEIR VOTING POWER

June 30, 1995

Executive director	Alternate	Casting votes of	IBRD		IDA	
			Total votes	% of total	Total votes	% of total
Appointed						
Jan Piercy	Michael Marek	United States	255,840	17.18	1,563,036	15.41
Atsuo Nishihara	Rintaro Tamaki	Japan	94,020	6.31	1,071,214	10.56
Fritz Fischer	(vacant)[b]	Germany	72,649	4.88	702,871	6.93
Marc-Antoine Autheman	Arnaud Chneiweiss	France	69,647	4.68	420,934	4.15
Huw Evans	David Stanton	United Kingdom	69,647	4.68	518,046	5.11
Elected						
Walter Rill (Austria)	Philippe Peeters (Belgium)	Austria, Belarus,[a] Belgium, Czech Republic, Hungary, Kazakhstan, Luxembourg, Slovak Republic, Slovenia, Turkey	75,410	5.06	439,996	4.34
Eveline Herfkens (Netherlands)	Sergiy Kulyk (Ukraine)	Armenia, Bulgaria,[a] Croatia, Cyprus, Georgia, Israel, Macedonia (former Yugoslav Republic of), Moldova, Netherlands, Romania,[a] Ukraine[a]	71,409	4.79	337,822	3.33
Leonard Good (Canada)	Winston Cox (Barbados)	Antigua and Barbuda,[a] The Bahamas,[a] Barbados,[a] Belize, Canada, Dominica, Grenada, Guyana, Ireland, Jamaica,[a] St. Kitts and Nevis, St. Lucia, St. Vincent and the Grenadines	61,989	4.16	422,394	4.16
Jorge Terrazas (Mexico)	Gabriel Castellanos[c] (Guatemala)	Costa Rica, El Salvador, Guatemala, Honduras, Mexico, Nicaragua, Panama, Spain, Venezuela[a]	59,017	3.96	223,664	2.21
Bimal Jalan (India)	Mushfiqur Rahman (Bangladesh)	Bangladesh, Bhutan, India, Sri Lanka	54,945	3.69	435,434	4.29
Enzo Grilli (Italy)	Helena Cordeiro (Portugal)	Albania, Greece, Italy, Malta,[a] Portugal	54,354	3.65	339,729	3.35
Abdul Karim Lodhi (Pakistan)	Kacim Brachemi (Algeria)	Afghanistan, Algeria, Ghana, Iran (Islamic Republic of), Morocco, Pakistan, Tunisia	50,875	3.42	220,397	2.17
Ruth Jacoby (Sweden)	Helga Jonsdottir[d] (Iceland)	Denmark, Estonia,[a] Finland, Iceland, Latvia, Lithuania,[a] Norway, Sweden	49,166	3.30	496,687	4.90
Marcos Caramuru de Paiva (Brazil)	Armando Montenegro (Colombia)	Brazil, Colombia, Dominican Republic, Ecuador, Haiti, Philippines, Suriname,[a] Trinidad and Tobago	46,593	3.13	285,334	2.81
Jean-Daniel Gerber (Switzerland)	Jan Sulmicki (Poland)	Azerbaijan, Kyrgyz Republic, Poland, Switzerland, Tajikistan Turkmenistan,[a] Uzbekistan	45,610	3.06	347,116	3.42

EXECUTIVE DIRECTORS AND ALTERNATES OF THE WORLD BANK AND THEIR VOTING POWER *(continued)*

June 30, 1995

Executive director	Alternate	Casting votes of	IBRD Total votes	IBRD % of total	IDA Total votes	IDA % of total
Zhang Shengman (China)	Zhu Guangyao (China)	China	45,049	3.02	205,683	2.03
Ibrahim A. Al-Assaf (Saudi Arabia)	Ibrahim M. Al-Mofleh (Saudi Arabia)	Saudi Arabia	45,045	3.02	353,707	3.49
Andrei Bugrov (Russian Federation)	Eugene Miagkov (Russian Federation)	Russian Federation	45,045	3.02	28,202	.28
Peter W. E. Nicholl (New Zealand)	Christopher Y. Legg (Australia)	Australia, Cambodia, Kiribati, Korea (Republic of), Marshall Islands, Micronesia (Federated States of), Mongolia, New Zealand, Papua New Guinea, Solomon Islands, Vanuatu, Western Samoa	45,024	3.02	289,308	2.85
Faisal A. Al-Khaled[e] (Kuwait)	Mohamed W. Hosny (Egypt)	Bahrain,[a] Egypt, Jordan, Kuwait, Lebanon, Libya, Maldives, Oman, Qatar,[a] Syrian Arab Republic, United Arab Emirates, Yemen (Republic of)	42,047	2.82	247,561	2.44
Harry M. Mapondo[f] (Malawi)	Joaquim R. Carvalho (Mozambique)	Angola, Botswana, Burundi, Eritrea, Ethiopia, The Gambia, Guinea, Kenya, Lesotho, Liberia, Malawi, Mozambique, Namibia,[a] Nigeria, Seychelles,[a] Sierra Leone, Sudan, Swaziland, Tanzania, Uganda, Zambia, Zimbabwe	38,566	2.59	430,645	4.25
Suwan Pasugswad (Thailand)	Khin Ohn Thant (Myanmar)	Fiji, Indonesia, Lao People's Democratic Republic, Malaysia, Myanmar, Nepal, Singapore,[a] Thailand, Tonga, Viet Nam	37,753	2.53	284,472	2.80
Julio Nogues (Argentina)	Carlos Steneri (Uruguay)	Argentina, Bolivia, Chile, Paraguay, Peru, Uruguay[a]	36,265	2.43	182,491	1.80
Ali Bourhane (Comoros)	Luc-Abdi Aden (Djibouti)	Benin, Burkina Faso, Cameroon, Cape Verde, Central African Republic, Chad, Comoros, Congo, Côte d'Ivoire, Djibouti, Equatorial Guinea, Gabon, Guinea-Bissau, Madagascar, Mali, Mauritania, Mauritius, Niger, Rwanda, São Tomé and Principe, Senegal, Togo, Zaire	23,537	1.58	295,362	2.91

In addition to the executive directors and alternates shown in the foregoing list, the following also served after October 31, 1994:

Executive director	End of period of service	Alternate director	End of period of service
John H. Cosgrove (Australia)	May 31, 1995	Alexander N. Doumnov (Russian Federation)	November 1, 1994
Yasuyuki Kawahara (Japan)	May 31, 1995	Ileana Ionescu (Romania)	May 31, 1995
		Harald Rehm (Germany)	May 31, 1995
		M. A. Syed (Bangladesh)	November 30, 1994
		Bong-Hee Won (Republic of Korea)	March 31, 1995

NOTE: *Iraq (3,058 votes in* IBRD *and 9,407 votes in* IDA*), Somalia (802 votes in* IBRD *and 10,506 votes in* IDA*), and South Africa (13,712 votes in* IBRD *and 30,089 votes in* IDA*) did not participate in the 1994 Regular Election of Executive Directors.*
a. Member of the IBRD *only.*
b. Erika Wagenhöfer (Germany) appointed effective July 1, 1995.
c. To be succeeded by Roberto Jimenez-Ortiz (El Salvador) effective July 1, 1995.
d. To be succeeded by Jorgen Varder (Denmark) effective August 1, 1995.
e. To be succeeded by Khaled Al-Saad (Kuwait) effective August 1, 1995.
f. To be succeeded by Leonard Mseka (Malawi) effective July 1, 1995.

Officers and Department Directors of The World Bank

June 30, 1995

President	James D. Wolfensohn
Managing Director	Richard H. Frank
Managing Director	Gautam S. Kaji
Managing Director	Sven Sandstrom
Vice President, Africa	Edward V. K. Jaycox
Vice President, Cofinancing and Financial Advisory Services	Hiroo Fukui
Vice President and Controller	Jules W. Muis
Vice President and Chief Economist, Development Economics	Michael P. Bruno
Vice President, East Asia and Pacific	Russell J. Cheetham
Vice President, Environmentally Sustainable Development	M. Ismail Serageldin
Vice President, Europe and Central Asia	Wilfried P. Thalwitz
Vice President, Finance and Private Sector Development	Jean-François Rischard
Vice President, Financial Policy and Resource Mobilization	Johannes F. Linn
Vice President, Human Resources Development and Operations Policy	Armeane M. Choksi
Vice President, Latin America and the Caribbean	S. Javed Burki
Senior Vice President and General Counsel	Ibrahim F. I. Shihata
Senior Vice President, Management and Personnel Services	S. Shahid Husain
Vice President, Middle East and North Africa	Caio K. Koch-Weser
Director-General, Operations Evaluation	Robert Picciotto
Vice President and Secretary	Timothy T. Thahane
Vice President, South Asia	D. Joseph Wood
Vice President and Treasurer	Jessica P. Einhorn

External Affairs

Director, External Affairs Department	Mark Malloch Brown

Legal

Deputy General Counsel, Administration, Finance, and Institutional Affairs	Daoud L. Khairallah
Deputy General Counsel, Operations	Andres Rigo Sureda
Assistant General Counsel, Administration and Institutional Affairs	Eva L. Meigher
Assistant General Counsel, Finance	Stephen A. Silard
Assistant General Counsel, Legal Reform and Advisory Services	Andrew N. Vorkink
Assistant General Counsel, Operations	Sherif Omar Hassan

Secretary's

Deputy Secretary, General Operations	Wadi D. Haddad (eff. 7/1)

Africa Regional Office

Director, Africa Regional Office	Stephen M. Denning
Director, Southern Africa Department: Angola, Botswana, Lesotho, Malawi, Mozambique, Namibia, South Africa, Swaziland, Zambia, Zimbabwe	Katherine Marshall
Director, Eastern Africa Department: Djibouti, Eritrea, Ethiopia, Kenya, Somalia, Sudan, Tanzania, Uganda	James W. Adams (eff. 7/1)
Director, Central Africa and Indian Ocean Department: Burundi, Cameroon, Central African Republic, Chad, Comoros, Congo, Equatorial Guinea, Gabon, Madagascar, Mauritius, Rwanda, Seychelles, Zaire	Andrew P. Rogerson
Director, West Central Africa Department: Benin, Burkina-Faso, Côte d'Ivoire, Ghana, Niger, Nigeria, Togo	Olivier Lafourcade
Director, Western Africa Department: Cape Verde, The Gambia, Guinea, Guinea-Bissau, Liberia, Mali, Mauritania, São Tomé and Principe, Senegal, Sierra Leone	Jean-Louis Sarbib
Director, Africa Technical Department	Kevin M. Cleaver

Asia Technical Department
Director   Harold W. Messenger

East Asia and Pacific Regional Office
Director, Country Department I: Cambodia, Republic of Korea, Lao PDR,   Callisto E. Madavo
    Malaysia, Mekong Committee, Myanmar, Philippines, Thailand, Viet Nam
Director, Country Department II: China, Mongolia   Nicholas C. Hope
Director, Country Department III: Fiji, Indonesia, Kiribati,   Marianne Haug
    The Marshall Islands, Micronesia, Papua New Guinea,
    Solomon Islands, Tonga, Vanuatu, Western Samoa

South Asia Regional Office
Director, Country Department I: Afghanistan, Bangladesh, Maldives,   Paul Isenman
    Pakistan, Sri Lanka
Director, Country Department II: Bhutan, India, Nepal   Heinz Vergin

Europe and Central Asia, Middle East and
North Africa Regions Technical Department
Director   Anil Sood

Europe and Central Asia Regional Office
Director, Country Department I: Bulgaria, Cyprus, Macedonia (former Yugoslav   Rachel J. Lomax
    Republic of), Portugal, Romania, Turkey
Director, Country Department II: Albania, Bosnia-Herzegovina,   Kemal Dervis
    Croatia, Czech Republic, Hungary, Poland,
    Slovak Republic, Slovenia
Director, Country Department III: Azerbaijan, Kazakhstan,   Yukon Huang
    Kyrgyz Republic, Russian Federation, Tajikistan, Turkmenistan, Uzbekistan
Director, Country Department IV: Armenia, Belarus, Estonia, Georgia,   Basil G. Kavalsky
    Latvia, Lithuania, Moldova, Ukraine
Director, Resource Mobilization and Private Sector Development   Ghassan El-Rifai

Middle East and North Africa Regional Office
Director, Country Department I: Algeria, Islamic Republic of Iran,   Daniel Ritchie
    Libya, Malta, Morocco, Tunisia
Director, Country Department II: Bahrain, Egypt, Iraq, Jordan,   Inder K. Sud
    Kuwait, Lebanon, Oman, Qatar, Saudi Arabia, Syria,
    United Arab Emirates, Yemen Republic

Latin America and the Caribbean Regional Office
Director, Country Department I: Argentina, Brazil, Chile, Paraguay, Uruguay   Gobind T. Nankani
Director, Country Department II: Costa Rica, Dominican Republic, El Salvador, Edilberto L. Segura
    Guatemala, Haiti, Honduras, Mexico, Nicaragua, Panama, Venezuela
Director, Country Department III: The Bahamas, Barbados, Belize,   Yoshiaki Abe
    Bolivia, Caribbean Development Bank, Colombia, Ecuador, Guyana,
    Jamaica, OECS Member States, Peru, Suriname, Trinidad and Tobago
Director, Technical Department   M. G. Sri-Ram Aiyer

Cofinancing and Financial Advisory Services
Director   Ram Kumar Chopra

Development Economics

Director, Development Policy	Mark W. Baird
Director, Economic Development Institute	Vinod Thomas
Director, International Economics Department	Masood Ahmed
Director, Policy Research Department	Lyn Squire
Administrator, Research Advisory Staff	Gregory K. Ingram

Environmentally Sustainable Development

Director, Agriculture and Natural Resources Department	Alexander F. McCalla
Director, Environment Department	Andrew D. Steer
Director, Transportation, Water, and Urban Development Department	Anthony Pellegrini
Director, Agricultural Research Group	Michel J. Petit
Executive Secretary, Consultative Group on International Agricultural Research	Alexander von der Osten

Finance and Private Sector Development

Director, Financial Sector Development Department	Gary L. Perlin
Director, Industry and Energy Department	Richard D. Stern
Director, Private Sector Development Department	Magdi R. Iskander

Human Capital Development and Operations Policy

Director, Poverty and Social Policy Department	Ishrat Husain (eff. 7/1)
Director, Operations Policy Department	Myrna Alexander (eff. 7/1)
Director, Human Development Department	David de Ferranti
Director, Public Sector Management	Alberto de Capitani

Financial Policy and Resource Mobilization

Director, Resource Mobilization Department	Paula Donovan
Director, Risk Management and Financial Policy Department	Mieko Nishimizu

Treasurer's

Director, Cash Management Department	Walter Peyerl
Director, Financial Operations Department	Hans M. Rothenbuhler
Director, Investment Department	Veronique Lavorel
Director, Pension Department	Afsaneh Mashayekhi Beschloss
Director, Tokyo Office	Satoru Miyamura (eff. 7/1)

Controller's

Director, Accounting Department	Michael E. Ruddy
Auditor-General, Internal Auditing Department	J. Graham Joscelyne
Director, Loan Department	V. S. Raghavan
Director, Planning and Budgeting Department	Richard B. Lynn

Management and Personnel Services

Director, General Services Department	Pilar J. San Jose
Director, Headquarters Construction Department	Ernesto E. Henriod
Director, Health Services Department	Bernhard H. Liese
Director, Organization and Business Practices Department	Ian A. Scott
Director, Personnel Management Department	Peter Karp
Director, Personnel Services and Compensation Department	Everardo C. Wessels

Operations Evaluation

Director, Operations Evaluation Department	Francisco Aguirre-Sacasa

Headquarters: 1818 H Street, N.W., Washington, D.C. 20433, U.S.A.

New York Office: The World Bank Mission to the United Nations/New York Office, 809 United Nations Plaza, Suite 900, New York, N.Y. 10017, U.S.A.

European Office: The World Bank, 66, avenue d'Iéna, 75116 Paris, France

London: The World Bank, New Zealand House, 15th Floor, Haymarket, London, SW1 Y4TE, England

Tokyo Office: The World Bank, Kokusai Building (Room 916), 1-1, Marunouchi 3-chome, Chiyoda-ku, Tokyo 100, Japan

Regional Mission in Eastern Africa: The World Bank, Hill Park Building, Upper Hill, Nairobi, Kenya
(mailing address: P.O. Box 30577)

Regional Mission in Western Africa: The World Bank, Corner of Booker Washington and Jacques AKA Streets, Cocody, Abidjan 01, Côte d'Ivoire
(mailing address: B. P. 1850)

Regional Mission in Thailand: The World Bank, 14th Floor, Diethelm, Tower A, 93/1 Wireless Road, Bangkok 10330, Thailand

Regional Mission in Latvia: The World Bank, Kalku Street, 15, Riga, Latvia 1050

Baltics Regional Mission Satellite in Estonia: The World Bank/Maailmapank, Kohtu 8, Tallinn EE0001, Estonia

Baltics Regional Mission Satelite in Lithuania: The World Bank, Vilniaus Str. 28, 2600 Vilnius, Lithuania

Albania: The World Bank, Deshmoret e 4 Shkurtit, No. 34, Tirana, Albania

Angola: Banco Mundial, Rua Alfredo Troni (Edifício BPC), 14° Andar, CP 1331, Luanda, Angola

Argentina: Banco Mundial, Avenida Leandro N. Alem 628-30, Piso 12, Buenos Aires, Argentina

Armenia: The World Bank, Republic Square, 2 Khorhertarani Street, Yerevan 10, Armenia

Bangladesh: The World Bank, 3A Paribagh, Dhaka 1000, Bangladesh
(mailing address: G.P.O. 97)

Belarus: The World Bank, 6A Partizansky Avenue, 5th Floor, Minsk 220033, Republic of Belarus

Benin: The World Bank, Zone Résidentielle de la Radio, Cotonou, Benin
(mailing address: B. P. 03-2112)

Bolivia: Banco Mundial, Edificio BISA, Piso 9, 16 de Julio 1628, La Paz, Bolivia
(mailing address: Casilla 8692)

Brazil: Banco Mundial , Setor Comercial Sul, Quadra 1, Bloco H, Edifício Morro Vermelho—8 Andar, Brasilia, DF 70399-900, Brazil

Brazil: Banco Mundial, Avenida Isaac Povoas, No. 1251, Edificio Nacional Palacios, Sala 603, Centro, 78.045–640 Cuiaba, Mato Grosso (MT), Brazil

Brazil: Banco Mundial, S/127, Edifício SUDENE, Cidade Universitária, 50670-900 Recife PE, Brazil

Bulgaria: The World Bank, World Trade Center–Sofia, 36 Dragan Tsankov Boulevard, Sofia, Bulgaria

Burkina Faso: The World Bank, Immeuble BICIA (3ème étage), Ouagadougou, Burkina Faso
(mailing address: B. P. 622)

Burundi: The World Bank, Avenue du 18 Septembre, Bujumbura, Burundi
(mailing address: B. P. 2637)

Cameroon: The World Bank, New Bastos, P. O. Box 1128, Yaoundé, Cameroon
(mailing address: B. P. 1128)

Central African Republic: Banque Mondiale, Rue des Missions, Bangui, C.A.R.

Chad: The World Bank, P.O. Box 146, N'djamena, Chad

China: The World Bank, No. 2 Fu Cheng Lu, Diaoyutai, State Guest House, Building No. 5, Beijing 100830, China
(mailing address: P.O. Box 802)

Colombia: Banco Mundial, Diagonal 35 No. 5-98, Bogotá, D.E., Colombia
(mailing address: Apartado Aéreo l0229)

Congo: Banque Mondiale, Immeuble Arc (5ème étage), Avenue Amilcar Cabral, Brazzaville, Congo
(mailing address: B. P. 14536)

Costa Rica: Regional Implementation Mission—Banco Mundial, Boulevard Rohrmoser, 150 mts. oeste Residencia ex-Presidente Oscar Arias, San José, Cosa Rica
(mailing address: P.O. Box No. 11925-1000)

Ecuador: Banco Mundial, Calle Juan Leon Mera 130 y Ave. Patria, Edificio Corporación Financiera Nacional, 6to Piso, Quito, Ecuador

Egypt: The World Bank, World Trade Center, 1191 Corniche El-Nil, 15th Floor, Cairo, Egypt

Ethiopia: The World Bank, Africa Avenue, Bole, Addis Ababa, Ethiopia
(mailing address: P.O. Box 5515)

Ghana: The World Bank, 69 Eighth Avenue Extension, Northridge Residential Area, Accra, Ghana
(mailing address: P.O. Box M27)

Guinea: Banque Mondiale, Immeuble de l'Archevêche, Face Baie des Anges, Conakry, Guinea
(mailing address: B. P. 1420)

Hungary: The World Bank, Suba Trade Center, 4th Floor, Nagymezo Utca 44, Budapest 1065, Hungary

India: The World Bank, 70 Lodi Estate, New Delhi 110003, India
(mailing address: P.O. Box 416, New Delhi 110001)

Indonesia: The World Bank, Lippo Life Building, Suite 301, J1. H. R. Rasuna Said, Kav. B-10, Kuningan, Jakarta 12940, Indonesia
(mailing address: P.O. Box 324/JKT)

Jamaica: The World Bank, Island Life Center, 6 St. Lucia Avenue, Suite 8–South, Kingston 5, Jamaica

Kazakhstan: The World Bank, Almaty Resident Mission, Samal-1, Bldg. No. 36, 3rd Floor, Almaty, Republic of Kazakhstan 480099

Kyrgyz Republic: The World Bank, Toktogula St. 98, Apt. 8, Bishkek, Kyrgyz Republic

Macedonia: World Bank Field Office, Kompleks Na Banki, B. Zgaada Na Bnt, IV Sprat, 91000 Skopje, former Yugoslav Republic of Macedonia

Madagascar: Banque Mondiale, 1 Rue Patrice Lumumba, Antananarivo 101, Madagascar (mailing address: B. P. 4140)

Malawi: The World Bank, Development House, Capital City, Lilongwe 3, Malawi (mailing address: P.O. Box 30557)

Mali: Banque Mondiale, Immeuble SOGEFIH, Quartier du Fleuve, Bamako, Mali (mailing address: B. P. 1864)

Mauritania: The World Bank, Villa No. 30, Ilot A, Quartier Socogim, Nouakchott, Mauritania (mailing address: B. P. 667)

Mexico: Banco Mundial, Plaza Nafin, Insurgentes Sur 1971, Nivel Paseo, Locales 71 y 72, Col. Guadalupe Inn, 01020 México, D.F.

Moldova: World Bank Field Office, Piata Marii Adunari Nationale 1, 277033 Chisinau, Moldova

Mozambique: The World Bank, Ave. Kenneth Kaunda, 1224, 2-Andar, Maputo, Mozambique (mailing address: Caixa Postal 4053)

Nepal: The World Bank, Lal & Yeti Hotel, Lat Dunbar, Kathmandu, Nepal (mailing address: P.O. Box 798)

Niger: Banque Mondiale, Rue des Dallols, Niamey, Niger (mailing address: B. P. 12402)

Nigeria: The World Bank, 1st Floor, Plot PC-10, Engineering Close, off Idowu Taylor Street, Victoria Island, Lagos, Nigeria (mailing address: P.O. Box 127)

Pakistan: The World Bank, 20 A , Shanhrah-e-Jamhuriat, Ramna 5 G-5/1 Islamabad, Pakistan (mailing address: P.O. Box 1025)

Peru: The World Bank, Avenida Pardo y Aliaga 640, Piso 16, San Isidro, Lima, Peru

Philippines: The World Bank, Central Bank of the Philippines, Multi-Storey Building, Room 200, Roxas Boulevard, Manila, Philippines

Poland: The World Bank, INTRACO I Building, 17th Floor, 2 Stawki Street, 00-193 Warsaw, Poland

Romania: The World Bank, Boulevard Dacia 83, Sector 2, Bucharest, Romania

Russia: World Bank Regional Office, Sadovo-Kudrinskaya No. 3, Moscow 123242, Russian Federation

Rwanda: The World Bank, Blvd. de la Révolution, SORAS Building, Kigali, Rwanda (mailing address: P.O. Box 609)

Saudi Arabia: The World Bank Resident Mission, UNDP Building, King Faisal Street, Riyadh, Saudi Arabia 11432
(mailing address: P.O. Box 5900)

Senegal: The World Bank, Immeuble S.D.I.H., 3 Place de l'Indépendance, Dakar, Senegal
(mailing address: B. P. 3296)

South Africa: The World Bank, Grosvenor Gate, First Floor, Hyde Park Lane, Hyde Park 2196, Johannesburg, South Africa
(mailing address: P.O. Box 41283, Craig Hall 2024)

Sri Lanka: The World Bank, Development Finance Corporation of Ceylon, (DFCC) Building, 1st Floor, 73/5 Galle Road, Colombo 3, Sri Lanka
(mailing address: P.O. Box 1761)

Tanzania: The World Bank, N.I.C. Building (7th Floor, B), Dar-es-Salaam, Tanzania
(mailing address: P.O. Box 2054)

Togo: Banque Mondiale, 169 boulevard du 13 Janvier, Immeuble BTCI (8ème étage), Lomé, Togo
(mailing address: B. P. 3915)

Turkey: The World Bank, Ataturk Bulvari, No. 211, Gama-Guris Building Kat 6, 06683 Kavaklidere, Ankara, Turkey

Uganda: EADB Building, Nile Avenue, Kampala, Uganda
(mailing address: P.O. Box 4463)

Ukraine: The World Bank, 26, Shovkovychna St. (Ex. K Liebknecht St.), Suites Two and Three, Kiev 252024, Ukraine

Uzbekistan: 43, Academician Suleimanova St., Tashkent, Uzbekistan

Venezuela: Banco Mundial, Edificio Parque Cristal, Torre Oeste, Piso 15, Oficina 15-05, Avenida Francisco de Miranda, Los Palos Grandes, Caracas, Venezuela

Viet Nam: The World Bank, 53 Tran Phu Street, Hanoi, Viet Nam

West Bank and Gaza: The World Bank, Gaza City, Gaza

Yemen: The World Bank, 14 Djibouti St., Sana'a, Republic of Yemen
(mailing address: P.O. Box 18152)

Zaire: World Bank Liaison Office, c/o UNDP, P. O. Box 7248, Kinshasa, Zaire

Zambia: The World Bank, Red Cross House, 2nd Floor, Long Acres, Lusaka, Zambia,
(mailing address: P.O. Box 35410)

Zimbabwe: The World Bank, Finsure House, 5th Floor, 84-86 Union Avenue, Harare, Zimbabwe
(mailing address: P.O. Box 2960)

COUNTRY ELIGIBILITY FOR BORROWING FROM THE WORLD BANK

(as of June 30, 1995)

COUNTRIES ELIGIBLE FOR IBRD FUNDS ONLY

Income category and country	1994 GNP per capita (US$)[a]	Income category and country	1994 GNP per capita (US$)
Per capita income over $5,055		Belarus[b]	2,160
Argentina	8,060	Namibia	2,030
Slovenia	7,140	Russian Federation[b]	1,910
Seychelles	6,210	Peru	1,890
Antigua and Barbuda	n.a.	Tunisia	1,800
		Algeria	1,690
Per capita income $2,896–$5,055		Colombia	1,620
Uruguay	4,650	Paraguay	1,570
Mexico	4,010	Ukraine[b]	1,570
Hungary	3,840	El Salvador	1,480
Trinidad and Tobago	3,740	Jamaica	1,420
Chile	3,560	Iran, Islamic Republic of	n.a.
Gabon	3,550	Lebanon	n.a.
Malaysia	3,520	Marshall Islands	n.a.
Brazil	3,370	Micronesia	n.a.
Czech Republic	3,210		
Mauritius	3,180	**Per capita income $726–$1,395**	
South Africa	3,010	Jordan	1,390
St. Kitts and Nevis	n.a.	Lithuania[b]	1,350
		Dominican Republic	1,320
Per capita income $1,396–$2,895		Ecuador	1,310
Estonia[b]	2,820	Romania	1,230
Botswana	2,800	Guatemala	1,190
Venezuela	2,760	Bulgaria	1,160
Panama	2,670	Papua New Guinea	1,160
Belize	2,550	Morocco	1,150
Croatia	2,530	Kazakhstan[b]	1,110
Poland	2,470	Philippines	960
Turkey	2,450	Uzbekistan[b]	950
Costa Rica	2,380	Moldova[b]	870
Fiji	2,320	Suriname	870
Latvia[b]	2,290	Indonesia	790
Slovak Republic	2,230	Swaziland	n.a.
Thailand	2,210	Syrian Arab Republic	n.a.
		Turkmenistan[b]	n.a.

COUNTRIES ELIGBLE FOR A BLEND OF IBRD AND IDA FUNDS[c]

Income category and country	1994 GNP per capita (US$)[a]	Income category and country	1994 GNP per capita (US$)
Per capita income $2,896–$5,055		**Per capita income $725 or less**	
St. Lucia[d]	n.a.	Egypt	710
		Armenia[b]	670
Per capita income $1,396–$2,895		Kyrgyz Republic[b]	610
Dominica[d]	n.a.	China	530
Grenada[d]	n.a.	Azerbaijan[b]	500
St. Vincent and the Grenadines[d]	n.a.	Zimbabwe	490
		Pakistan	440
Per capita income $726–$1,395		India	310
Macedonia, FYR of	790	Nigeria	280
		Georgia[b]	n.a.

(as of June 30, 1995)

COUNTRIES ELIGIBLE FOR IDA FUNDS ONLY[c]

Income category and country	1994 GNP per capita (US$)[a]	Income category and country	1994 GNP per capita (US$)
Per capita income $1,396–$2,895		Nicaragua	330
Tonga[d]	n.a.	Lao People's Democratic Republic	320
		Togo	320
Per capita income $726–$1,395		Burkina Faso	300
Vanuatu[d]	1,150	Yemen, Republic of	280
Western Samoa[d]	970	Mali	250
Cape Verde	910	São Tomé and Principe	250
Maldives	900	Guinea-Bissau	240
Bolivia	770	Bangladesh	230
Angola	n.a.	Madagascar	230
Djibouti	n.a.	Niger	230
Kiribati	n.a.	Haiti	220
Solomon Islands	n.a.	Nepal	200
		Uganda	200
Per capita income $725 or less		Chad	190
Cameroon	680	Viet Nam	190
Congo	640	Burundi	150
Sri Lanka	640	Sierra Leone	150
Senegal	610	Malawi	140
Honduras	580	Ethiopia	130
Guyana	530	Mozambique	80
Comoros	510	Afghanistan	n.a.
Côte d'Ivoire	510	Bhutan	n.a.
Guinea	510	Cambodia	n.a.
Mauritania	480	Eritrea	n.a.
Equatorial Guinea	430	Kenya	n.a.
Ghana	430	Lesotho	n.a.
Benin	370	Liberia	n.a.
Central African Republic	370	Myanmar	n.a.
Albania	360	Rwanda	n.a.
Gambia, The	360	Somalia	n.a.
Tajikistan[b]	350	Sudan	n.a.
Zambia	350	Tanzania	n.a.
Mongolia	340	Zaire	n.a.

n.a. Not available.

a. World Bank Atlas *methodology; base period 1992–94; per capita* GNP *figures are in 1994 U.S. dollars.*

b. *Estimates for these countries are preliminary.*

c. *Countries are eligible for* IDA *on the basis of (a) relative poverty and (b) lack of creditworthiness. The operational cutoff for* IDA *eligibility for FY96 is a 1994* GNP *per capita of $865, using* Atlas *methodology (base period 1992–94). To receive* IDA *resources, countries also meet tests of performance. In exceptional circumstances,* IDA *extends eligibility temporarily to countries that are above the operational cutoff and are undertaking major adjustment efforts but are not creditworthy for* IBRD *lending. An exception has also been made for small island economies (see footnote d).*

d. *During the* IDA-10 *period (FY94–96), an exception to the* GNP *per capita operational cutoff for* IDA *eligibility ($865 for FY96) has been made for specific small island economies, which otherwise would have little or no access to Bank Group assistance because they lack creditworthiness. For such countries,* IDA *funding is considered case by case for the financing of projects and adjustment programs designed to strengthen creditworthiness.*

(millions of US dollars)

Term	Actual			1996 Program
	1993	1994	1995	
Expense Category				
Staff costs	771.2	851.8	874.8	862.2
Consultants	104.8	113.7	111.9	102.2
Contractual services/representation	42.9	66.3	62.9	57.8
Operational travel	122.0	129.8	127.5	121.9
Overhead	209.1	230.8	232.2	213.7
Direct contributions to Special Grants Program[a]	80.7	103.4	110.9	105.2
President's contingency[b]	—	—	—	13.7
Reimbursements	(95.3)	(107.3)	(111.2)	(99.6)
Allocation for pending benefit initiatives[c]	—	—	—	5.2
Total	1,235.6	1,388.4	1,409.0	1,382.2
Administrative Program[d]				
Regional	582.0	612.2	652.4[d]	635.6[d]
Financial	92.4	98.5	107.7	107.4
Development and advisory[e]	172.3	216.6	235.3	221.3
Administrative support	106.0	119.3	136.6	124.0
Corporate management, and legal services	40.6	45.1	55.6	52.8
Total	993.3	1,091.7	1,187.5	1,141.1
Overhead/benefits[f]	193.8	233.6[g]	143.3	133.4
President's contingency	—	—	—	13.7
Reimbursements	(95.3)	(107.3)	(111.2)	(99.6)
Net administrative programs	1,091.7	1,218.0	1,219.6	1,188.6
Special programs[h]	88.8	109.7	119.1	113.2
Boards	43.1	46.9	54.6	59.5
Operations evaluation	12.0	13.8	15.7	15.7
Allocation for pending benefit initiatives[c]	—	—	—	5.2
Total budget	1,235.6	1,388.4[i]	1,409.0	1,382.2

— Not applicable.

NOTE: Details may not add to totals because of rounding.

a. Includes Institutional Development Fund in FY93–95.

b. Allocations from president's contingency have been included in respective categories/programs for FY93–95.

c. Provisional allocations, subject to board approval of the policy initiatives.

d. FY95 expenses and FY96 budget include decentralized office occupancy costs.

e. Includes FAO Cooperative Program.

f. FY93–94 expenses include office occupancy costs of Bank units that were managed centrally. FY95 expenses and the FY96 budget exclude these costs, which now have been allocated to the units.

g. Includes $23 million in accrual for resettlement grants on termination due to accounting changes (Financial Accounting Standards–112).

h. Includes direct contributions to and administrative costs of the Special Programs.

i. Excludes $20 million for Somalia relief.

(millions of US dollars)

Borrowing countries[a]	Local procurement	Foreign procurement	Total amount	Percentage of total disbursements[b]
Algeria	51	†	52	0.29
Argentina	247	53	299	1.69
Bangladesh	114	9	123	0.69
Bolivia	48	1	49	0.27
Brazil	791	120	911	5.14
Burkina Faso	35	†	35	0.20
Chile	82	12	94	0.53
China	1,130	212	1,342	7.58
Colombia	319	18	338	1.91
Côte d'Ivoire	23	37	60	0.34
Cyprus	16	18	35	0.20
Ecuador	98	22	120	0.68
Egypt	51	12	63	0.36
Ghana	80	8	88	0.49
Guinea	20	21	40	0.23
Hungary	128	24	152	0.86
India	1,402	121	1,524	8.60
Indonesia	761	37	799	4.51
Jordan	28	3	31	0.18
Kazakhstan	29	24	53	0.30
Kenya	41	40	81	0.46
Korea, Republic of	105	266	371	2.09
Madagascar	32	†	32	0.18
Malaysia	132	23	154	0.87
Mexico	937	27	964	5.44
Morocco	182	2	184	1.04
Nigeria	159	48	207	1.17
Pakistan	302	5	308	1.74
Peru	39	3	43	0.24
Philippines	108	4	112	0.63
Poland	50	48	98	0.55
Romania	3	36	39	0.22
Russia	5	241	245	1.38
Senegal	26	10	36	0.20
South Africa	—	185	185	1.05
Sri Lanka	65	2	67	0.38
Tanzania	43	4	47	0.26
Thailand	55	23	78	0.44
Tunisia	107	4	111	0.63
Turkey	199	76	275	1.55
Turkmenistan	—	35	35	0.19
Uganda	50	†	50	0.28
Ukraine	†	49	49	0.28
Uruguay	22	23	44	0.25
Venezuela	9	28	37	0.21
Viet Nam	57	5	62	0.35
Others	463	217	679	3.83
Total	8,644	2,122	10,765	61.00

— Zero, † *less than $0.5 million*

NOTE: *Disbursements for debt reduction and net advance disbursements are excluded. Details may not add to totals because of rounding.*
a. *Based on the fiscal 1995–98 lending program as of June 30, 1995.*
b. *Refers to the share of all IBRD and IDA payments for fiscal 1995 (excluding disbursements for debt reduction), which totaled $17,720 million.*

(amounts in millions of US dollars)

Supplying country	IBRD cumulative to June 30, 1995		IBRD fiscal 1995		IDA cumulative to June 30, 1995		IDA fiscal 1995	
	Amount	%	Amount	%	Amount	%	Amount	%
Argentina	792	0.77	42	0.72	103	0.27	10	0.32
Australia	1,053	1.03	30	0.5	601	1.57	212	6.63
Austria	1,461	1.43	212	3.59	221	0.58	8	0.24
Azerbaijan	†	*	†	*	10	*	10	0.31
Bahamas, The	92	0.09	13	0.21	8	*	—	*
Bahrain	68	0.07	2	*	127	0.33	2	*
Bangladesh	15	*	2	*	46	0.12	7	0.23
Belarus	26	*	26	0.44	1	*	†	*
Belgium	1,501	1.47	66	1.13	980	2.57	45	1.4
Brazil	1,775	1.74	95	1.6	307	0.8	26	0.81
Bulgaria	28	*	15	0.25	11	*	3	0.1
Canada	2,327	2.28	123	2.09	682	1.79	48	1.49
Chile	368	0.36	11	0.18	31	0.08	1	*
China	1,266	1.24	76	1.29	1,012	2.65	136	4.26
Colombia	222	0.22	15	0.25	18	*	4	0.12
Costa Rica	37	*	6	0.11	20	0.05	9	0.29
Côte d'Ivoire	40	*	5	0.08	218	0.57	32	1.0
Cyprus	41	*	17	0.28	32	0.08	1	*
Czech Republic	49	*	15	0.25	5	*	1	*
Denmark	691	0.68	58	0.98	281	0.74	20	0.61
Ecuador	132	0.13	19	0.32	5	*	3	0.11
Equatorial Guinea	†	*	—	*	14	*	8	0.26
Finland	435	0.43	36	0.62	120	0.31	5	0.17
France	7,288	7.13	516	8.75	3,973	10.41	420	13.14
Germany	11,560	11.31	667	11.31	3,346	8.76	155	4.86
Ghana	10	*	†	*	14	*	8	0.24
Greece	197	0.19	15	0.26	69	0.18	5	0.16
Guatemala	19	*	2	*	18	*	6	0.19
Guinea	3	*	—	*	22	0.06	21	0.65
Hungary	276	0.27	21	0.36	25	0.07	2	0.06
India	359	0.35	32	0.55	713	1.87	89	2.79
Indonesia	149	0.15	5	0.08	104	0.27	33	1.03
Iran, Islamic Republic of	144	0.14	†	*	194	0.51	10	0.31
Iraq	459	0.45	—	*	30	0.08	—	*
Ireland	138	0.14	13	0.23	87	0.23	10	0.31
Israel	244	0.24	14	0.23	96	0.25	10	0.3
Italy	5,999	5.87	651	11.04	1,636	4.28	104	3.24
Japan	13,958	13.66	485	8.22	4,021	10.53	131	4.11
Jordan	49	*	†	*	131	0.34	3	0.08
Kazakhstan	17	*	17	0.29	7	*	7	0.22
Kenya	28	*	—	*	260	0.68	40	1.24
Korea, Republic of	1,512	1.48	171	2.91	699	1.83	95	2.96
Kuwait	257	0.25	5	0.08	240	0.63	36	1.12
Lao People's Democratic Republic	12	*	—	*	6	*	6	0.2
Lithuania	18	*	17	0.29	2	*	1	*
Malaysia	330	0.32	8	0.14	229	0.6	14	0.45
Mexico	517	0.51	24	0.41	97	0.25	3	0.1
Netherlands	1,963	1.92	119	2.02	1,054	2.76	158	4.95
New Zealand	163	0.16	13	0.22	99	0.26	10	0.31
Nigeria	389	0.38	†	*	348	0.91	48	1.49
Norway	327	0.32	18	0.3	134	0.35	14	0.44
Pakistan	110	0.11	2	*	168	0.44	4	0.12
Panama	380	0.37	10	0.16	49	0.13	2	0.07
Philippines	71	0.07	1	*	80	0.21	3	0.08
Poland	210	0.21	46	0.78	43	0.11	2	0.06
Portugal	57	0.06	5	0.08	243	0.64	31	0.98
Romania	283	0.28	31	0.52	69	0.18	5	0.16
Russia	356	0.35	206	3.49	44	0.11	35	1.09
Saudi Arabia	575	0.56	18	0.31	221	0.58	5	0.16

(amounts in millions of US dollars)

Supplying country	IBRD cumulative to June 30, 1995		IBRD fiscal 1995		IDA cumulative to June 30, 1995		IDA fiscal 1995	
	Amount	%	Amount	%	Amount	%	Amount	%
Senegal	23	*	†	*	80	0.21	10	0.32
Singapore	986	0.96	77	1.31	668	1.75	45	1.42
South Africa	400	0.39	14	0.25	836	2.19	171	5.35
Spain	1,148	1.12	73	1.24	260	0.68	32	0.99
Sri Lanka	22	*	1	*	17	*	1	*
Sweden	1,582	1.55	62	1.06	424	1.11	28	0.87
Switzerland	4,240	4.15	189	3.2	1,002	2.62	61	1.9
Thailand	144	0.14	2	*	339	0.89	21	0.66
Togo	29	*	—	*	26	0.07	4	0.13
Turkey	270	0.26	52	0.88	65	0.17	24	0.75
Ukraine	42	*	13	0.22	38	0.1	36	1.12
United Arab Emirates	546	0.53	10	0.16	344	0.9	11	0.35
United Kingdom[a]	7,795	7.63	414	7.03	5,070	13.28	266	8.31
United States	20,123	19.69	742	12.59	3,808	9.97	197	6.16
Uruguay	110	0.11	23	0.39	5	*	†	*
Venezuela	473	0.46	8	0.13	186	0.49	20	0.62
Yemen, Republic of	†	*	-	*	207	0.54	—	*
Yugoslavia (former)[b]	856	0.84	2	*	172	0.45	3	0.08
Zambia	30	*	†	*	110	0.29	4	0.11
Zimbabwe	34	*	†	*	93	0.24	8	0.26
Other	2,510	2.46	197	3.34	1,011	2.65	138	4.32
Total	102,206	100	5,896	100	38,181	100	3,197	100

— *Zero, † than $0.5 million, * less than 0.05 percent*

NOTE: *Disbursements for debt reduction and net advance disbursements are excluded.*

Details may not add to totals because of rounding.

a. *United Kingdom includes Hong Kong.*

b. *Figures represent payments to subcontractors in respect to contracts awarded to suppliers from Yugoslavia (former).*

IBRD AND IDA PAYMENTS TO SUPPLYING COUNTRIES FOR FOREIGN PROCUREMENT, BY DESCRIPTION OF GOODS, FISCAL 1995

(amounts in millions of US dollars)

	Equipment		Civil works		Consultants		All other goods		Total disbursements	
	Amount	%	Amount	%	Amount	%	Amount	%	Amount	%
Argentina	31	0.45	11	1.19	1	0.1	9	3.13	53	0.58
Australia	216	3.05	2	0.25	15	1.94	8	2.9	242	2.66
Austria	211	2.98	3	0.33	5	0.69	†	0.06	219	2.41
Bahamas, The	6	0.09	6	0.66	—	*	—	*	13	0.14
Bangladesh	6	0.08	2	0.26	†	*	1	0.47	9	0.1
Belarus	26	0.37	—	*	—	*	—	*	26	0.29
Belgium	90	1.28	5	0.53	11	1.37	5	1.75	111	1.22
Brazil	107	1.51	6	0.62	5	0.66	3	0.92	120	1.32
Bulgaria	18	0.26	—	*	—	*	—	*	18	0.2
Canada	106	1.5	8	0.82	52	6.59	5	1.73	171	1.88
China	127	1.8	72	7.59	6	0.79	7	2.36	212	2.33
Colombia	4	0.05	4	0.42	4	0.47	7	2.51	18	0.2
Costa Rica	9	0.13	—	*	6	0.76	†	*	16	0.17
Côte d'Ivoire	17	0.24	15	1.57	1	0.1	4	1.42	37	0.4
Cyprus	3	*	6	0.65	1	0.12	8	2.78	18	0.2
Czech Republic	16	0.22	—	*	†	*	—	*	16	0.18
Denmark	32	0.46	31	3.33	13	1.6	1	0.32	77	0.85
Ecuador	4	0.05	1	0.12	13	1.61	5	1.58	22	0.24
Egypt	9	0.12	2	0.18	2	0.25	†	*	12	0.13
Finland	30	0.43	1	0.14	10	1.27	†	0.1	42	0.46
France	743	10.51	99	10.53	87	11.02	6	2.22	936	10.29
Germany	666	9.42	101	10.72	38	4.82	17	6	822	9.04
Greece	20	0.29	†	*	†	*	—	*	20	0.22
Guinea	20	0.29	†	*	†	*	—	*	21	0.23
Hungary	22	0.31	1	0.14	†	*	—	*	24	0.26
India	89	1.26	16	1.71	9	1.09	8	2.75	121	1.34
Indonesia	34	0.49	—	*	—	*	3	1.03	37	0.41
Ireland	7	0.1	†	*	16	2.01	†	*	23	0.26
Israel	14	0.2	—	*	9	1.13	†	0.17	23	0.26
Italy	394	5.57	346	36.62	7	0.88	8	2.93	755	8.3
Japan	565	8	14	1.44	12	1.47	26	8.95	616	6.78
Kazakhstan	24	0.34	—	*	—	*	—	*	24	0.27
Kenya	15	0.21	†	*	5	0.59	20	6.89	40	0.44
Korea, Republic of	199	2.81	53	5.65	8	1.07	5	1.84	266	2.92
Kuwait	40	0.57	—	*	†	*	†	*	40	0.44
Lebanon	†	*	2	0.18	3	0.36	†	*	5	0.05
Lithuania	18	0.26	—	*	—	*	—	*	18	0.2
Malaysia	23	0.32	†	*	†	*	†	*	23	0.25
Mauritius	2	*	†	*	†	*	1	0.21	3	*
Mexico	23	0.33	2	0.16	†	*	2	0.62	27	0.3
Netherlands	205	2.89	43	4.54	26	3.3	4	1.33	277	3.05
New Zealand	18	0.25	†	*	6	0.7	†	*	23	0.26
Nigeria	48	0.67	†	*	†	*	†	*	48	0.53
Norway	23	0.33	—	*	8	1.02	1	0.23	32	0.35
Pakistan	4	0.06	†	*	1	0.07	1	0.27	5	0.06
Panama	9	0.13	2	0.17	—	*	1	0.22	12	0.13
Paraguay	1	*	2	0.2	†	*	1	0.21	3	*
Philippines	1	*	—	*	3	0.4	—	*	4	*
Poland	45	0.64	3	0.27	†	*	—	*	48	0.53
Portugal	12	0.18	8	0.89	15	1.9	†	*	36	0.4
Romania	34	0.49	2	0.17	†	*	†	*	36	0.4
Russia	241	3.4	†	*	†	*	—	*	241	2.65
Saudi Arabia	23	0.32	—	*	†	*	†	0.14	23	0.26
Senegal	4	0.06	4	0.45	†	*	2	0.53	10	0.11
Singapore	117	1.65	1	0.07	†	0.06	5	1.64	123	1.35
South Africa	174	2.46	†	*	9	1.07	3	0.97	185	2.04
Spain	83	1.17	18	1.91	4	0.45	†	0.07	104	1.15
St. Lucia	7	0.1	†	*	—	*	1	0.37	8	0.09
Sweden	81	1.15	1	0.1	6	0.71	2	0.8	90	0.99

(amounts in millions of US dollars)

	Equipment		Civil works		Consultants		All other goods		Total disbursements	
	Amount	%	Amount	%	Amount	%	Amount	%	Amount	%
Switzerland	224	3.18	2	0.17	19	2.43	4	1.42	249	2.74
Tanzania	2	*	†	*	†	*	2	0.69	4	*
Thailand	22	0.31	†	*	1	0.11	†	0.11	23	0.26
Togo	3	*	†	*	†	*	2	0.53	4	*
Turkey	75	1.07	—	*	—	*	†	0.09	76	0.83
Turkmenistan	35	0.49	—	*	—	*	—	*	35	0.38
Ukraine	48	0.67	—	*	—	*	1	0.38	49	0.54
United Arab Emirates	18	0.26	—	*	—	*	3	0.95	21	0.23
United Kingdom[a]	513	7.26	27	2.81	125	15.82	14	5.02	680	7.48
United States	748	10.59	2	0.25	160	20.16	29	10	939	10.33
Uruguay	21	0.3	—	*	†	*	1	0.49	23	0.25
Venezuela	25	0.35	—	*	1	0.14	2	0.72	28	0.3
Yugoslavia (former)[b]	†	*	5	0.48	—	*	—	*	5	0.05
Zambia	2	*	†	*	†	*	1	0.47	4	*
Other	215	3.04	14	1.48	68	8.57	49	17.01	347	3.81
Total	7,068	100	944	100	793	100	288	100	9,094	100

— Zero, † less than $0.5 million, * less than 0.05 percent.

NOTE: *Disbursements for debt reduction and net advance disbursements are excluded.*

Details may not add to totals because of rounding.

a. *United Kingdom includes Hong Kong.*

b. *Figures represent payments to subcontractors in respect to contracts awarded to suppliers from Yugoslavia (former).*

IBRD and IDA Foreign Disbursements, by Description of Goods, for Investment Lending, Fiscal 1993–95

Item	1993			1994			1995		
	OECD	Non-OECD	Total	OECD	Non-OECD	Total	OECD	Non-OECD	Total

Millions of US Dollars

Item	OECD	Non-OECD	Total	OECD	Non-OECD	Total	OECD	Non-OECD	Total
Civil works	337	176	513	317	209	526	706	229	937
Consultants	612	105	717	615	124	739	626	140	766
Goods	2,851	556	3,408	2,519	593	3,112	2,758	424	3,183
All other	72	66	138	60	65	125	82	73	155
Total	3,873	903	4,776	3,512	991	4,502	4,173	867	5,040

Percent[a]

Item	OECD	Non-OECD	Total	OECD	Non-OECD	Total	OECD	Non-OECD	Total
Civil works	66	34	11	60	40	12	76	24	19
Consultants	85	15	15	83	17	16	82	18	15
Goods	84	16	71	81	19	69	87	13	63
All other	52	48	3	48	52	3	53	47	3
Total	81	19	100	78	22	100	83	17	100

NOTE: *Disbursements for debt reduction and net advance disbursements are excluded. Disbursements for structural adjustment loans, sector adjustment loans, and hybrids (loans that support policy and institutional reforms in a specific sector by financing both a policy component disbursed against imports and an investment component) are also excluded. Mexico became an OECD member in May 1994. For consistency of comparison, Mexico is included as an OECD country for all periods covered by this table.*
a. All of the percentages are based on the dollar amounts shown under the total disbursements section. These percentages show both the breakdown between OECD and non-OECD countries for individual goods categories and the share of each goods category compared with total disbursements.

LOW- AND MIDDLE-INCOME ECONOMIES: GROWTH OF GDP AND GDP PER CAPITA, 1983–94

(average annual percentage change unless otherwise noted)

Region or income group	GDP					GDP per capita				
	1983-91	1992-94	1992	1993	1994	1983-91	1992-94	1992	1993	1994
Low- and middle-income economies	3.3	3.9	3.6	4.3	4.0	1.3	2.1	1.6	2.3	2.2
By regional group										
Sub-Saharan Africa[a]	2.1	0.8	1.3	0.2	1.2	-0.9	-2.1	-1.6	-2.7	-1.7
East Asia and Pacific[b]	7.9	9.3	9.0	9.4	9.6	6.3	7.9	7.5	7.9	8.3
South Asia[c]	5.3	4.4	5.1	3.5	4.7	3.1	2.3	2.9	1.3	2.7
Middle East and North Africa[d]	1.7	0.6	3.6	1.6	-3.3	-1.3	-2.0	1.0	-1.1	-5.8
Europe and Central Asia[e]	0.9	-9.6	-13.1	-6.4	-9.2	0.1	-10.1	-13.6	-7.1	-9.6
Latin America and the Caribbean[f]	1.9	3.6	2.7	3.8	4.2	-0.2	1.6	0.7	1.7	2.4
Memo items										
Low-and middle-income economies, excluding Europe and Central Asia transitional economies	3.8	4.5	4.7	4.7	4.1	1.7	2.6	2.7	2.7	2.3

a. Excludes South Africa.
b. American Samoa, Cambodia, China, Fiji, Guam, Indonesia, Kiribati, Rep. of Korea, Lao People's Democratic Republic, Macao, Malaysia, Mongolia, Myanmar, New Caledonia and Pacific Islands' Trust Territory, Papua New Guinea, the Philippines, Solomon Islands, Thailand, Tonga, Vanuatu, Viet Nam, and Western Samoa.
c. Afghanstan, Bangladesh, Bhutan, India, Maldives, Nepal, Pakistan, and Sri Lanka.
d. Algeria, Bahrain, Egypt, Islamic Republic of Iran, Iraq, Jordan, Lebanon, Libya, Morocco, Oman, Saudi Arabia, Syrian Arab Republic, Tunisia, and Yemen.
e. Republics of the former Soviet Union, republics of former Yugoslavia, Albania, Bulgaria,Czechoslovakia (through 1992; the Czech Republic and the Slovak Republic thereafter), Gibraltar, Greece, Hungary, Isle of Man, Malta, Poland, Portugal, Romania, and Turkey.
f. Except Cuba.
Source: World Bank.

LONG-TERM FINANCIAL FLOWS TO DEVELOPING COUNTRIES, 1987–94

(billions of US dollars)

Item	1987	1988	1989	1990	1991	1992	1993	1994[a]
Long-term aggregate net resource flows	68.5	77.4	84.5	103.5	124.7	153.0	213.1	227.3
Official development assistance	43.4	42.4	42.6	57.9	61.8	50.3	53.9	54.4
Official grants	16.9	18.4	19.2	28.7	32.6	29.9	30.1	30.5
Net official loans	26.4	24.1	23.4	29.2	29.2	20.4	23.8	23.9
Bilateral	11.5	12.9	11.6	14.0	14.2	7.7	9.3	n.a.
Multilateral	14.9	11.1	11.7	15.2	15.0	12.7	14.5	n.a.
Net private loans	9.8	12.7	12.8	15.1	18.6	41.5	45.7	55.6
Commercial banks	1.0	2.9	5.3	3.4	12.5	12.9	42.0	n.a.
Bonds	3.0	7.3	0.9	0.1	4.0	12.8	-2.2	n.a.
Others	5.8	2.5	6.6	11.5	2.1	15.7	5.8	n.a.
Foreign direct investment	14.6	21.2	25.7	26.7	36.8	47.1	66.6	77.9
Portfolio equity investment[b]	0.8	1.1	3.5	3.8	7.6	14.2	46.9	39.5
Long-term aggregate net transfers[c]	-1.6	-1.1	7.2	26.2	45.8	74.4	132.2	137.5

n.a. Not available.
a. Preliminary.
b. World Bank staff estimates.
c. Long-term aggregate resource flows minus interest payments and reinvested and remitted profits.
Source: World Bank.

LOW- AND MIDDLE-INCOME ECONOMIES:
LONG-TERM DEBT AND DEBT SERVICE, SELECTED YEARS, 1989–94
(billions of US dollars; percentages)

Item	All low- and middle-income economies			Severely indebted middle-income economies			Sub-Saharan Africa		
	1989	1993	1994[a]	1989	1993	1994[a]	1989	1993	1994[a]
Debt outstanding	1,150.6	1,424.0	1,537.7	323.6	361.8	377.9	142.7	155.9	165.2
Official (%)	47.9	51.2	50.8	46.2	50.2	50.5	64.0	74.9	76.2
Private (%)	52.1	48.8	49.2	53.8	49.8	49.5	36.0	25.1	23.8
Debt as % of GNP	27.8	31.2	32.2	48.2	34.3	33.3	59.4	57.0	64.9
Debt service	146.1	167.6	174.8	30.2	26.7	28.4	10.0	10.2	8.1
Interest payments	60.0	57.6	64.5	11.1	11.4	13.6	5.2	3.9	4.2
Official (%)	30.9	42.6	42.0	36.4	51.8	49.2	38.3	53.5	60.3
Private (%)	69.1	57.4	58.0	63.6	48.2	50.8	61.7	46.5	39.7
Principal payments	86.1	110.0	110.3	19.1	15.4	14.9	4.8	6.3	3.9
Official (%)	28.9	28.0	32.2	32.1	39.7	41.3	36.3	34.5	70.6
Private(%)	71.1	72.0	67.8	67.9	60.3	58.7	63.7	65.5	29.4
Debt-service ratio (%)[b]	17.2	15.9	15.0	24.2	22.0	19.3	13.6	12.9	9.7
Average interest rate on new commitments (%)[c]	6.8	5.8	n.a.	7.3	6.9	n.a.	4.2	2.9	n.a.
Official (%)	5.3	4.9	n.a.	5.8	7.1	n.a.	3.6	2.5	n.a.
Private (%)	8.4	6.5	n.a.	9.1	6.8	n.a.	8.3	5.7	n.a.
Disbursements	122.3	179.5	189.8	19.7	32.1	26.0	11.0	7.6	10.2
Official (%)	39.5	30.4	31.3	42.9	32.5	37.6	64.4	81.3	77.4
Private (%)	60.5	69.6	68.7	57.1	67.5	62.4	35.6	18.7	22.6
Net resource flows on long-term lending[d]	36.1	69.4	79.5	0.6	16.7	11.1	6.2	1.3	6.3
Net transfers on long-term lending[e]	-23.9	11.8	15.0	-10.5	5.4	-2.5	1.0	-2.6	2.2

NOTE: Stock, flow, and economic data cover 154 countries of which 137 report to the World Bank Debtor Reporting System.
n.a. Not available.
a. Preliminary.
b. Debt service as a percentage of exports of goods and services.
c. Covers only the countries reporting to the World Bank Debtor Reporting System.
d. Disbursements minus (actual) principal payments.
e. New resource flows minus (actual) interest payments.
Source: World Bank.

SELECTED TRADE-PERFORMANCE INDICATORS, 1971–94
(average annual percentage change)

Country group and indicator	1971-81	1981-91	1992	1993	1994
Low- and middle-income countries					
Import volume	2.9	1.2	9.3	9.5	9.0
Export volume	2.9	3.4	5.9	6.7	8.8
Terms of trade	0.5	-2.7	-1.8	-0.7	1.3
Sub-Saharan Africa[a]					
Import volume	-0.8	-4.0	-1.1	0.9	4.4
Export volume	1.3	1.4	-0.2	-0.8	3.0
Terms of trade	-1.1	-4.0	-4.1	0.0	2.0
Asia					
Import volume	7.3	6.7	8.9	18.4	16.4
Export volume	8.2	9.5	12.9	13.4	15.1
Terms of trade	-0.7	-1.5	-1.2	0.6	2.0
Europe and Central Asia[b]					
Import volume	1.8	0.4	7.5	3.0	3.1
Export volume	2.2	0.2	0.1	-4.0	5.7
Terms of trade	0.3	-0.2	0.1	-0.9	1.1
Middle East and North Africa					
Import volume	3.0	-2.7	6.1	-4.2	-2.3
Export volume	-2.3	0.5	-3.4	4.1	0.8
Terms of trade	4.1	-2.7	-1.5	-5.2	-4.3
Latin America and the Caribbean					
Import volume	1.2	0.4	19.4	12.3	8.7
Export volume	4.7	4.3	10.8	10.9	7.0
Terms of trade	-0.4	-2.6	-5.5	-1.9	1.7
Memorandum item					
World export volume	4.4	4.7	4.7	3.4	8.6

a. Excluding South Africa.
b. Including republics of the former Soviet Union.
Source: World Bank.

COMMODITY PRICES, 1987–94
(average annual percentage change)

Commodity price	1987-92	1992	1993	1994
In current-dollar terms				
Food	4.0	0.8	-1.4	8.3
Beverages	-9.8	-15.4	6.9	77.1
Agricultural raw materials	1.8	-0.8	12.2	14.1
Metals and minerals	3.8	-3.0	-14.2	14.3
Fertilizers	0.6	-6.4	-12.6	11.6
Total nonfuel	0.3	-3.6	-0.5	22.2
Petroleum	2.7	-1.9	-11.4	-5.7
In real terms[a]				
Total nonoil	-3.4	-7.5	-0.2	18.4
Petroleum	-0.8	-5.8	-11.2	-8.5
In special drawing rights (SDRs)				
Total nonoil	-1.4	-6.3	0.3	19.1
Petroleum	1.1	-4.7	-10.7	-8.0

NOTE: *The World Bank Price Index for the Primary Commodities was revised in April 1995. The revised index has been updated with 1987-89 developing country exports earnings as its weights, previously for 1979–81 period. Country coverage has been broadened to include the republics of the former Soviet Union.*
 a. *Deflated by unit-value index of manufactures exports from the G-5 countries (France, Germany, Japan, the United Kingdom, and the United States) to the developing countres.*
Source: *World Bank.*

COMMUNIQUE

October 3, 1994

1. The 49th meeting of the Development Committee was held in Madrid, Spain on October 3, 1994 under the chairmanship of Mr. Mourad Cherif, Minister of Finance and Investment of Morocco. On its own 20th Anniversary, the Committee joined in congratulations to the World Bank and IMF on the 50th Anniversary of the Bretton Woods agreement, and welcomed the World Bank's publication "Learning from the Past—Embracing the Future."

Transfer of Resources

2. The Committee's main task is to keep under review the transfer of resources to developing and transition countries. It therefore welcomes the continued high level of total flows to these countries. It notes the slow rate of growth in official development assistance and calls on donor countries to enhance their aid as soon as possible and to increase its focus on the poorest countries. Where appropriate, the Committee favors a reduction in the stock of debt and an increase in concessionality for the poorest countries facing special difficulties. The Committee recognizes the special needs and problems of countries emerging from economic and political disruption and also of the poorest, most indebted countries and requests the Executive Boards to examine proposals in these areas.

3. The Committee welcomes the increased volume of private flows in recent years to a growing number of countries that are implementing economic reforms. It notes uncertainties about the sustainability of such flows in changing world conditions and the fact that they continue to be concentrated in a small number of countries. It urges countries not currently receiving such flows to improve their creditworthiness through macroeconomic reform and to create a climate favorable to sound private sector development; these measures will attract more foreign portfolio and direct investment. The Committee asks the World Bank Group, the IMF and industrial countries to continue their efforts to facilitate and encourage private flows to all developing and transition countries.

Aid Effectiveness

4. Effective aid requires closer collaboration between receiving countries, international organizations and donors. For aid to be most effective it has to be adequate and to operate in a favorable environment. Prime responsibility for domestic policies that contribute to aid effectiveness rests, of course, with the recipient countries themselves. The guiding principles for recipients are:

a. Appropriate domestic economic policies tailored to local conditions are essential if aid is to be effective.

b. The effective use of aid requires strong administrative and institutional capacity.

c. "Ownership" by the government and participation by other stakeholders, including beneficiaries, are essential.

5. The guiding principles for donors and international agencies are these:

a. The best conditions and policies for aid cannot substitute for strong "ownership" by the recipient government and good governance. Donors and recipients must collaborate to make these the basis for effective aid.

b. Donors should support participation by relevant stakeholders (especially women, the poor and other disadvantaged groups); this helps to improve the design of projects and ensure that they are properly implemented and operated. The Bank should strengthen its skill mix and incentive system for these purposes.

c. Technical assistance (TA) is likely to be most effective when it responds to clearly-defined needs and the absorptive capacity of the recipient. TA should work within and, if necessary, seek to strengthen the institutional environment along the lines approved by the OECD Development Assistance Committee (DAC).

d. Multilateral agencies, including the IMF, the World Bank Group and the regional development banks, work closely to support countries' own efforts to put in place a sound framework for macroeconomic and structural policies that foster the private sector and strengthen public sector management. Aid programs should be consistent with this framework and with the country's own development priorities. Innovative approaches to achieve this objective are to be encouraged. The World Bank will strengthen its consultations with other donors who in turn will collaborate in this approach.

e. Efforts to coordinate and simplify donor aid procedures and practices should be accelerated. Aid operations should be made more transparent to improve accountability. Donors should avoid setting up mechanisms that are inconsistent with the recipients' own efforts to manage their own budgets and implement aid. Ministers support recent efforts in the DAC to reduce the use of tied aid credits. They also urge donors to minimize the additional costs associated with trade-distorting tied aid where this can be done without reducing volume.

f. The DAC principles provide an appropriate framework for improving aid coordination. Consultative groups and roundtable meetings are more effective when preceded by active involvement of the recipient government and consultation with other donors. The agenda for consultative groups should cover issues of development strategy, aid utilization, aid coordination and technical assistance in addition to mobilization of financial resources.

g. Recent efforts to improve the effectiveness of the World Bank and other development agencies, focusing on their development impact and on results in the field, need to be sustained and extended. Particular attention should be given to: shifting the focus from projects to country programs; improving the "quality at entry" of projects; strengthening evaluation and disclosure policies; streamlining procedures; addressing urgently the adequacy of field office networks; and changing staff incentives to focus on development impact.

h. Aid can also help to stimulate private investment; institutions such as the IFC and MIGA can play a valuable role but must pay due attention to development effectiveness.

i. Many of these principles apply with equal force to the countries in transition. However,

more attention needs to be given in these countries, in differing degrees, to informing both policymakers and public opinion at large of the workings of a market economy and the complementary roles of the public and private sectors.

6. The Committee will follow up these issues carefully at future meetings and particularly looks forward to the report of its Task Force on the Multilateral Development Banks.

The Uruguay Round and the Developing and Transition Countries

7. The Committee reviewed the results of the recently completed Uruguay Round negotiations and their impact on the developing and transition countries. At this stage it was only possible to make a preliminary assessment of the likely effects. The Committee also considered the implications for the future work of the World Bank and the IMF. It believes that:

a. In addition to its global effects, the successful conclusion of the Uruguay Round will bring significant benefits to developing countries over time through increased market access, the integration of new areas into the system, and strengthened rules and institutions. Early ratification and implementation are therefore essential.

b. These benefits will accrue particularly to countries that pursue sound macroeconomic policies and adopt market-based reforms.

c. A number of developing countries should benefit in particular from the phased integration of textiles and clothing into the multilateral system, although the timetable for liberalization will delay these benefits.

d. Some countries may need help to adjust to higher world food prices and the erosion of preferences, although most of them will gain from the reduction of agricultural subsidies. Initial studies made by the Bank and the IMF indicate that the negative effects are likely to be fairly small and that existing instruments seem adequate to deal with them. Further research may refine these findings. Meanwhile, the Bank and the IMF must be ready to address these problems.

e.   In the longer run it is important to keep up the momentum of mutually advantageous trade liberalization and to avoid new forms of protectionism.

f.   The task of the Bank and the IMF is to assist developing and transition countries to ease the change to the new trading system by providing policy advice, financial support and technical assistance in order to maximize the gains from new market opportunities.

g.   It will also be necessary to bring the transition countries (many of whom are not yet members of GATT) into the multilateral process as quickly as possible so that they can fully share the benefits of trade liberalization and enlarged market access without discrimination. The Bank and the IMF should encourage and assist these countries in their efforts to become more fully integrated into the multilateral trading system and to adopt policies that will facilitate their accession to the new World Trade Organization (WTO).

8.   The Committee believes it is essential for both institutions to collaborate closely with the WTO and notes that the ministerial declaration at the end of the Uruguay Round calls for early talks between the Director-General of the WTO and the heads of the Bank and IMF.

Population

9.   Ministers from the participating countries welcomed the outcome of the recent United Nations Conference on Population and Development, which it discussed at its last meeting. The Committee called on the Bank and conference participants to play an active part in implementing the Programme of Action approved by the conference.

Desertification

10. It also welcomed the agreement on the antidesertification convention, called for its early ratification, and encouraged the Bank to continue its active support for development and environmental management in dryland areas.

COMMUNIQUE

April 27, 1995

1.   The 50th meeting of the Development Committee was held in Washington, D.C. on April 27, 1995, under the chairmanship of Mr. Mohamed Kabbaj, Minister of Finance and Investment of Morocco. The Committee expressed its deep regret at the departure of Mr. Lewis T. Preston and recorded its great appreciation of his distinguished leadership as President of the World Bank. It offered its congratulations to his successor, Mr. James D. Wolfensohn.

Resource Flows to Developing and Transition Countries

2.   The Committee welcomed the continued high level of total resource flows and the increase since 1990 in various forms of private finance, especially foreign direct investment, which does not add to debt-servicing burdens. At a time of rapid globalization and liberalization of financial markets, it noted the recent high volatility of financial flows, as exemplified by currency movements. But portfolio flows have declined, and Ministers recognized that markets are likely to be more selective in their provision of such capital. This emphasizes the need for recipient countries to follow sound macroeconomic policies to gain or maintain access to private markets and to mobilize significant domestic savings. They should avoid excessive reliance on short-term flows to finance longer-term development needs. The strong policy base and solid long-term prospects of many developing and transition countries suggest that they should be able to attract continued foreign direct investment.

3.   The Committee expressed its concern about the prospect of a fall in total official development assistance. Given the pressing needs of the poorest countries, it urged continued strong support for the International Development Association (IDA) and for the Special Program of Assistance for Africa (SPA). It welcomed the recent agreement in the Paris Club to implement "Naples Terms" for the poorest and most heavily indebted countries and called for them to be applied flexibly. The Committee noted that some of these countries have a heavy burden of debt owed to multilateral institutions. It invited the Executive Boards of the World Bank and the IMF to continue their review of this sub-

ject so that Ministers can return to it at the next meeting.

Trade

4. The Committee welcomed the establishment on January 1 of the World Trade Organization and urged close collaboration between the WTO and the Bretton Woods institutions. It called on the Bank and IMF to assist those countries that are not yet members of the WTO to join the organization and to become more fully integrated into the multilateral trading system. It noted the Bank's new estimates of the likely impact of the Uruguay Round upon the trade of developing countries. It welcomed evidence of the positive effect the Round will have on most developing countries, especially on those taking this opportunity to reform their own policies. It noted the Bank's view that the adverse impact upon food-importing countries and those that will lose preferential access to industrial markets is likely to be small. It asked the Bank and IMF to monitor the impact on individual countries and to be prepared to help as necessary. It agreed that further liberalization of the agricultural and service sectors would provide important additional gains.

Infrastructure

5. The Committee noted that developing countries currently invest over $200 billion a year in infrastructure, more than 90 percent of it in the public sector. Adequate, efficient and carefully designed infrastructure with full regard to the environment is crucial to sustainable development. More investment and improved performance in infrastructure will require a series of reforms in the structure and delivery of services. Governments have a continuing responsibility, whether as providers or regulators of infrastructure. In particular, efficiency requires prices that reflect all long-run economic costs, more businesslike management, increased involvement of the private sector, and better-targeted subsidies. Such reforms should be designed to increase incentives to devote suffi-

cient resources to maintenance in order to make best use of existing assets and reduce the need for expensive replacements.

6. Improvement will also involve more use of private finance in various forms. The options chosen will vary for each country and service depending on conditions such as level of domestic savings and the depth of financial markets. Private participation can be encouraged through build-own-operate and build-own-operate-transfer concessions, leases, operating contracts, partial guarantees from the public sector, and privatization. The aim must be to pass the commercial risks to the private sector and to reduce the call on public funding and public guarantees.

7. The Committee agreed that the poor stand to gain directly and quickly from better infrastructure, which can also help to improve environmental conditions. Donor countries can help the poorest countries by providing financial and technical support and investment guarantees for the development of infrastructure within a policy framework that encourages efficient operation, maintenance, and responsiveness to users. The multilateral institutions (including IDA) have a major responsibility for providing advice and financial support. They can also play a catalytic role in mobilizing funds from a wider range of private sector sources, using all the means available, including World Bank guarantees, and IFC and MIGA resources.

Social Summit

8. The Committee generally welcomed the outcome of the recent Social Summit in Copenhagen and agreed to discuss the implications for the developing and transition countries and for donors and the Bank and the IMF, at its next meeting in Washington, D.C. on October 9, 1995.

Executive Secretary

9. The Committee expressed its deep appreciation to Peter Mountfield, the retiring Executive Secretary, for his dedicated service to the Committee over the past four years.